Poles in the UK

CW01239449

For Simon – my English Friend
Thank You for your friends...P...
Pawek B.

Eastleigh 18.11.2016

Poles in the UK

A Story of Friendship and Cooperation

By Brin Best and Maria Helena Żukowska

With specialist contributions from
Amanda Best, Joanna Ewa Bieniek, Katarzyna Dejewska, Maja Karpowicz, Kinga Kreffta, Teresa Hough, Kathryn Needham, Marcin Wielicki and Simona Żukowska

And literary contributions from
B.E. Andre and Maria Jastrzębska

THE BRITISH POLONIA FOUNDATION

Published 2016 by The British Polonia Foundation
9 Throstle Nest Close
Otley
LS21 2RR
West Yorkshire
UK

ISBN 978-0-9954956-1-6

© Copyright in text
Brin Best & Maria Helena Żukowska, with the exception of the following:
Mariam Al-Janabi (p. 184–185); B.E. Andre (p. 143–147); Amanda Best (p. 109); Joanna Ewa Bieniek (p. 114–116); Marek Bucholc (p. 165); Anna Cieśluk (p. 164); Idalia Maria Cruz (p. 165); Kasia Dejewska (p. 159, 186–188); Barbara Domzal-Karpowicz (p. 88–95); Adrianna Green (p. 161); John Green (p. 232); Zygmunt Green (p. 178–179); Soham Handa (p. 227); Jane Harvey-Berrick (p. 233); Teresa Hough (p. 160, 182–183); Maria Jastrzębska (p. 33, 148–150); Maja Karpowicz (p. 40, 43, 47, 55, 58, 60, 64, 67–69); Zbig Karpowicz (p. 110–113); Radosław Kolator (p. 164); Michalina Kulikjan (p. 162); Agnieszka Kulmaczewska & Rafał Kulmaczewski (p. 170–172); Kinga Kreffta (p. 166–169); Aleksandra Lepczyńska (p. 202); Kasia Madera (p. 151–152); Zuzanna Malka (p. 165); Kathryn Needham (p. 84–85, 87, 155, 157); Roxana Panufnik (p. 138); Ben Parker (p. 231); Zuzanna Sawicka (p. 173–175); Emilka Solny (p. 163); Wiktoria Szykuła (p. 162); Dominika Szymańska (p. 164); Laura Tubacka (p. 163); Marcin Wielicki (p. 208); Renata Wroniecka (p. 215–217); Simona Żukowska (p. 205).

© Copyright in images
This rests with the named individuals for each image. Images without a credit are believed to be in the public domain.

Proof-reader: Gill O'Donnell
Picture consultant: Kathryn Needham

The publisher has made every effort to trace the copyright holders of all the material printed in the book. Should any items have been overlooked, it would be happy to make the necessary arrangements at the earliest opportunity.

A CIP record for this publication is available from the British Library.

Design by erte

Printed and bound in the UK by Hart & Clough (The Amadeus Press), Cleckheaton, West Yorkshire.

The companion Facebook page for this book can be viewed at
www.facebook.com/polesintheuk

This publication supports the
Wrocław 2016 European Capital of Culture Programme

This book was supported by a grant from
The Polonia Aid Foundation Trust

Contents

Acknowledgements 7

Introduction 10

Pronouncing Polish Sounds 12

PART ONE POLAND IN THE WORLD

CHAPTER 1
A Short History of Poland 15

The tumultuous history of Poland over the centuries, charting the important people, powerful groups and bloody wars that have – quite literally – shaped the country of Poland for over a thousand years. The chapter also presents a timeline of the key historical events of Poland which have led to its people settling in the UK, over the centuries.

CHAPTER 2
The Geography of Poland 39

The diverse physical and human geography of Poland, highlighting some of the key landmarks, habitats and settlements of the country. The chapter also presents many of the highly distinctive features of Poland, while demonstrating its links with neighbouring countries and cultures.

PART TWO POLES IN THE UK

CHAPTER 3
World War II 77

The vital contribution of Polish people to the successful Allied campaign during World War II. The chapter also outlines the many reasons why British people today owe a debt to the Polish men and woman who fought alongside British forces, or made other essential contributions to the war effort, often at great personal sacrifice to themselves.

CHAPTER 4
Science 101

The many ways in which Polish people have made key contributions to science in the UK and worldwide, over the centuries. The chapter includes the important sixteenth century astronomical breakthroughs of Nicolaus Copernicus, alongside many more recent contributions, which continue to impact on British society today.

CHAPTER 5
The Arts 117

The numerous ways in which Polish people – and those with Polish heritage – have made significant contributions to the arts in Britain, including the fields of literature, music, new media and broadcasting. The chapter also includes interviews with people who are highly respected in their fields, or whose work is well known in the UK.

CHAPTER 6
Public Services 153

An overview of the profound influence that Polish people – and those with Polish heritage – have had, and continue to have, on Britain's public service industries. The chapter also includes a special section showcasing the work of children from one of the many Polish Saturday Schools in the UK.

CHAPTER 7
Business 189

Provides many examples illustrating the various ways in which Polish people have made an important contribution to business and retail activity in the UK. The chapter also includes some of the pioneers of Anglo-Polish business collaboration, such as Michael Marks, whose company would eventually become one of the most famous British brands in history.

CHAPTER 8
Food and Drink 203

Presents some of the food and drink classics from Poland, as well as providing examples of the many ways in which Polish people are involved in the UK food and drink sector today. It includes step by step recipes which will allow you to create authentic Polish dishes, from ingredients now sold in UK shops.

PART THREE THE BRITISH ON THE POLES

CHAPTER 9
The Polish Contribution to the UK 225

Showcases the personal perspective of British people of all ages on the many Polish contributions to the UK. The chapter also includes some general conclusions, looking back over the other chapters of the book, on what Poles have done for Britain. It demonstrates, in a powerful and often personal way, why Polish people and culture are valued by so many across Britain today.

Index 235
Further reading and information 241

Acknowledgements

When we started out writing *Poles in the UK* over a year ago, we had no idea that it would grow into the substantial work that is currently in your hands. What began as a concise overview, aimed mainly at younger readers, grew into the most comprehensive book ever written about the contribution of Polish people to the UK.

Such a work was only possible thanks to the generous support of well over 100 people, who freely gave their time to help make the book a success. We are very grateful to them all and also touched by their willingness to support our project so passionately. Their various contributions to the book are outlined below.

We would like to offer our special thanks to the trustees of the Polonia Aid Foundation Trust, who awarded us an important grant towards the publication costs for the book (and for follow-up educational work). In particular, Dr Jan Mokrzycki provided us with very helpful advice as we prepared our grant application.

The book has been enormously enriched through the interviews with, and contributions from, all those whose stories are included. We are extremely grateful for their participation, which in many cases required both time engaged in interviews and extensive correspondence, in order to tell their stories fully and accurately.

Eleven additional people, whose profiles are featured on p. 244–246, have made special written contributions to the book on themes that are close to their hearts. Their contributions have helped to make the text more comprehensive and engaging, and we thank them warmly for their efforts. We also very grateful to B.E. Andre and Maria Jastrzębska for their literary contributions.

The highly illustrated, and often deeply personal, character of the book has only been possible due to the generous support of the people who kindly provided photographs for inclusion. In many cases the inclusion of these photographs required extensive research in family albums and other places, and liaison with other family members. Each image used in the book is credited to the person who provided it – except for those which are public domain.

We wish to give special thanks to Chris Ottewell (Chairman of the Anglo Polish Society) who has been a wonderful ally at every stage in the production of the book. Chris played a pivotal role in helping us locate many of the interviewees featured in these pages. He was also an enthusiastic advocate for our project, both locally and nationally, helping us gain the vital support we needed for the book to be a success. We also thank fellow Anglo Polish Society member Paweł Komorowski, who was especially meticulous in suggesting people and topics to include. Clare Mulley provided some helpful historical information which improved the accuracy of the text about Krystyna Skarbek, and we also thank Andrew Hay, Sofia Iqbal, Chris Hudson, Sukbir Kaur and Kinga Ewa Plinch, who provided helpful information and useful contacts.

We are very grateful to Teresa Hough and Magda Ions, from the Polish Catholic Centre in Leeds, who have provided extensive support and encouragement over a long period. This included the opportunity to work with children and young people from the Centre as we planned the book, and to promote our project in various other ways. Zygmunt Green and Roman Paszel from the Centre provided additional assistance with IT support and photography respectively, and the Centre librarian Anita Skwierawska helped us find suitable publications during our research.

Thirty-eight children from the Leeds Polish Saturday School played an important role in the planning of the book. This occurred both through the workshop we ran at the school in October 2015, and by providing thoughtful written work on the topics explored in the workshop. The children provided hundreds of ideas for content, which have improved the book considerably. Their names appear on p. 246, and a selection of photographs from the workshop day is included in Chapter 6.

As well as being featured in the book, and providing a contributing interview, Kinga Kreffta helped at various points in the planning stages. She also cooked some delicious Polish dishes, which helped provide sustenance at key points during the long writing process.

In addition to giving a very detailed interview, Anna Collins provided much additional support by putting us in touch with interviewees and other helpful contacts, providing additional ideas and dealing with our various requests extremely efficiently. Her contribution to the book has been significant.

We would like to thank Gill O'Donnell who kindly proof-read portions of the book, helping to improve its readability and accuracy. We also worked with a team of younger readers to help ensure that the text is accessible to the widest possible age range – namely Charlotte Davis, Thomas Fawell, Soham Handa and Emily Rizzo. These youngsters read over key parts of the text and made numerous helpful suggestions. Despite these people's input, any errors in the text that remain are, of course, our own. As well as providing a written contribution, Ben Parker provided expert advice on social media issues, helping us find interviewees and promoting the book more generally.

We give special thanks to our expert designer, Luiza Pindral, who in addition to producing a stunning design, provided us with invaluable, kind support during the whole design and print process.

Brin Best's acknowledgements
I wish to thank Michał Bryś, whose interest in my writing project about Polish people in the UK eventually led to an introduction to my wonderful co-author Maria Żukowska.

Maria's influence on the project has been very profound, in so many ways, and I know the book is immeasurably better because of her involvement. I feel truly fortunate that our paths have crossed in order to write this important book. I have so many things to thank her for: her incredible professionalism, her hard work over many months, her creativity, her extraordinary attention to detail and her tireless good humour at every stage in the production of the book. I know Maria is going to achieve great things in this world and I consider it a privilege to have worked with her on this project.

I would also like to give special thanks to Karolina Iskra, who I first met in Leeds almost three years ago. I don't think this book would ever have come about had she not been so generous in sharing her inspiring story of moving to the UK as a teenager, 11 years ago. It was Karolina's story, building on my awareness of the vital historic links between my home country and Poland, which convinced me that a book about Polish people in the UK was long overdue.

My dear friend Alex Gilbert provided me with the opportunity, over several years, to work with many Polish children at her Harrogate primary school. These visits, and the conversations with Polish children that they allowed, fuelled my interest in the fascinating lives of Polish people who had arrived in the UK since EU enlargement.

I would like to thank Debbs Lait, who was my health and fitness coach during much of the writing of this book. She helped to keep me fresh and clear my mind for writing, and also shared some valuable stories from her own work with Polish people. Many thanks also to Jane Holmes, whose expertise and advice has enabled me to stay in tiptop condition mentally during the writing process.

The Polish and non-Polish staff of the Leeds Bridgewater Place and Albion Street Starbucks stores looked after me very well during my writing days in Leeds. Their stores also provided the ideal venue for several of the interviews featured in the book, as well as numerous planning sessions.

Finally, huge thanks to my wife Amanda who provided so much love and support as this project grew and grew. She was endlessly patient when I disappeared to carry out interviews and spend hours at the computer. She kept me fed, watered and healthy and was always on hand for hugs and sympathy when things got tough. I could, quite simply, not have written this book without her.

Maria's acknowledgements

I would like to thank my co-author, Brin Best, for giving this young writer a truly extraordinary opportunity – for believing in me straight from the start, and for inviting me on board this unique project with no hesitation. His support, guidance and expert advice were invaluable and made it possible for me to tell this Anglo-Polish story.

I would like to thank my mum, Simona, for her loving support and for helping me in all sorts of ways during the writing process; for being my greatest fan, and for providing lots of invaluable content suggestions (especially relating to Polish art, industry, geography, and the story of Marek Kamiński). And, of course, for all the delicious cheesecakes she baked in aid of this project. You are my expert on everything, mum!

Michał Bryś has patiently and lovingly supported me in many, many ways for all the months when I was completely immersed in the world of writing. Thank you for all your thoughtful advice and suggestions, further content ideas, pertinent comments and fact-checking, pasta-and-tomato sauces, teas and coffees, for all the laughs, and for being my greatest fan, too.

A huge thank you to Greg Stecki, who has been my personal expert on Polish and European history, helping me with the structure and content of the history chapter. I could not have written a short history of Poland without his impressive knowledge, advice and fun fact ideas.

Thank you to my grandparents, Jadwiga and Kazimierz, for being my faithful supporters, for their suggestions relating to Polish geography and for sharing traditional Polish items from their personal collection to be photographed and used as illustrations to Chapter 2.

I would also like to thank Michał Kunik for putting us in contact with our designer, Luiza Pindral, as well as for all his additional, technical advice, content suggestions regarding the history and geography of Poland, and for fact-checking. Thank you for acting as the self-appointed *dobry duch* for my part of this project.

I would also like to take this opportunity to express my gratitude to my wonderful educators – Pani Jarosława Makus and Pan Adam Franiuk from *Gimnazjum Nr 7* in Wrocław, as well as my tutors from Leeds Beckett University, especially Dr Joanne Watkiss. My becoming an author is in no small part due to their support and inspirational approach to teaching. You saw and encouraged the writer in me long before I did myself.

And finally, to all my friends at home and abroad – wherever our 'at-homes' might be – for always keeping me inspired, for all these years.

Introduction

Polish people, or those with Polish heritage, now make up a significant part of the population of the United Kingdom. At the time of writing there are thought to be at least 800,000 Polish nationals living in the UK, with Polish now the second most commonly spoken language on British soil. Although many Poles return home from the UK every year, thousands continue to leave Poland to start a new life in Britain.

This population movement, and the cultural changes which have accompanied it, represents the most significant population shift in the UK since World War II. Yet most British people know very little about Poland and the important historic links between the two countries over the centuries. Fewer still realise that Polish service personnel and civilians carried out vital roles in some of the key events of World War II, including the decoding of the German Enigma machine and the iconic Battle of Britain. During the latter, over one hundred Polish Spitfire pilots flew alongside their British counterparts to defend British shores against Germany's aerial firepower.

A first of its kind
Poles in the UK is the first book to tell the amazing story of the positive contribution that Polish people, and those with Polish heritage, have made to the UK over the years. In the book you will find details of scientific advances, information on artistic contributions, tales of heroism, acts of compassion and everyday stories from the lives of Polish people living and working in the UK today. These are all set against the backdrop of the historic ties between the two countries and the many ways in which these successful nations are still linked today.

Our book, therefore, aims to provide both a historical perspective on the contributions of Polish people to the UK, and an important insight into the many ways in which they form part of a modern, vibrant and multicultural Britain in the twenty-first century.

The book is collaboration between a British and a Polish author, both of whom have been fascinated by each other's country and language since childhood. The fall of communism in Poland and neighbouring countries, which took place in the late 1980s and early 1990s, came between their births, paving the way for the enlargement of the European Union. This would be the trigger for the current generation of Poles moving to the UK, which included the Polish co-author of this book.

We have taken special care to make sure that the book is accessible to the widest possible range of readers, both British and Polish. It is our hope that readers of all ages will enjoy reading the book and learning all sorts of things they never knew about Poland, Polish people and culture.

A wider project

The book is just one part of a wider project which is being run through the UK charity The British Polonia Foundation, which has published the book. The authors and the project team have also provided, or are planning, the following additional resources and activities:

- A companion Facebook page to the book, with educational resources, additional stories, information and updates.
  www.facebook.com/polesintheuk
- School and college workshops, where children and young people at primary, secondary and post-16 level will have the chance to learn more about the shared history of Poland and the UK, and the many contributions of Polish people to this country.

Get in touch

We realise that any project such as this is never truly 'finished', as new stories and information are always coming forward to add to what has already been recorded. In recognition of this we encourage you to contact the project team, using the contact details on p. 247, if you wish to share your own perspective on the contribution of Poles to the UK.

Dziękujemy i życzymy Państwu przyjemnej lektury!

Brin Best & Maria Helena Żukowska
Leeds, West Yorkshire – July 2016

Pronouncing Polish Sounds
A simplified guide

A, a   short 'ah', as in the English word 'tap'
Ą, ą   nasal sound, similar to 'om' or 'on'
C, c   'ts', as in the English word 'bats'
Ć, ć   soft 'ch', similar to that in the English word 'cheese'
E, e   'eh', as in the English word 'text'
Ę, ę   another nasal sound, similar to 'em' or 'en'
G, g   'gh', as in the English word 'group'
H, h   'kh', similar to the 'h' in English, but it is always pronounced, and slightly harder
I, i   'ee', as in the English word 'teeth'
J, j   'y', as in the English word 'you'
Ł, ł   'w', as in the English word 'wood'
Ń, ń   slightly softer 'n', similar to the 'n' sound in the English word 'need'
O, o   short 'oh', as in the English word 'top'
Ó, ó   'oo', as in the English word 'too'
R, r   hard, rolling 'r' sound
Ś, ś   soft 'sh'
U, u   'oo', as in the English word 'too'; the same as 'ó'
W, w   'v', as in the English word 'vest'
Y, y   similar to the English 'i' in words such as 'bill', 'till'.
Ź, ź   'zh', but a slightly softer version of 'ż' (see below)
Ż, ż   hard 'zh', similar to the sound in the English word 'leisure'.

The following combination of letters produce the following sounds:

Ch, ch   same as 'h'
Cz, cz   'ch' or 'tch', similar to 'ć' but harder, as in the English word 'switch'
Sz, sz   hard 'sh', as in the English word 'shark'
Dz, dz   best described as a 'z' pronounced immediately after the 'd'.
Dź, dź   soft 'j', similar to 'dż', but softer (see below)
Dż, dż   'j', as in the English word 'junction'
Rz, rz   the same as 'ż'

Usually, whenever there is an 'i' after a consonant, it makes the preceding consonant sound softer. For example, the 'c' in the Polish word 'cena' reads like a 'ts' – 'tseh-na'. But, when an 'i' appears after the 'c', for example in the Polish word 'ciasto', it becomes a soft 'ch' – 'chah-sto'.

The remaining letters, b, d, f, k, l, m, n, p, s, t and z, are all pronounced in the same way as in English.

PART ONE
POLAND IN THE WORLD

CHAPTER 1

A Short History of Poland

This chapter describes the tumultuous history of Poland over the centuries, charting the important people, powerful groups and bloody wars that have – quite literally – shaped the country of Poland for over a thousand years. The chapter also presents a timeline of the key historical events of Poland which have led to its people settling in the UK, over the centuries.

Poland in the World

An ancient legend has it that three mythical brothers founded their respective countries: Lech (representing Poland), Czech (symbolising Czech Republic) and Rus (standing for today's Ukraine, Belarus and Russia). Looking for a place to settle, the brothers separated. Czech left to the south, Rus went east and Lech departed to the west.

Lech arrived in a land full of forests, rivers and fertile fields. He even spotted a white eagle's nest at the top of an ancient oak, and he liked it so much he decided to build his settlement in the shade of the tree. According to the myth, this is why the white eagle is the symbol of Poland – and it is always portrayed against a red backdrop, because in the legend Lech saw the eagle in the red light of a sunset.

Lech called his new settlement Gniezno (from Polish *gniazdo* – 'a nest'). This is where our myth ends and history begins, as Gniezno, a town in central Poland, was the country's first historical capital.

Lech, Czech, Rus and the White Eagle, in an artwork by Walery Eljasz-Radzikowski [1841–1905]

THE BEGINNINGS

Polish people belong to the **Slavic** ethno-linguistic group, the largest branch of the Indo-European group of peoples in Europe.

Our short history of Poland will begin in the tenth century, with the Polans (*Polanie*) tribe, native to the areas which constitute much of today's Poland. Even though various Slavic tribes inhabited these areas for many centuries before them, it is the Polans who are often credited as being the forefathers of the modern Polish nation.

Their name originated, most probably, from the Polish word *pole*, meaning 'field'. One reason for this might be that the Polans' livelihood depended heavily on farming and agriculture.

CHAPTER 1: A Short History of Poland

The Polans incorporated many other local groups and tribes. Their culture was Slavic, with a well-developed mythology celebrating nature and the elements. They formed villages which, in turn, made up larger settlements. Each such network of settlements had its chief.

One such chief, Prince **Mieszko I of Poland** [c.930–992], became the first documented ruler of Poland, from c.960 until his death. He unified the various tribes inhabiting the Polish lands, which was the first step towards the formation of Poland as a country.

Many sources seem to suggest that Mieszko I was the grandfather of Cnut the Great, also known as Canute, the king of England in the early eleventh century, thus hinting at a very early Anglo-Polish link.

In 966, the **Baptism of Poland** took place, when Prince Mieszko accepted the Christian belief through a ceremonial baptism. The symbolic baptism of the ruler gave way to the Christianisation of Poland, as paganism was increasingly pushed out.

The Baptism of Poland is also commonly regarded as the starting point for the country's statehood. The year 1025 saw the coronation of Prince Mieszko's successor, Bolesław I the Brave (*Bolesław Chrobry* in Polish), as the first king of the now officially Christian Poland.

However, Poland did not remain a unified country for long. In 1138, Prince Bolesław III the Wrymouth (*Bolesław Krzywousty* in Polish) decided to divide Poland into separate dukedoms – one for each of his then four sons. This was in an attempt to stop his sons fighting over who should inherit and rule the

An imagined portrait of Prince Mieszko I, Poland's first documented ruler (painted by Jan Matejko some time in the 1800s)

The millennium of Christianity in Poland (in 1966) was celebrated through special stamps in several countries

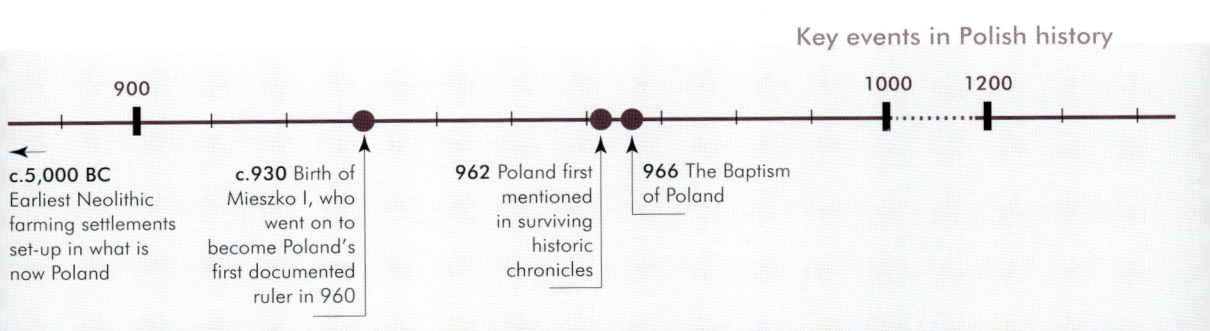

Key events in Polish history

- **c.5,000 BC** Earliest Neolithic farming settlements set-up in what is now Poland
- **c.930** Birth of Mieszko I, who went on to become Poland's first documented ruler in 960
- **962** Poland first mentioned in surviving historic chronicles
- **966** The Baptism of Poland

17

Poland in the World

CNUT THE GREAT – AN ANGLO-POLISH MONARCH?

King Canute, also called Cnut the Great, was the son of Sweyn Forkbeard (king of Denmark, England and Norway). While we cannot be entirely clear as to who Canute's mother was, most sources point to Sigrid, also referred to as Gunhild. Some medievalists have proposed that the name of Sigrid could have been an alternative, Scandinavian version of Świętosława – the daughter of Mieszko I of Poland and his wife, Dobrawa. Świętosława's name was likely changed by the Norse chronicle writers. Some early Scandinavian chronicles suggest that Sweyn Forkbeard's wife was a Polish princess, or a sister of the Polish king Bolesław I the Brave (Mieszko and Dobrawa's son). This seems to show that Sigrid and Świętosława were the same person – meaning that King Canute's mother was Polish and that he was the grandson of a Polish monarch.

country after their father's death. This was called 'feudal fragmentation' and lasted for over 180 years.

Feudal fragmentation lessened the influence of the monarchy over townships, which in turn enabled the development of a prototype local government structure. However, it also meant that the fragmented country appeared weaker to its neighbours, and it soon lost some territories to the **Margraviate of Brandenburg** (a separate kingdom at the time, and one of the German states today), as well as to the **Teutonic Knights**. The Teutonic Knights were a powerful Catholic military and religious order, with whom Poland would have much trouble until the fifteenth century, as will be explained later.

What is more, in 1241 Poland was also attacked in a Mongolian invasion, started earlier in the thirteenth century by Emperor Genghis Khan himself – the founder and long-term ruler of the Mongol Empire. The invasion that reached Poland was led by Genghis Khan's grandson, Batu Khan. One significant battle during this invasion was the Battle of

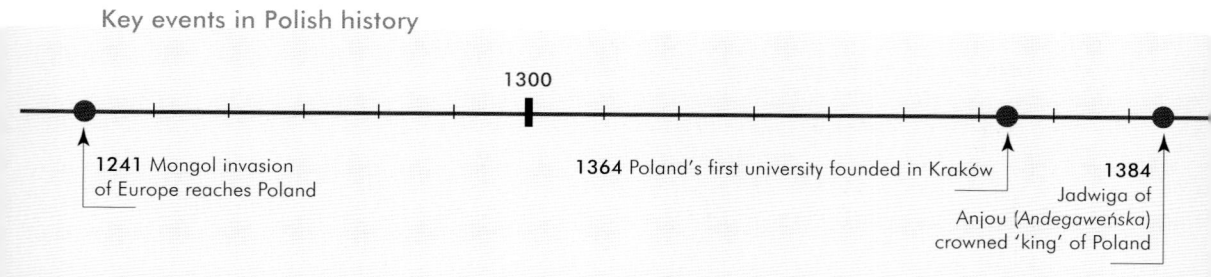

Key events in Polish history

1241 Mongol invasion of Europe reaches Poland

1300

1364 Poland's first university founded in Kraków

1384 Jadwiga of Anjou (Andegaweńska) crowned 'king' of Poland

Legnica (1241), a town in today's Lower Silesia region, which was won by the Mongol army.

THE MIDDLE AGES

The country was unified again in early fourteenth century, and in 1335 the first Congress of Visegrád (a historic town in northern Hungary) took place. Attended by the Czech, Hungarian and Polish rulers, its aims were to discuss matters relating to land, as well as the disagreements with the Teutonic Order.

In the latter part of the fourteenth century, the reign of **Kazimierz the Great** (*Kazimierz Wielki* in Polish) brought some much-needed developments. Poland's first higher education institution, today's Jagiellonian University, was founded in Kraków in 1364; it is one of the world's oldest universities. Castles were built and expanded, towns were modernised and the first written codes of law were formally introduced and defined. What is more, peace with the Czech and Teutonic states was established after some earlier turmoil.

A portrait of Queen Jadwiga by the Polish-Italian painter Marcello Bacciarelli, painted 1768–1771

When Kazimierz died in 1370 without a legitimate son, his nephew Louis I of Hungary (*Ludwik Węgierski* in Polish) became the king of Poland – Hungary was, at the time, Poland's main ally. However, Louis did not have any sons, either. He took care of the issue of succession by offering the nobility (*szlachta*) many new privileges, in exchange for recognising his daughter, Jadwiga, as lawful heir to the throne. And so, with the nobility successfully persuaded, Jadwiga was crowned king of Poland at the age of 10 or 11, after Louis's death. Because of the law of primogeniture, she could not formally use the title of 'queen'.

THE VISEGRÁD GROUP

Over five centuries after the first congress, the leaders of Czech Republic, Hungary and Poland would meet again in Visegrád for another summit, in 1991. This was to discuss political issues which arose following the collapse of the Soviet Union earlier that year. Today, the term 'Visegrád Group' is still used with reference to the four Central European countries of the Czech Republic, Hungary, Poland and Slovakia. These nations continue to maintain and promote their cultural, economic and political partnership.

Poland in the World

Did you know?
Nowadays, every July the village of Grunwald is transformed into a medieval town, complete with a fair and an annual historic battle re-enactment. For its 600th anniversary in 2010, the battle was re-enacted by over 2,200 actors and medieval enthusiasts, and attracted over 100,000 spectators from around the globe. The medieval show at Grunwald came top of the list of Poland's main tourist attractions in 2016, based on a poll conducted by the Polish Tourism Organisation.

Jadwiga was married two years later to Władysław II Jagiełło, the Grand Duke of Lithuania, who automatically became the king of Poland as part of an agreement sealed by the Union of Krewo in 1385. The aim of the agreement was to create the **Polish-Lithuanian Union** – a unified country incorporating Poland and the Grand Duchy of Lithuania. This was meant to strengthen the status of both nations in the eyes of their common threat, the Teutonic Order.

Meanwhile, the Teutonic Knights were extending their influence over Poland. They were initially invited by High Duke Konrad I of Masovia (*Konrad Mazowiecki* in Polish) to help the Polish army invade and Christianise the pagan Baltic Prussians (or Old Prussians), who inhabited the north-east of the country. This was endorsed by Pope Gregory IX.

During this period, the Teutonic Knights were expanding **Malbork Castle**, which is still the world's largest fortress in terms of surface area (▶ p. 53). With such impressive headquarters, the Knights began setting up their own, independent

An early engraving of Malbork Castle

CHAPTER 1: A Short History of Poland

The Battle of Grunwald (Bitwa pod Grunwaldem) by the Polish painter Jan Matejko, painted 1878

state. Once they assumed significant power, they declared war with Poland and invaded Polish Pomerania, a large region in the north of the country, which stretches along the Polish coast of the Baltic Sea.

The peak of these troubles dates to 1410, when Europe witnessed one of its largest battles of medieval times – the **Battle of Grunwald** – which saw approximately 60,000 soldiers on the battlefield. The battle

Key events in Polish history

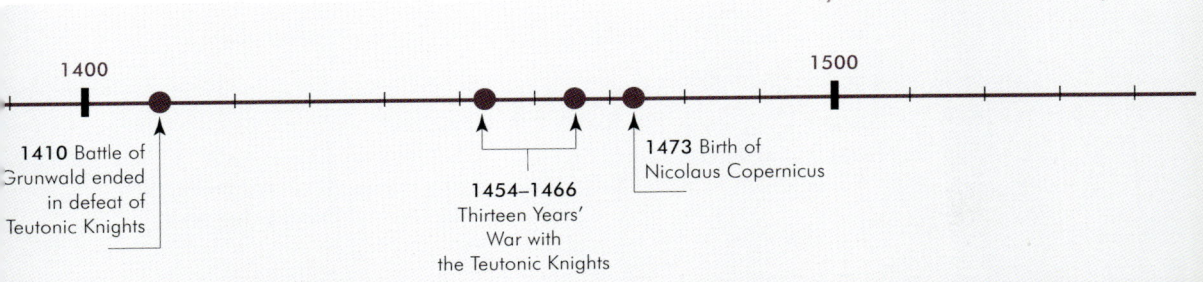

1400 — 1500

1410 Battle of Grunwald ended in defeat of Teutonic Knights

1454–1466 Thirteen Years' War with the Teutonic Knights

1473 Birth of Nicolaus Copernicus

21

Poland in the World

resulted in a resounding victory of the Polish-Lithuanian army over the Teutonic Order. It is safe to say that the Battle of Grunwald is, for Polish schoolchildren, the equivalent of the Battle of Hastings – every student knows the date.

THE GOLDEN AGE

In the years following their defeat at Grunwald, and after some further conflicts with the Kingdom of Poland, the Teutonic Knights' influence over Pomerania gradually diminished. This allowed Poland to regain access to the Baltic Sea and the mouth of the Vistula (*Wisła*) river. This development was of strategic importance, as the river was a major route for exporting grain to the rest of Europe – including to Britain. This breakthrough helped to develop trade in Poland and contributed to the country's significant economic growth in this period.

The sixteenth century is referred to as the **Golden Age** in the history of Poland. The country was among the largest in Europe, with significant partnerships with, and influence over, other countries. Poland was also the continent's main exporter of agricultural produce and timber.

SCOTS IN POLAND

Many Scottish merchants spotted the opportunity to trade on the flourishing Polish market. Reputable Polish-Scottish trading routes were established, such as the Gdańsk-Aberdeen route, dealing mostly with commodities such as wool products, various types of cloth and household ironware items. Numerous Scots accumulated significant wealth from their trade with Poland, took on Polish citizenship and settled permanently in Polish cities, such as Gdańsk, Kraków and Lublin.

It seems that Poland's religious freedom laws might have been another reason why Scottish people saw the country as particularly attractive. Poland offered them protection from discrimination or persecution on the grounds of their beliefs, be they Calvinist, Catholic, Episcopal or any others.

The Scottish population in Poland became substantial for the time, and was organised into well-established communities. According to the website www.scotland.org: 'by the 1600s, there were an estimated 30,000 Scots living in Poland'. Today, traces of this ancient Scottish presence in Poland can still be found in the form of Scots place names and surnames.

Find out more

The Polish-Scottish Heritage website: **www.polishscottishheritage.co.uk**

CHAPTER 1: **A Short History of Poland**

The Baltic coast city of Gdańsk was at that time one of Europe's most important market towns and also a **Hanseatic League city**. The League was an international union of trade towns and merchant guilds, located on the coasts of the North Sea and the Baltic Sea, which supported one another economically and politically. This included several ports in England such as London, King's Lynn and Hull. In King's Lynn it is still possible to see the last surviving Hanseatic building in England, a warehouse dating to 1475.

This was also a time of political development. In 1493 the first session of the General *Sejm*, the prototype of the Polish Parliament, took place. The king was joined by two chambers in making decisions: the Senate (*Senat*) and the Lower House (*Sejm*). This meant that the king could no longer pass laws without parliament's approval. **Democracy** continued to develop, gradually pushing out the monarchy.

It was also a Golden Age for science, especially mathematics and astronomy, with the likes of Nicolaus Copernicus (*Mikołaj Kopernik* in Polish) making their revolutionary discoveries (▶ p. 103). Humanism was now the dominant philosophy, and Poland became a progressive multi-ethnic, multi-faith country where Calvinism, Islam, Judaism, Lutheranism and the Orthodox Church co-existed with Catholicism.

In 1569 the Polish-Lithuanian Commonwealth was formed, and in 1573 the Commonwealth held the **Warsaw Confederation**. This Confederation was very important,

Did you know?

Over the course of its long history, Poland has had some of the world's most unusually-named rulers. Here are some creative, strange and undoubtedly unique examples:

- Władysław I the Elbow-high (*Władysław I Łokietek*)
- Mieszko I the Tanglefoot (*Mieszko I Plątonogi*)
- Bolesław IV the Curly (*Bolesław IV Kędzierzawy*)
- Bolesław II the Generous (*Bolesław II Szczodry*)
- Władysław II the Exile (*Władysław II Wygnaniec*)
- Henry the Bearded (*Henryk I Brodaty*)
- Henry II the Pious (*Henryk II Pobożny*)
- Bolesław V the Chaste (*Bolesław V Wstydliwy*)
- Bolesław III the Wrymouth (*Bolesław III Krzywousty*)
- Bolesław II the Horned (*Bolesław II Rogatka*)
- Władysław III the Spindleshanks (*Władysław III Laskonogi*).

Key events in Polish history

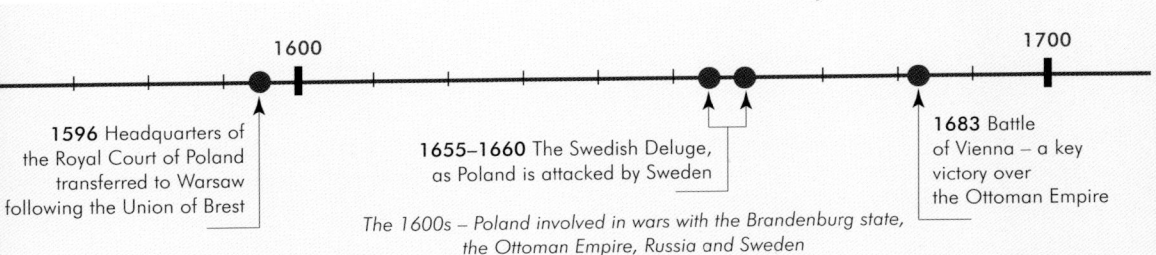

1596 Headquarters of the Royal Court of Poland transferred to Warsaw following the Union of Brest

1655–1660 The Swedish Deluge, as Poland is attacked by Sweden

The 1600s – Poland involved in wars with the Brandenburg state, the Ottoman Empire, Russia and Sweden

1683 Battle of Vienna – a key victory over the Ottoman Empire

23

Poland in the World

Did you know?

Polish people played an important role in the founding of Jamestown, the first English settlement on the east coast of North America. The practical skills of the Polish artisans who travelled there (first arriving in 1608) were focussed especially on glass-making and other essential materials. It helped the early settlers develop and expand their presence in what is now Virginia, USA. The earliest Polish travellers helped contribute to the development of the first settlements in North America by the English, which has resulted in the distant family links to England which millions of citizens of the USA still have to this day.

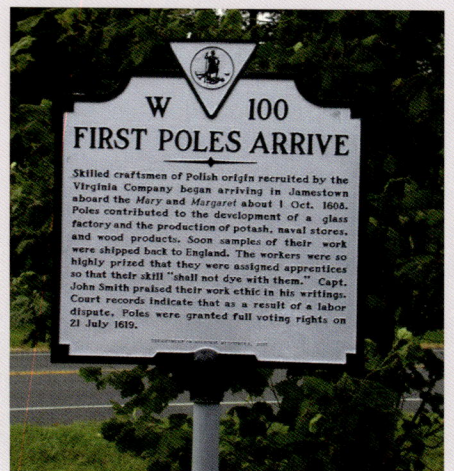

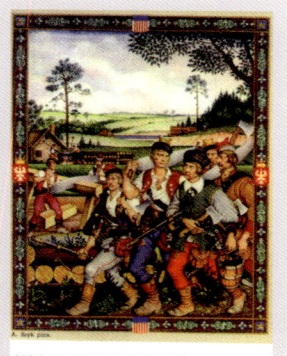

because it granted, by law, the freedom of religion and equal rights for the followers of all faiths – the first ever declaration of this kind in Europe. Poland soon became a safe haven for people fleeing religious persecution in other European countries.

After Zygmunt II Augustus (*Zygmunt II August* in Polish), the last of the Jagiellons Dynasty, died without heirs, the 'free election' system was introduced – whereby the monarchy was not hereditary anymore, but kings were elected by the nobility.

THE TURBULENT SIXTEENTH AND SEVENTEENTH CENTURIES

In late sixteenth and early seventeenth centuries, Poland was involved in various wars with Sweden (following a Swedish invasion known as the Swedish Deluge), Russia, the Cossacks (the East-Slavic inhabitants of today's Ukraine and parts of Russia) and the Turkish Empire, also known as the Ottoman Empire.

CHAPTER 1: A Short History of Poland

In 1683, when the Ottoman army attacked Vienna (the capital of today's Austria), the Habsburg court asked the Polish king, Jan III Sobieski, for military help. Although the exact figures remain unknown, the Ottoman army was substantial – estimates from different sources range from about 90,000 to 300,000 soldiers. For the **Battle of Vienna**, Jan III Sobieski mobilised approximately 27,000 soldiers and joined the Austrian and German armies, taking leadership of an estimated 90,000 troops overall.

Despite its large number of troops, the Ottoman Army was defeated at Vienna. As the Supreme Commander of the battle, Jan III Sobieski is commonly credited for the victory. As a result of the battle, the Ottoman Empire retreated from Central Europe and eventually lost control over the previously-invaded south of Hungary and Transylvania (a region in today's central Romania). Crucially, this stopped the Ottoman Empire's expansion into Europe.

THE PARTITIONS AND STRUGGLE FOR INDEPENDENCE

Despite the joint Austro-German-Polish efforts at Vienna nearly a century earlier, in 1772 the Kingdom of Prussia (today's Germany), Habsburg Austria and Russia made a pact to carry out the **First Partition of Poland**. This forcefully divided some of its lands between these three states.

The invaders were able to partition Poland because it was by then a much weakened state. The country could not afford to carry out the necessary reforms as the nobility, magnates and clergy refused to pay higher taxes for this purpose. This problem was meant to be addressed

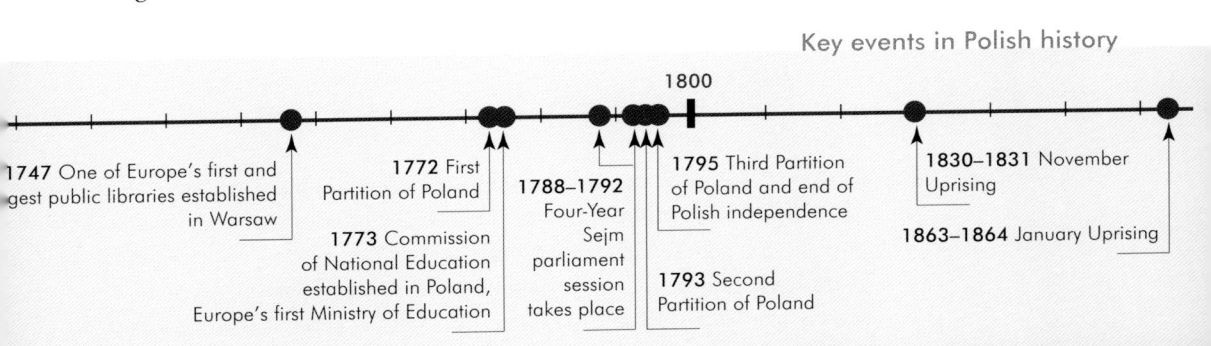

Key events in Polish history

1747 One of Europe's first and largest public libraries established in Warsaw

1772 First Partition of Poland

1773 Commission of National Education established in Poland, Europe's first Ministry of Education

1788–1792 Four-Year Sejm parliament session takes place

1793 Second Partition of Poland

1795 Third Partition of Poland and end of Polish independence

1830–1831 November Uprising

1863–1864 January Uprising

25

Poland in the World

The Passing of the 3rd of May Constitution, 1791 (Uchwalenie Konstytucji 3 Maja 1791) – painted by Kazimierz Wojniakowski, 1806

by the Great *Sejm* between 1788 and 1792 (a specially called four-year parliament session). It introduced economic and educational reforms in order to aid the development of the country and to regain its lost lands.

In 1791 the *Sejm* put forward the **Constitution of May 3** – Europe's first constitution. It introduced a range of important advancements, such as offering the peasants state protection and guaranteeing their rights. Unfortunately, despite the reformist nature of the constitution, further partitions of Poland took place, with the second in 1793 and third in 1795.

The **Third Partition** resulted in all of the remaining Polish lands becoming completely incorporated into Austria, Prussia and Russia. Poland would disappear from the maps of Europe for a long time.

The **Polish Legions** were then set up in Italy by refugee soldiers and volunteers. These groups later joined Napoleon Bonaparte's war efforts in exchange for his promise to create the Duchy of Warsaw – this would help Poland regain its independent territory.

Further developments were halted by Napoleon's defeat in Russia in 1812. Rather than being independent, the Duchy entered Russia's sphere

CHAPTER 1: A Short History of Poland

of influence. In 1815 it was divided again between Prussia and Russia, while Austria still held on to the Polish lands it captured in the first partition. As a result of this, there was a series of Polish uprisings against foreign rule and control.

> **Did you know?**
> As a result of the partitions, Poland disappeared completely from the maps and **ceased to exist as an independent country for 123 years**. Therefore, it could be said that five generations of Poles lived without a country. During this time, speaking Polish and cultivating Polish traditions was largely persecuted, but Poles still managed to maintain and preserve their culture and language.

THE FIGHT FOR FREEDOM AND THE FIRST WAVE OF MIGRATION FROM POLAND

Throughout the years of the partitions, the Polish insurgents opposed the forced Russification and Germanisation of the Polish people, as well as ethnic discrimination of the Poles. After each of the main uprisings, Russia tightened its grip on the Polish territories, attempting to put a stop to any pro-independence activities.

Existing restrictions were gradually increased to include laws prohibiting Polish citizens from speaking their mother tongue in public, teaching children the Polish language in schools, or cultivating Polish traditions. The Russian and German invaders were the strictest in this respect, while in the Austrian Partition Poles were allowed slightly more freedom from persecution.

The 1830 **November Uprising** led to the first major wave of emigration from Poland. Soldiers, the nobility, poets and artists started to leave for France, Belgium and, in smaller numbers, for Britain. Fryderyk Chopin (▶ p. 120), who emigrated to Paris, is one notable example. This is also when the Anglo Polish Society (which is still active today) was founded by the British poet Thomas Campbell, 'to offer sympathy and support to Polish insurgents'.

In 1863, the **January Uprising** began (and lasted for over a year, until October 1864), the largest in the history of the country. Throughout the course of the uprising, approximately 200,000 Polish soldiers and volunteers took part in around 1,200 different battles. Many prominent independence activists and artists were among the volunteers, including the playwright Apollo Korzeniowski, father of the Polish-British novelist Joseph Conrad (▶ p. 132).

The uprising was unsuccessful and resulted in even harsher treatment of the Polish citizens by Russia. Insurgents were later persecuted, and most of them were executed or deported to Siberia. The failure of the January Uprising was a shock to the Polish people, however they did not lose hope of regaining their country.

Throughout the nineteenth century, Polish volunteer troops often joined other countries' independence struggles, most notably fighting alongside Hungarian and Italian insurgents. The Polish motto **'For Our Freedom and Yours'** became iconic to independence fighters in many European countries and it is still sometimes quoted today.

INDEPENDENCE AND THE INTERWAR YEARS

Even though none of the uprisings proved successful, the efforts of the Polish people without a country succeeded in one very important way. The underground activities and unofficial schooling helped to maintain a strong Polish community, together with its traditions and language, despite the laws which tried to suppress them.

As Poland was not an independent state, it did not have an official army. Therefore, it could not play a large role in **World War I**. However, the Armistice Day on 11 November 1918 was especially significant to Poland, as it brought the country its independence.

Polish independence happened at the same time that the whole of Europe saw large-scale political changes following World War I. The

THE 'MIRACLE OF THE VISTULA'

In 1919 the border had still not been agreed between the newly-independent Poland and the yet-to-be internationally recognised Soviet state. This sparked the Polish-Soviet war, which culminated, in August 1920, with the **Battle of Warsaw**, sometimes referred to as the 'Miracle of the Vistula'. The Polish forces defeated the Red Army, in what was one of the most significant military victories in twentieth century Europe.

After the Bolsheviks rose to power, their radical plan was to extend their interpretation of a socialist revolution on to the west of Europe. This was cut short by their defeat in the Battle of Warsaw. Success in the battle also enabled Poland to maintain its independence, by retaining control of its eastern border.

Two months after the 'Miracle of the Vistula', Polish and Soviet officials signed the Treaty of Riga – a peace agreement which also settled the issue of the Polish-Russian border.

CHAPTER 1: A Short History of Poland

The evolution of the Polish national coat of arms over the centuries, as depicted on a set of stamps

Habsburg Empire collapsed, Germany was declared defeated and Russia was significantly weakened by its own internal troubles of the Russian Civil War. The latter saw a series of violent revolutions in which the Bolsheviks, a political and military faction in favour of a radical kind of socialism, had overthrown the Russian monarchy.

The Bolsheviks then came to power with the help of their Red Army, led by Vladimir Lenin, Joseph Stalin and Leon Trotsky. As a result of the Civil War, the Russian Empire was overthrown and eventually the Soviet Union was established. This would mark the beginning of a long and troublesome communist era in Russia and much of the east of Europe.

Various Polish activists and politicians worked internationally to bring the Polish cause to the attention of other countries. As a result of all these factors, Poland regained most of its former lands.

The three politicians who are the most celebrated and credited with reinstating Polish statehood were Józef Piłsudski (later Poland's Chief of State), Roman Dmowski and Ignacy Jan Paderewski OBE (diplomat and world-famous pianist and composer, who performed for Queen Victoria herself).

Soon the **Republic of Poland** was founded, which was not a monarchy anymore, and equal voting rights for all men and women were introduced later in November 1918. The Republic was a multi-party system. This is a system typical of democratic countries, in which political parties are able to run for the national election and potentially form a government. Poland was also a diverse state, with minority groups such as Belarusians, Germans, Jews, Ukrainians and others constituting around 30% of the population.

The interwar period was a time of unification, when all the lands previously incorporated into Austria, Prussia and Russia during the partitions were brought together to form Poland, once again. This involved introducing a new single currency for the whole country, and

Poland in the World

unifying railway systems, roads and traffic rules. This was no easy feat, since at the time vehicles on Austrian roads drove on the left, unlike in the other two partitions.

It was also a time of significant economic development, with the major port city of Gdynia built from scratch, and Poland's largest industrial complex of Silesia created and named the Upper Silesian Industrial Region. It became the heart of the country's mining and heavy industries, comparable to the north of England.

WORLD WAR II AND THE COMMUNIST STATE

Poland's further economic development was stopped by the beginning of **World War II**. The war started in the small hours of 1 September 1939, on what would have been the first day of school for Polish

The 'Little Insurgent' statue in Warsaw

THE TRAGEDY OF THE NAZI DEATH CAMPS

The death camps and concentration camps, sometimes wrongly referred to as 'Polish camps', were camps set up by the Nazi German forces in Germany and in German-occupied lands, including Poland. People sent to the camps, from within Poland and from other countries, were forced to carry out heavy labour, while imprisoned in inhumane conditions and denied their basic human rights.

The purpose of the camps was also to round up, isolate and kill people who were seen by the Nazi authorities as 'undesirable' in society. The camps were one of the most shocking instruments of the **Holocaust**, one of the worse examples in history of the inhumanity of people.

People suspected of being involved in the Polish resistance force, Polish civilians (especially those with a Jewish background), Romani people, gay people, people with disabilities, as well as those who were mentally ill, were all persecuted by the Nazi German forces and sent to the death camps.

Many of the people sent to the camps were random civilians, who were rounded up and captured in German raids as they were going about their daily routines in Polish towns and cities.

The setting up of the death and concentration camps by the Nazis on Polish soil was a great tragedy for the Polish nation. Among the victims of the camps, Polish Jews were the largest affected group. The total number of Polish prisoners killed in the Nazi death camps, of all religions and groups, numbered in the millions, although the true number will never be known.

CHAPTER 1: A Short History of Poland

students. Nazi Germany's attack on Gdańsk, Poland's historic northern city, marked the start of hostilities.

Just 16 days later, while the Polish army struggled with the German aggression in the west of the country, the Soviet Union unexpectedly invaded the east of Poland. This was secretly agreed earlier in the year by the German and Soviet rulers, who signed the Molotov–Ribbentrop Pact, sometimes referred to as the 'fourth partition of Poland'.

With two invasions, one on each side of the country, and without military help from the Allied forces, the situation in Poland was very serious. Despite this, the army and the various voluntary resistance groups, such as the underground **Home Army**, fought bravely to defend the country against the occupation. It was common for teenagers to enlist as soldiers and join the war effort as resistance activists, as was the case in the **Warsaw Uprising** (▶ p. 32).

Later, the Polish military struggles extended onto many other European front lines. Examples include the Polish army joining the Allies, including the British forces, in the Battle of Monte Cassino in Italy and, perhaps most notably, in the Battle of Britain (▶ p. 82). A unique soldier, Wojtek the Bear, helped during the Monte Cassino battle, as described on p. 84.

The war finally ended in 1945 following the defeat of the Nazis, and the Soviet troops crossed through Poland to march as far west as

An image from the forced resettlement of the citizens of Warsaw following the Uprising

Key events in Polish history

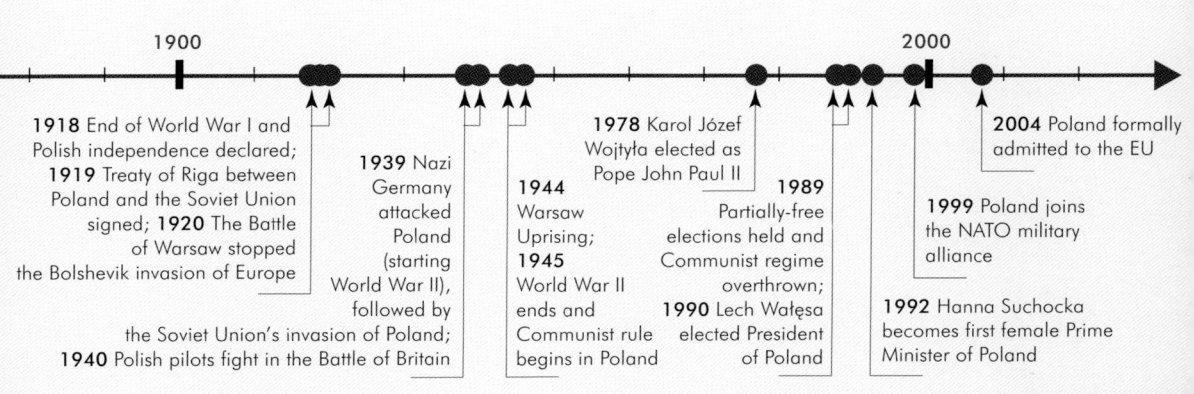

1900 — 2000

1918 End of World War I and Polish independence declared; **1919** Treaty of Riga between Poland and the Soviet Union signed; **1920** The Battle of Warsaw stopped the Bolshevik invasion of Europe

1939 Nazi Germany attacked Poland (starting World War II), followed by the Soviet Union's invasion of Poland; **1940** Polish pilots fight in the Battle of Britain

1944 Warsaw Uprising; **1945** World War II ends and Communist rule begins in Poland

1978 Karol Józef Wojtyła elected as Pope John Paul II

1989 Partially-free elections held and Communist regime overthrown; **1990** Lech Wałęsa elected President of Poland

1992 Hanna Suchocka becomes first female Prime Minister of Poland

1999 Poland joins the NATO military alliance

2004 Poland formally admitted to the EU

31

Poland in the World

THE WARSAW UPRISING

One important example of the young Poles' fight for freedom during World War II was the Warsaw Uprising of 1944. The operation was organised by the Polish Resistance force (the Home Army) and was Europe's largest military operation of its kind of the whole war.

The uprising begins

The uprising started on 1 August and lasted just over two months. Its aim was to free the capital from the hostile German occupation, but it had very limited support from the Allies. The fighters, many of them teenagers, were poorly and insufficiently armed, as well as vastly outnumbered by the Germans. Food shortages were also an issue.

The Nazi German forces retaliated against the Home Army's actions with great strength, destroying much of Poland's capital city in the process. The captured fighters, as well as thousands of civilians, including women and children, were executed by the Nazis. The German forces even attacked hospitals and residential districts.

Despite their brave efforts, after 63 days of dramatic struggle the fighters had to capitulate. The resistance did not have enough resources and could no longer sustain further military action. Over 10,000 soldiers of the Home Army and upwards of 150,000 civilians lost their lives in the Warsaw Uprising (although some sources suggest that the number of civilians killed was closer to 200,000).

The 'Planned Destruction of Warsaw'

In the aftermath of the uprising, the German forces carried out the 'Planned Destruction of Warsaw'. In addition to the damage which resulted from the uprising itself, the planned destruction aimed at tearing down what was left of the Polish capital.

Approximately 84% of the city on the western bank of the Vistula river, and an estimated 65% of the city overall, was completely destroyed by the end of the war. This included the planned burning of libraries and national archives, the destruction of key industrial buildings and plants, and the demolition of churches and places of worship. Many priceless and unique manuscripts and archival materials were lost, as were monuments and objects of particular historical and architectural significance.

As part of the destruction plan, large numbers of people were forcefully resettled from Warsaw. Over half a million inhabitants of Warsaw and its suburbs were forced to leave their homes. Some were transported to other areas of Poland and Germany. Others were sent to labour camps in Germany (around 90,000) or to the Nazi death camps (approximately 60,000; ▶ p. 30).

CHAPTER 1: A Short History of Poland

Leaving Warsaw at Candlemas

Didn't take a last look at our street.
We lived opposite
the old Gestapo prison
at number seven.
Why would I think
this was my last ride on a tram,
last game of hide and seek
in the courtyard?

It was February, willow buds
barely in view, the month when
candles are lit and snow
comes right up to the flats.

        Somewhere
on a frosty road
        wolves stop
to gaze in awe
at a girl holding a flame
who stamps her feet
to shake off the cold.

This poem first appeared in *At the Library of Memories*
by Maria Jastrzębska, published by Waterloo Press.
© Maria Jastrzębska

Berlin, in eastern Germany. Although it brought an end to the war, the involvement of the Soviet Union in post-war Poland was turbulent and violent. While Poland regained some of its western lands, it lost most of its eastern territories to the Soviet Union (parts of today's Belarus, Lithuania and Ukraine).

THE COMMUNIST ERA

After the war, the Soviet intrusion resulted in the implementation of a Communist regime in Poland. Although the Communist Government introduced some positive changes, such as free, compulsory state education for all, on the whole it was a repressive and often violent regime.

Warsaw's boy soldiers

The Home Army soldiers defending the city

The Uprising's Girl Scout post officers

An insurgent's grave, with the ruins of the capital city in the background

33

Poland in the World

A Polish milk ration coupon from 1983

The wartime resistance activists and soldiers were seen as a threat to the system, so they were persecuted, imprisoned and often executed, or forced to leave the country. Many of them were already in the UK at the end of the war, as they were involved in supporting the British forces – and these Poles found they could not go back home.

Back in Poland, state censorship and surveillance were common practice and civil rights were severely restricted, including freedom of speech and freedom to leave the country. The Polish economy kept declining, and in the 1970s and 1980s ration coupons were re-introduced for the majority of products, including bread, meat, chocolate, petrol, soap and even toilet roll. Poland's citizens were thrown back into economic hardship.

INTO DEMOCRACY, INTO THE FUTURE

Eventually, the 1980s brought a culmination of underground anti-communist activity. The system favoured the officials and those involved in some way in the Communist Party, which deepened social inequalities.

The people of Poland were also tired of the rapid economic decline and of not being able to express their views. Many people started to join or support the trade union **Solidarity** (*Solidarność* in Polish)**, led by the activist Lech Wałęsa** – an electrician at the Gdańsk Shipyard. The union called for less restrictive laws and increased civil rights.

With more and more people supporting Solidarity's protests, the union managed to arrange for discussions with the Communist Government. This was called the **Round Table Agreement**, and it eventually led to the non-violent overthrowing of Communist rule in 1989.

Poland's success in peacefully restoring democracy was the inspiration for other European nations living under communism to overthrow their respective governments. It soon resulted in a snowball of political changes, the fall of the Berlin Wall between East and West Germany being the most iconic.

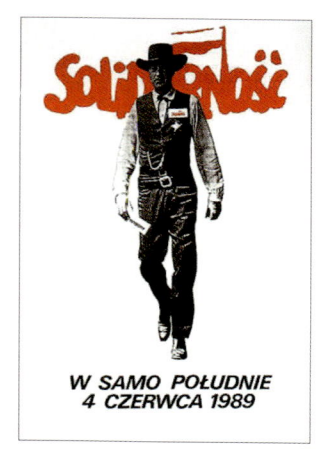

Lech Wałęsa, the second President of Poland (1990–1995)

A political poster from 1989 by Solidarity, featuring the actor Gary Cooper in his role in the famous movie *High Noon*

CHAPTER 1: A Short History of Poland

SUCCESS STORY

The worldwide leader of the Catholic church from 1978 to 2005 was a Polish man called **Karol Józef Wojtyła** [1920–2005] – better known to the world as Pope John Paul II. He was the second longest-serving pope in modern history, after Pope Pius IX. His wish was to place his church at the heart of a new religious alliance which would bring together Jews, Muslims and Christians. He was one of the most widely travelled leaders in history, visiting 129 different countries whilst pope. His visits to his home country of Poland were always greeted with huge joy and enormous crowds in this predominantly Catholic country. Pope John Paul II was made a saint in 2014, after two 'miracles' he carried out were formally recognised by the Catholic church.

The transition from a communist system to free-market capitalism in the 1990s was not easy. It resulted in an initial period of financial hardship and a temporary worsening of living conditions for many Polish citizens.

However, this eventually gave way to steady economic growth, with developments in all areas of governance and much social improvement. Today, Poland is one of the fastest-developing economies in Europe.

The historic centre of Kraków is a World Heritage Site and attracts hundreds of thousands of tourists from across the world every year

THE EUROPEAN POLAND – A NEW, HOPEFUL DESTINATION

Poland joined the European Union (the EU) in 2004. This was also when many Polish people decided to move to other European countries, including the UK. They travelled to work, study, improve their foreign language skills, or simply in search of a new challenge.

Some British people also went to work in Poland as a result of it joining the EU, with hundreds of international businesses setting up operations in the country. Furthermore, many British citizens found employment in Poland as English language teachers.

With the expansion of the EU, Europe saw a rise in cheap airline connections, including many budget

Poland in the World

POPULATION OF POLAND 1900–2010

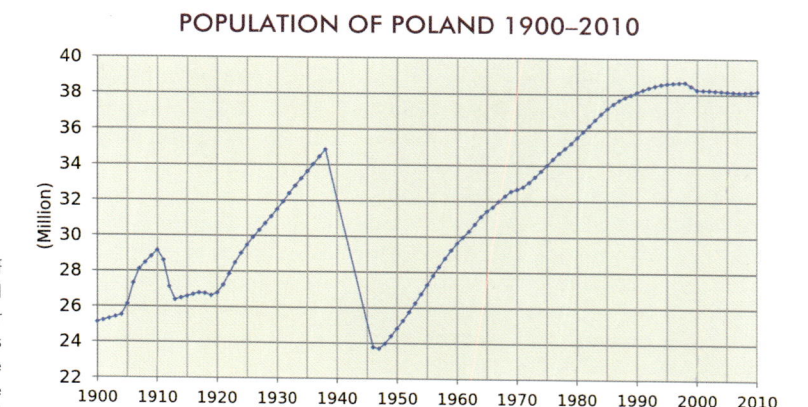

The population of Poland has risen and fallen dramatically over the last hundred years or so. Note the decline since Poland joined the EU in 2004.

This version of Poland's national flag, complete with the national coat of arms, is reserved for official use overseas and at sea.

UK-Poland flights, which became increasingly popular with British tourists. This made Polish cities and towns more accessible for weekend breaks and longer holidays.

Today, international tourism in Poland not only focusses on the buzzing capital, Warsaw, or the ever-popular and historic settlement of Kraków. It also encompasses such places as Wrocław, which holds the title of European Capital of Culture for 2016 (▶ p. 63), rural regions like the Masuria Lake District (▶ p. 45) and various upland locations such as the charming Bieszczady Mountains. All these places are now served by cheap flights from the UK, and British holiday makers – of all different kinds – now make an important contribution to the Polish tourist industry.

The Polish countryside, coastline, lake districts and mountainous regions attract more and more sightseers, beachgoers, hikers, climbers, bikers, watersports fans and ecotourists from around the world each year.

CHAPTER 1: A Short History of Poland

The territories of the Polish-Lithuanian Commonwealth in the early seventeenth century, as they would appear on a map of modern Europe

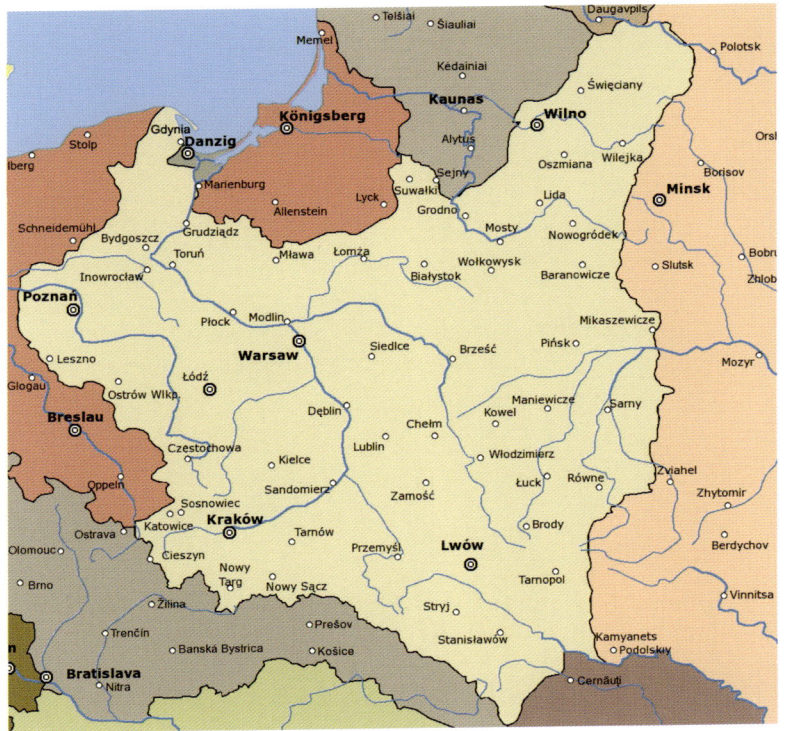

The lands of the Second Polish Republic, from 1921 to the start of World War II in 1939

Poland in the World

Poland's place within twenty-first century Europe

CHAPTER 2

The Geography of Poland

This chapter explores the diverse physical and human geography of Poland, highlighting some of the key landmarks, habitats and settlements of the country. The chapter presents many of the highly distinctive features of Poland, while also demonstrating its links to neighbouring countries and cultures.

Poland in the World

Poland is a medium-sized country in Central Europe, which is significantly larger than the UK in terms of land area (the UK covers only two thirds the land area of Poland). It is Europe's ninth largest country.

Poland has a very varied geography, with access to the Baltic Sea in the north-west, numerous mountainous regions in the south and everything from lake districts to forests and lowlands in between.

The Polish climate is temperate and combines maritime and continental characteristics. This means that the seasons are changeable. For example, winters tend to be frosty and snowy, but can quickly turn mild and wet. On the other hand, summers are usually hot and dry, although rain and thunderstorms are common. Spring and autumn are mild and comparable with those in the UK.

> **Did you know?**
> The highest ever recorded temperature in Poland was 40.2°C (Prószków, July 1921), and the lowest was -41.0°C (Siedlce, January 1940).

NATURAL WONDERS

Seaside fun

The **Polish Baltic coastline** is approximately 480 miles (773 kilometres) long. It boasts plenty of sandy beaches, dunes and cliffs, all usually bordered by woodland slightly further inland. These are starting to prove attractive to British holidaymakers looking for something completely different from (and significantly less expensive than) the traditional beach resorts of the Mediterranean coast countries.

The water in the Polish Baltic is always on the cool side (its average temperature in the summer months stays at approximately 18°C). However, this is no deterrent for those who love to swim and play in the sea, dip their toes in the water while walking along the shore, or build sandcastles.

> *If you search among the washed-up seaweed, or dig deep in the sand where the tide breaks, you may find pieces, or if you're lucky, large nuggets of amber.*
>
> Maja Karpowicz

40

CHAPTER 2: **The Geography of Poland**

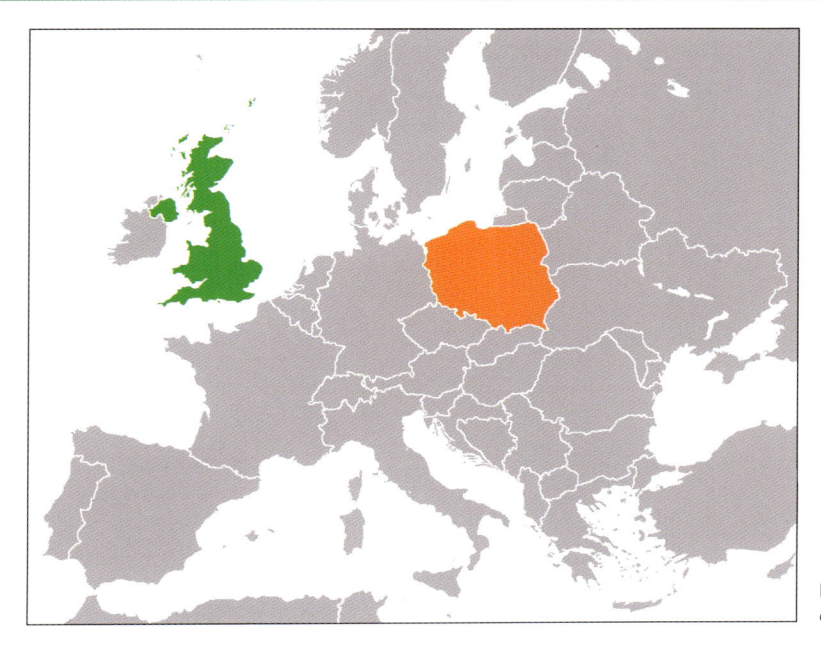

Poland and the UK in context, within Europe

Every summer seaside resorts buzz with water sports events, sand sculpture competitions, live music and arts festivals. Smaller, quieter villages offer a chance to enjoy unspoilt nature, while still tempting holidaymakers with homemade ice-cream, fresh *gofry* (a type of waffle) and local produce. Arts and crafts markets are also an integral part of coastal life. Their main attraction is usually jewellery made with Polish **amber** – the Baltic Sea's most beautiful resource.

Tourists who are up for adventure can go on a hunt for their very own pieces of amber. Amber is ancient, hardened tree resin that is occasionally found with insect 'inclusions', making it a real-life time capsule. It is used extensively in the jewellery industry.

Pieces of amber can often be found in the sand along the Baltic coast, the morning after a squall at sea. Those eager to find their own amber are encouraged to start looking at daybreak, before other explorers get there!

Amber jewellery comes in different shades and forms. Sometimes the gemstones are polished, at other times they are left in their more natural, rougher and irregular form, to reflect the gem's unique character

IMAGE: Maria H. Żukowska

41

Poland in the World

This topographic map shows some of the principal physical features of Poland, including the mountains in the south, the lake districts in the north and the major rivers traversing the country

POLISH GEOGRAPHY IN A NUTSHELL

Total area	120,726 square miles (312,679 square kilometres).
Population	approximately 38.5 million (2014 estimate), making Poland Europe's eighth most populous country.
Time zone	Central European Time, one hour ahead of the UK, and the same as Western European countries such as Spain, France, Germany and Italy.
Capital	Warsaw, in the central-east part of the country, with a population of over 1.7 million.
Neighbouring countries	(clockwise from the north-east): Russia (the exclave of Kaliningrad Oblast), Lithuania, Belarus, Ukraine, Slovakia, the Czech Republic and Germany.
Highest point	Rysy peak in the Tatra Mountains (*Tatry*), at 8,198 feet (2,499 metres).
Largest lake	Śniardwy in the Masuria Lakeland, at 43.9 square miles (113.8 square kilometres).
Deepest lake	Hańcza in the Masuria, with a maximum depth of 355 feet (110 metres).
Forest area	forests constitute around 30% of Poland's overall land area.

CHAPTER 2: **The Geography of Poland**

BAŁTYK

Soft, silken, yellow and white sands are not just found in Southern Europe, but in Poland, too. On hot summer days, the Baltic coast offers the best relief from the sun's rays in the sea's turquoise and navy depths.

In the seaport of **Świnoujście**, situated between the islands of Usedom (*Uznam*) and Wolin, there are plenty of seaside attractions, from bungee trampolines to inflatable slides and bouncy castles, all set up on the beach itself. Mini concerts are also staged here on platforms, allowing beachgoers to dance alongside the musicians — way into the night!

In addition to all this activity, there are restaurants and cafés located within walking distance of (or directly on) the sands, selling fresh Baltic fish, not unlike British fish and chips. At night, the typical seaside funfairs come alive with neon lights.

Maja Karpowicz

The soft, fine sand of the Polish Baltic coastline makes sunset walks along the shore especially pleasant

IMAGES: Maria H. Żukowska

Did you know?

One very unique place at the Polish seaside is the village of Łeba, one of the gateways to the **Słowiński National Park**. Tourists from all over Europe flock here to see the famous 'moving dunes'. The sand dunes of Łeba change their position throughout the year, moving as far as 32 feet (10 metres) per year. This is possible because of the processes of sand accumulation and relocation, in which the wind plays a key role. Łeba's beaches are also known for their near-white, soft and fine sand. They are considered among the most beautiful on the continent.

43

Poland in the World

THE SEVEN WONDERS OF POLAND

The following Seven Wonders were selected by the Polish public in a popular vote in 2007 (with the most popular first):

1. Wieliczka Salt Mine (in the Kraków metropolitan area).
2. Old Town in Toruń.
3. Malbork Castle.
4. Wawel Castle and Cathedral (in Kraków).
5. Elbląg Canal.
6. Old Town in Zamość.
7. Old Town and Market Square in Kraków.

All of these places, with the exception of the Elbląg Canal, are UNESCO World Heritage Sites. UNESCO stands for the United Nations Educational, Scientific and Cultural Organisation. The World Heritage Sites it promotes are places 'considered to be of outstanding value to humanity'. UNESCO-listed historical monuments in the UK include sites such as Stonehenge, the model industrial village of Saltaire (▶ p. 220) and the Tower of London.

The pristine Masuria Lakeland is an oasis of calm and tranquillity

CHAPTER 2: **The Geography of Poland**

Masuria is a first-rate destination for water sports

The Land of a Thousand Lakes

Other popular holiday destinations for Poles and visitors from the UK are the many **Polish lake districts**, notably Masuria, or Masurian Lakeland (*Mazury*). This region in the north-east of Poland is often referred to as the Land of a Thousand Lakes. It is the country's water sports, sailing and yachting hotspot. Many of the lakes are interconnected through canals, and together they form the Trail of the Great Masurian Lakes. The trail is approximately 80 miles (129 kilometres) long and navigable by boat.

Some of the lakes operate a quiet zone, where motorboats are prohibited, so that nature can thrive, while holidaymakers enjoy undisturbed peace and tranquillity. Fragrant forests, rich in wild mushrooms and berries, are never far away and ring out with the songs of exotic bird species which are completely new to British visitors. Many of the lakes also have their own little secret islands, waiting for sailors brave enough to reach and explore them.

Did you know?

In Masuria, you can keep sailing even when you have reached the end of a canal and just see dry land in front of you! For those wishing to sail the 51 miles (82 kilometres) of the **Elbląg Canal**, patches of grassy land on the way are not a problem. Built between 1844 and 1860, Elbląg Canal is fitted with an ingenious system of inclined planes and special boat carriers on rails, so you can skip between lakes without ever leaving your vessel. This even includes 'sailing' uphill on many parts of the route. The Canal is open to visitors all summer, and is a well-known historic monument because of its technological significance.

45

Poland in the World

Sailing along Elbląg Canal and watching its ingenious boat carrier system in action makes for a unique adventure

From the Sudetes to the Carpathians

The Polish mountainous regions in the south attract countless walkers, hikers and climbers from around the world all year round. Dramatic peaks, pastures on gently sloping hills, forests, lakes, streams, as well as picturesque refuges and shelters dotted along the path are all awaiting the visitor to this majestic part of Poland.

The gentle landscape of the **Sudetes** and the **Bieszczady Mountains**, in the westernmost and easternmost parts of Poland respectively, offer plenty of hill walks. In between them, the impressive peaks of the Tatra Mountains (also known as the Tatras) in central-southern Poland are an ideal destination for experienced hikers and mountaineers. There are also easier paths for those who just want to admire the stunning scenery.

Polish forests are home to countless natural monuments, such as this magnificent ash tree (*jesion*), known as Jesion Bolko, near Duszniki Zdrój in the Sudetes

IMAGE: Maria H. Żukowska

46

CHAPTER 2: **The Geography of Poland**

IMAGE: Jerzy Opioła

TATRA MOUNTAINS – ZAKOPANE

The **Tatras**, which surround the idyllic town of **Zakopane**, are snow-topped in winter and emerald-green in summer, when they offer an unparalleled hiking experience. There are crystal clear lakes in the area, and boats can be rented to explore and enjoy the sights the waters have in store. In the winter the town is a skiing resort. When covered in snow, it feels truly magical, with horse-drawn sleighs, glowing lights in the streets and warm log-fires inside the wooden restaurants.

Going to the summit of Giewont massif (at 6,217 feet, or 1,895 metres) at sunset to watch the peaks shine with rosy light is a breath-taking experience. After the climb, sipping on especially thick, rich hot chocolate in one of the cosy, rustic inns is equally as memorable.

The inhabitants of the Tatras, known as Highlanders or *Górale*, are very devoted to preserving their rich cultural heritage. The region is famous for its unique style of Polish folk art, traditional dress and music. The Highlanders' traditional songs and dances are always very sprightly and exciting to watch, let alone be involved in. So, if you come across a wedding on one of your hikes, then be prepared for a rare and captivating experience.

Maja Karpowicz

The Tatras straddle the Polish-Slovakian border. The Rysy summit towers over the Polish side of this dramatic range – at 2,499 metres (8,144 feet)

Poland in the World

The charming Samotnia mountain hut, located in the picturesque Karkonosze mountains (part of the Sudetes range), has a long history of offering shelter and hot food and drink to hikers

The Pieniny mountain range is part of the Polish Carpathians, in the south of the country. It attracts hikers with its green meadows and a highly varied flora and fauna, including many endemic plant species (plants which can only be found in this particular region)

Heathers can be found in the undergrowth of woodlands across Poland, such as here in the sandy ground of a coastal forest in Pomerania. Early autumn is the best time for forest walks in Poland, when heathers are in full bloom. This is also the peak of the wild mushroom-picking season in Polish forests

IMAGES: Maria H. Żukowska

CHAPTER 2: **The Geography of Poland**

The interior of the Białowieża Forest, one of Europe's most important protected areas

Did you know?

Poland has an extensive network of **protected areas** which support some of Europe's most important places for nature. As well as providing a haven for special habitats such as primeval forests, floodplain wetlands and pristine lakes, these protected areas are also home to many rare and threatened species of flora and fauna. Such species as European bison, elk, bear, wolf, lynx and beaver can all still be readily found in Poland. Of special note are Poland's 23 national parks, with the following area particularly important on a European and even a global scale.

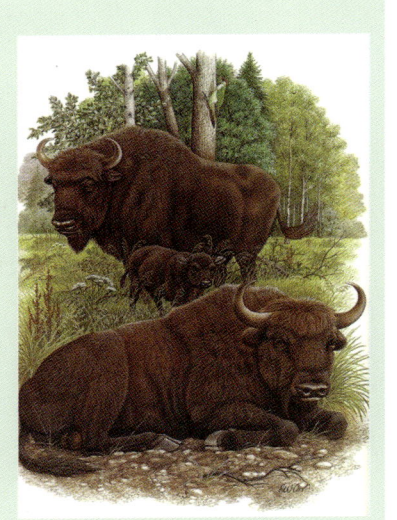

The world's largest surviving population of European bison (*żubr* in Polish), the continent's heaviest land mammal, lives inside the Białowieża Forest

Białowieża National Park

This huge protected area (over 40 square miles or 105 square kilometres in size) in the far east of Poland is Europe's last primeval forest. It is considered so important that it was declared a UNESCO World Heritage Site for its biological value. The **Białowieża Forest** provides a home for the world's largest population of European bison, and played a vital role in preventing this species from going extinct in the twentieth century.

49

Poland in the World

The Vang church is an authentic Scandinavian treasure located in the hills of the Karkonosze mountains, in the Sudetes range (south-western Poland)

Poland's calming rural landscapes leave a lasting impression on visitors

THE *REAL* NARNIA

Poland's stunning natural landscapes are known to filmmakers from around the world, including those behind *The Chronicles of Narnia* film series. Both *The Lion, the Witch and the Wardrobe* and *Prince Caspian* were partly shot in the Stołowe Mountains and near the Karpacz resort in the Sudetes, making Poland the likely real-life Narnia.

VIKINGS IN SOUTHERN POLAND?

A hidden gem awaits walkers in the southern mountainous resort of Karpacz. **The Vang** is an ancient Norwegian stave church, built at the beginning of the thirteenth century. However, it is not a remnant of some long lost Nordic colony. The Vang was originally built in Norway and bought by a German museum in the nineteenth century. It changed hands a few more times before it was eventually moved to an elevated site in Karpacz, overlooking the village, and lovingly restored. This intricate church was constructed entirely from wood, without a single nail.

   All of the walks and ascents are clearly marked out and colour-coded according to their difficulty level, so walkers of all abilities can easily choose the trail that is most appropriate for them, without the need to understand the Polish language.

CHAPTER 2: **The Geography of Poland**

ARCHITECTURE AND CULTURE

For the body and the soul

There are numerous **spa towns** in Poland, with one of the most popular resorts being Ciechocinek (near Toruń). It is famous for its saline graduation towers, a historical monument dating back to the mid-nineteenth century. The towers are carefully designed wooden walls, along which mineral waters run, in special troughs, and then trickle down a system of blackthorn twigs.

With the help of a little breeze and evaporation, the saline waters improve the air quality in the area. People with cardiovascular and respiratory conditions are often prescribed a stay in Ciechocinek, where they can inhale the healing mineral vapours while taking a stroll in the gardens.

The Sudetes are also rich in spa resorts, which boast their own mineral springs, such as Kudowa Zdrój and Duszniki Zdrój. The microclimate in these picturesque resorts, hidden among gentle

> **Did you know?**
> Kudowa Zdrój is also famous for a unique, yet grim monument. This is the **Skull Chapel**, built at the end of the eighteenth century. It was constructed following the discovery of a former village cemetery for victims of wars and plagues. The internal walls of this small chapel are inlaid with around 3,000 human skulls and bones. This decoration was intended to commemorate the deceased, and to make the living ponder at the mysteries of life and death. It is one of very few such chapels in Europe. It is open to visitors and even hosts an annual church service.

The well room in Kudowa Zdrój was built at the beginning of the twentieth century. Inside, there is a medicinal water drinking point, as well as a café and shops selling local crafts

IMAGE: Maria H. Żukowska

51

Poland in the World

Duszniki Zdrój is a peaceful spa town, complete with a quaint old town, a well room offering medicinal waters, and mature gardens perfect for regenerative strolls

hills and forests, is said to be highly curative. Medicinal waters are available to drink in the historic well rooms, usually set in mature parks. In these parks, visitors can take time to relax and breathe in the mineral-rich air in the many romantic gazebos and bandstands.

A stone-paved trail near Karpacz in the Sudetes, perfect for less experienced hikers

IMAGES: Maria H. Żukowska

CHAPTER 2: **The Geography of Poland**

A woodland near Łódź, Greater Poland, in late summer

IMAGE: Maria H. Żukowska

> ### Did you know?
> One of the world's largest castles can be found at Malbork in northern Poland, 90 miles (145 kilometres) north of Toruń. Here, on the bank of the Nogat river, the Gothic **Malbork Castle** proudly stands. It was built by the Teutonic Knights, who started its contruction in the late thirteenth century. It is the world's largest fortress in terms of surface area and a UNESCO protected site. Its overall area is around 49 acres (20 hectares).

53

Poland in the World

Toruń – home of astronomy and gingerbread

What do a Polish astronomer and gingerbread cakes have in common? The historic city of Toruń! The medieval complex of the Old Town has many fascinating sights in store: the ruins of a Teutonic castle, Gothic tenement houses and Toruń's very own Leaning Tower.

However, Toruń is best known as the birthplace of **Nicolaus Copernicus** (▶ p. 103). Today, his family home operates as a museum. To recognise the city's astronomical heritage, a planetarium was founded in Toruń in the 1990s. Here, visitors can enjoy an astronomical show, projected onto the domed ceiling of the specially constructed building.

Toruń is also famous for its **artisan gingerbread**, baked here since the fourteenth century. The Toruń gingerbread cakes come in all shapes and sizes, with different fillings and decorations to satisfy even the most demanding of connoisseurs. Cake masters from Toruń work to traditional, secret recipes – and legend has it that they are Europe's finest.

The bronze Nicolaus Copernicus Monument in the historic Market Square in Toruń

The famous Toruń gingerbread cakes come in an array of flavours and shapes

IMAGES: Karolina Bryś

CHAPTER 2: **The Geography of Poland**

A tale of four cities

Poland is alive with thriving cities which, thanks to the now excellent and cost-effective air links, attract hundreds of thousands of visitors from the UK every year. Four Polish cities of special note are the capital city of Warsaw, the bohemian Kraków, the coastal city of Gdańsk and Wrocław, also known as 'the meeting place'.

Warsaw

Warsaw (*Warszawa*) is the capital and the largest city in Poland, with over 1.7 million inhabitants (making it the ninth largest city in the European Union). As Warsaw was almost completely destroyed in World War II, it had to be rebuilt from scratch in the post-war years.

TOP TOURIST SITES IN WARSAW

Explore the beautiful **Old Town** (*Stare Miasto*) with its colourful Baroque houses and bronze statue of Warsaw's own legendary mermaid, Sawa. She is surrounded by a flowing pool of water which you can dip your toes into, and she carries a sword and shield to protect her beloved city.

The **Łazienki Park** is perfect for a Sunday stroll, when works by Poland's famous composer Fryderyk Chopin (▶ p. 120) are played live beneath his statue. You can also feed the red squirrels and peacocks which inhabit the gardens, straight from your hand.

The **Copernicus Science Centre** (*Centrum Nauki Kopernik*) is a unique attraction. The interactive exhibitions provide a hands-on experience, making science fun and fascinating. The museum is a real treat, where you can experience the optical illusions of light, learn more about a cheetah's speed and enjoy the physics behind your very own magic carpet ride.

Whether you like history or not, the **Warsaw Uprising Museum** is also a must, since its interactive exhibitions put you in the shoes of the brave child and teenage insurgents of the Warsaw Uprising in 1944 (▶ p. 32 for more details on this dramatic period in Poland's history). It was during this period that they fought for their freedom against the brutal Nazi occupation during World War II. Its powerful, eye-opening history will show Warsaw in a new and inspiring light, which will leave a lasting impression for years to come. Warsaw was rebuilt after World War II by its citizens, like a phoenix from the ashes, with the help of historic paintings by famous artists, notably the eighteenth century Italian painter Bernardo Bellotto (who also borrowed his uncle's name of Canaletto).

Maja Karpowicz

Poland in the World

Warsaw Castle Square by night

The Chopin monument in the Łazienki Park in Warsaw

IMAGE: Karolina Bryś

In the warmer months, the bars and restaurants located in the tenements of the Warsaw Old Town attract locals and visitors with their beer gardens and patios

IMAGE: Maja Karpowicz

CHAPTER 2: **The Geography of Poland**

The Palace on the Water (left) in the Łazienki Park, as well as the Wilanów Palace in the south of the city (dubbed the 'Polish Versailles'; below) are among Warsaw's most interesting sights

IMAGES: Karolina Bryś

Today, Warsaw is a cosmopolitan capital that has it all: from historic monuments (such as the lovingly restored Old Town, the Royal Castle and the Presidential Palace) to the walks along the Vistula river, beautiful parks and cutting-edge interactive museums. There is also a vibrant cultural scene, many shopping opportunities and extensive nightlife.

Kraków

The historic southern city of Kraków has always been the favourite city of Polish artists, actors and musicians. Its bohemian cultural legacy is reflected in the many art galleries, independent cafés, quirky shops and

Poland in the World

The Wawel complex incorporates the Royal Castle and the Wawel Cathedral, as well as many towers, gates, chapels and gardens

IMAGE: Jennifer Boyer

MORE TOURIST SITES IN KRAKÓW

Make sure you visit the **Cloth Hall** (*Sukiennice*), in the centre of the Market Square, where stallholders sell a range of Polish souvenirs. These include amber jewellery, intricately carved wooden boxes, dolls, wooden swords and traditional folk costumes.

From the tower of **St. Mary's Basilica**, which stands prominently over the Main Market Square, a trumpeter plays to mark every hour, in four directions. As legend has it, when the Mongols were approaching Kraków to conquer it in 1241, the trumpeter on watch played the St. Mary's Trumpet Call (*Hejnał Mariacki*) to warn the guards at the gates of the invasion. However, the trumpeter was shot in the throat before he could complete the anthem, which is why it ends abruptly.

The interior of the Basilica is truly stunning, with its bright colours and the largest carved Gothic altarpiece in the world, the **Altarpiece of Veit Stoss** (*Ołtarz Wita Stwosza*), made entirely of wood.

Maja Karpowicz

Kraków's famous Wawel Dragon statue, breathing fire

intimate music venues scattered around the historic Market Square and Old Town.

One of Kraków's main attractions is the **Wawel Castle**, the resting place of Polish kings and queens. The castle is still 'guarded' by the **Wawel Dragon** (*Smok Wawelski*), a creature from a well-known Polish legend. Its bronze statue at the Wawel Hill is a major tourist highlight

58

CHAPTER 2: **The Geography of Poland**

The Cloth Hall, or *Sukiennice*, encapsulates the romantic atmosphere of Kraków

Situated in the heart of Kraków's Old Town, St. Mary's Basilica is home to the world's largest Gothic altarpiece

59

Poland in the World

> It feels like you've stepped into the dwarf mines of The Lord of the Rings, with stalactites hanging from high ceilings and statues carved from the silvery, saline surroundings. It's a fantastic, once in a lifetime experience.
>
> Maja Karpowicz

of Kraków, especially as it breathes real fire every few minutes – and, in a modern twist, it can now even do so on request. Anyone can wake the vicious beast by sending a text message.

In Kraków's southern district, just 10 miles (17 kilometres) south of the Old Town, there is another architectural wonder: **Wieliczka Salt Mine**, the world's oldest mine of its kind. Operating continually since the middle ages, the mine is a mesmerising complex of corridors, chambers, underground lakes and chapels illuminated with dazzling chandeliers. Everything inside the mine is cut from blocks of salt (yes, including the chandeliers). But do not take our word for it – licking the walls is allowed, so you can verify this yourself!

Tricity

The Tricity metropolitan area, in the very north of the country, is an urban complex of three coastal cities: Gdańsk, Gdynia and Sopot.

TOP TOURIST SITES IN GDAŃSK

One of Gdańsk's must-see sites is the incredible market square, known as the **Long Market** (*Długi Targ*), which is lined with tall, colourful houses. There is also a fountain of Neptune here, with the whole scene reminiscent of something from a fairy tale.

Through the **Green Gate** (*Brama Zielona*), you will find yourself at the Motława river, where you can get another scenic view of the towering, colourful buildings, all with intricate designs on their facades.

The recently built **European Solidarity Centre** (*Europejskie Centrum Solidarności*) depicts the rise of Poland's Solidarity Movement, which brought an end to Communist rule in the country and, later, across Europe. It is not only worth a visit for its engaging exhibitions and architecture, but also for the moving way in which it portrays Lech Wałęsa, the former union leader who later became the President of Poland.

Gdańsk is also the centre of the Polish amber trade. The city hosts an **Amber Museum** and many jewellery trade fairs that glisten with these fossilized, multi-hued gems that were formed nearby over 40 million years ago.

Maja Karpowicz

CHAPTER 2: **The Geography of Poland**

The characterful Old Town in Gdańsk is buzzing in July and August each year during its world-famous St. Dominic's Fair. It lasts around three weeks and boasts a rich cultural programme, plus hundreds of stalls selling local art and craft items, amber jewellery, speciality food and drink, collectors' items, bric-a-brac and more. The Fair dates its origins all the way back to the thirteenth century

Neptune's Fountain is one of Gdańsk's iconic sights

61

Poland in the World

A view along the Motława river in Gdańsk, with the historic wooden port crane in the background

Once the heart of European commerce and trade, with ancient trading links to Britain, **Gdańsk** used to be one of the thriving and multicultural **Hanseatic** port towns (▶ p. 22 for some more information on its long and fascinating history). The architecture of Gdańsk reflects its culturally rich past, as the Old Town is full of impressive examples of Germanic and Dutch-style architecture. These include city gates, a medieval port crane, royal courts and chapels, and an array of stunning churches.

Gdańsk and its famous shipyard are also known for being the birthplace of the **Solidarity** (*Solidarność*) trade union. You can find out more about how the Solidarity movement helped trigger major political changes (and the fall of communism) in Europe on p. 34.

Gdynia started off as a modest fishing village, but it was expanded and developed into a major port city in the 1920s. Apart from its maritime heritage, it is home to one of Europe's largest international music events, the Open'er Festival (▶ p. 121). **Sopot** is an attractive spa town famous for its city beach and romantic, wooden pier (which, at 1,678 feet or 511.5 metres, is the longest in Europe).

CHAPTER 2: **The Geography of Poland**

Wrocław

The attractive settlement of **Wrocław**, the home city of one of the authors of this book, is set on the Oder (*Odra*) river, and is the largest city in western Poland. As well as the main river, numerous smaller water courses also flow through the city, enriching its landscape. The rivers and canals make Wrocław a city of bridges (with no less than 117, some of which are pedestrian-only bridges) and islands (12 principal ones).

The Old Town, the Cathedral Island (also referred to as *Ostrów Tumski*) and Market Square boast beautiful historic architecture and plenty of romantic cobbled streets, characterful cafés and galleries.

Because the city is a thriving cultural hub and an architectural gem, it was selected as the **European Capital of Culture for 2016**. As part of

Did you know?

Wrocław is also known for its **dwarves** – over 300 of them and growing each year! The charming statuettes can be found across the city, each representing a different aspect of the settlement's heritage. For example, the Blacksmith can be found in the historic blacksmiths' quarter, off the Market Square. Although playful the figurines, which started to appear in 2001, are inspired by the student-led anti-communist opposition movement, Orange Alternative (*Pomarańczowa Alternatywa*), which was active in the 1980s. Founded in Wrocław, they were an underground group who organised peaceful protests. A dwarf was their humorous trademark, and so they often drew it in various locations across the city.

Some of the most well-known dwarf sculptures in Wrocław are the Blacksmith, the Syzyfki ('the two Sisyphuses', a reference to the Greek myth of Sisyphus) and the Guardian of the Gate to the Dwarf City

Poland in the World

Wrocław is attractively situated over a number of islands, making for charming city walks by the waterside

IMAGE: Maria H. Żukowska

Red squirrels are common and much loved in Poland. This one lives in one of Wrocław's city parks

MORE TOURIST SIGHTS IN WROCŁAW

In addition to the city's cute dwarves, look out for a range of remarkable **bronze statues**. They range from farm animals to a thought-provoking piece featuring figures sinking into and rising from the pavements of the Piłudskiego and Świdnicka streets. They appear to be descending underground and emerging from it, on the other side of the street. This is the 'Statue of the Anonymous Passerby', revealed on the twenty-fourth anniversary of the introduction of martial law in Poland in 1981. According to some interpretations, the statue symbolises the struggle of the anonymous Polish people who fought the oppressive regime through their involvement in the anti-communist underground.

The **University of Wrocław's Botanical Gardens** have been described as a 'live museum' and offer a day of bliss as you get lost in this secret garden, complete with fountains, bridges, fragrant wild plants and artistically cut hedges.

Don't miss out on **Wrocław Zoo**, set up in sections for monkeys; animals from the Sahara, Madagascar and South Africa; the Safari; the aviary and much more – even a butterfly house! All the animals are well looked after and kept humanely in spacious, five-star conditions, which adds to the enjoyment of the visit.

Maja Karpowicz

CHAPTER 2: The Geography of Poland

the programme, Wrocław will be hosting many international events throughout 2016, such as concerts (including a performance by Pink Floyd's David Gilmour), exhibitions and festivals. Previously, the UK cities of Glasgow and Liverpool were selected for this prestigious award, while the country's official candidates for the 2023 edition are Leeds and Dundee.

Wrocław is the capital of the **Lower Silesia** region – home to the sleepy, mysterious hills of the Sudetes. Lower Silesia is still alive with the ghosts of old Slavic legends, their ancient shrines and long-lost Celtic settlements. The area is also rich in Czech and Germanic influences. All of these have shaped the region's history and culture.

The rich heritage of the region led to Wrocław adopting the slogan of 'Wrocław, the Meeting Place'. This catchphrase, as well as referring to the fact that today's Wrocław is a friendly and welcoming city, also conveys a deeper historical meaning. After World War II Wrocław (historically Polish, Czech, German and now Polish again) became a new home for countless people from all over Poland, mostly the displaced people from the east of the country (today's Ukraine). Wrocław therefore became a city bringing together, once again, people from countless other places – a meeting place.

IMAGE: Maja Karpowicz
The bronze Memorial Monument for the Farm Animals at *Jatki* (the historic shambles) in Wrocław

The Market Square in Wrocław is rich in restaurants, shops, bars, pop-up open-air art installations and concert venues. It is the city's cultural heart

IMAGE: Maria H. Żukowska

65

Poland in the World

> **Did you know?**
> Traditional Polish ceramics are now popular in homeware and craft shops across the UK, with their beautiful designs appealing to both British buyers and Poles wanting a reminder of home. This display, in a trendy Edinburgh shop, has proven popular with locals (both Poles and Scots), as well as the many international visitors to this cosmopolitan capital city. Elsewhere, at Hebden Bridge in West Yorkshire, a whole shop is filled with the stunning patterns of Polish traditional ceramics.

IMAGE: Brin Best

The painted village of Zalipie

In Polish folk art the more colour and flowers, the better. No one knows this as well as the inhabitants of **Zalipie, the 'painted village'**, situated around 60 miles (96.5 kilometres) north-east of Kraków.

The houses (both externally and internally), wells, benches and wayside shrines in Zalipie and the surrounding villages are all adorned with colourful floral patterning. Each year, the decorations are brought

One of the traditional painted cottages in Zalipie

CHAPTER 2: **The Geography of Poland**

DISCOVERING SANDOMIERZ

Sandomierz is a beautiful and historic town near the Świętokrzyskie Mountains (meaning Holy Cross Mountains), in the south-east of Poland. Its charming scenery and architecture are most famously featured in an entertaining Polish television series about a crime-solving priest, who cycles around the scenic local landmarks in his black cassock. Tourists flock not only to explore this pretty little town but also to witness filming in progress.

The town has a picturesque Town Hall, complete with a bell tower, which is situated in the ancient main square dating back to the fourteenth century. You can also take a pleasant walk through the cobbled streets and green pastures surrounding the town. Just like Rome, the town is set on seven hills!

Maja Karpowicz

IMAGE: Maja Karpowicz

back to life as the villagers compete for the title of the most beautifully decorated house.

The competition takes place in the summer, but one of the cottages is open to visitors all year round as a museum dedicated to the house painting tradition. Handmade folk art and crafts are also on display.

Czocha Castle – School of Witchcraft and Wizardry

There are many castles in Poland, some of which are quite fairy tale-like. But only Czocha Castle, not far from Wrocław, had the chance to become a real-life Hogwarts.

Poland in the World

Książ Castle is one of Poland's most famous fortresses and an excellent day out. The castle and its impressive grounds are the subject of many legends and thrilling stories — just like the Sudetes mountain range, where the castle is situated

IMAGE: Maria H. Żukowska

IMAGE: Manfred Heyde

Poland supports Europe's largest population of white storks

The Castle was recently chosen to host a series of **Harry Potter**-inspired LARP sessions (Live Action Role Playing games). The College of Wizardry events attracted hundreds of Harry Potter fans from all over Europe, including many from the UK. Participants had the opportunity to stay in Czocha Castle-turned-Hogwarts as 'students' and become characters inspired by their beloved book series (complete with gowns, wands and other magical paraphernalia).

EXPLORING ŁÓDŹ

The city of **Łódź**, pronounced 'Woodj', is located in central Poland. It was the hub of the nineteenth century Polish **textile industry**, and is often dubbed the 'Polish Manchester'. Many of its beautiful old factories have been renovated and converted into offices, hotels and shopping centres. One example of Łódź's restored industrial landmarks is the famous Manufaktura, a contemporary arts and leisure complex, which is certainly worth a visit.

Łódź is also the home of the famous **National Film School**, where Poland's brightest and most highly celebrated film directors studied. Piotrkowska Street, the city's main road and one of Europe's longest high streets, is paved with Hollywood-style stars bearing the names of famous Polish film stars and producers. This is why the city is sometimes humorously referred to as 'Holly-Łódź'.

Maja Karpowicz

CHAPTER 2: **The Geography of Poland**

ŁOWICZ'S BUTTON MUSEUM

Have you ever been to a button museum? Well, you can visit one in Łowicz, near Warsaw. The **Museum of Buttons** is definitely one of a kind, as you learn the intriguing backgrounds of the exhibits' owners, all of whom were prominent Polish figures who changed the face of the country's history, fashion or culture.

Łowicz is the home of the famous striped, woollen folk costumes, with skirts that form a pretty bell as they spin. It's worth visiting in May or June (during the Corpus Christi celebrations) to watch the procession of the colourful Łowicz costumes in the street. By experiencing this spectacle, you will get a true taste for Polish culture, which is deeply woven into Catholic devotion and the ongoing celebration of Poland's customs and traditions.

Maja Karpowicz

The Polish LARP sessions were so popular in 2015 that the Danish organisers are planning to continue the tradition. In fact, a fundraising campaign has been launched to buy a similar Polish fortress. The aim is to set up permanent LARP headquarters in Poland for fantasy-themed games – and could there be a better location for this than an historic castle in scenic surroundings?

POLISH INDUSTRY AND FOLK ART

High quality Polish goods are proudly exported in large quantities to the UK and other countries. This section presents some notable examples of Poland's trademark food and drink, key industries and exquisite folk art, known the world over.

Food and fresh produce

Poland is famous for its agricultural wealth and irresistible cuisine. Some traditional Polish recipes, to get your taste-buds tingling, appear in Chapter 8. Many mouth-watering specialities can be discovered in Poland (and in Polish food shops in the UK), including traditional Polish bread, cheeses, cold meats and delicious confectionery. What

IMAGE: Maria H. Żukowska

Fresh Polish foods are of exceptional quality. Here are some typical products as seen during a hiker's outdoor lunch – fresh bread rolls and sweet pastries, plums, redcurrants and a home-grown 'raspberry' tomato, a variety known for its sweet taste

69

Poland in the World

The historic Spiż Brewery (Browar Spiż) and pub in Wrocław

is more, the general stock in UK supermarkets now also features significant amounts of fresh produce imported directly from Poland. Some of the most commonly exported fresh foods include berries, plums, apples, mushrooms, root vegetables, tomatoes, garlic and many more. Look out for the 'Country of Origin: Poland' labels in your local chain store.

Craft alcohols

Poland has a long tradition of alcohol production. Several brands of high quality Polish vodka are celebrated internationally (one even has a strand of 'bison grass' submerged in the contents of the bottle!). Polish vodkas are usually dry in taste and distilled from rye, but varieties are also made from potatoes, wheat or herbs. The country is also known for its brewing industry, which produces and exports numerous kinds of beers, including lager, dark ales, wheat brew, honey beers and pale ales. Many of these Polish craft beers are widely available in UK shops. Finally, large quantities of Poland's fresh produce end up in Polish cider and an array of exquisite liqueurs made from fruit, herbs and even hazelnuts or walnuts.

CHAPTER 2: **The Geography of Poland**

Glassware

The Polish glassware industry is well-established and known for products such as tumblers, artisan cocktail and wine glasses, jugs, vases, as well as hand-painted Christmas baubles and decorative pieces. This glassware is commonly available in shops across Europe.

Glass baubles with handcrafted lace decorations, by master embroideress Zofia Radna

Stoneware, pottery and ceramics

Pottery is one of the trademark exports of Poland. Several Polish workshops produce some of Europe's most unique, hand-crafted ceramics. The products are distinct in their style and their designs, and often incorporate traditional Polish folk elements. Among the most popular are dining sets; tea sets with beautiful, hand-painted teapots; serving bowls; mugs; decorative plates and tiles; and ovenproof baking dishes and cake stands.

Textiles

Łódź, a city in central Poland, is the historic heart of the country's textile industry (▶ p. 68). Today, workshops in Poland still produce large quantities of excellent quality cotton, satin, lace, flannel and damask cloths. Polish linen and other household fabrics, including

Traditional, hand-painted Polish pottery

Each major region of Poland has its own distinct folk patterns, unique in terms of colour scheme, detail and style

71

Poland in the World

intricate net curtains, are also popular. All kinds of Polish cloth come in thousands of colours and patterns, contemporary and traditional.

Clothing and leatherware

Polish contemporary fashion brands are on the rise, and although they sell their products internationally online, they often take pride in making their clothing locally, in Polish studios, from home-made textiles. In addition to the modern Polish haute couture, traditional items of clothing are ever-popular with locals and tourists alike. These include natural sheepskin and leather garments, handmade according to the Highlanders' method, such as shoes, slippers, hats, gloves, vests, coats, belts and bags. These accessories are usually decorated beautifully with folk patterns, and available in resorts like Zakopane, as well as from charming wooden stands in most cities and towns in Poland.

Polish crafts: two examples of embroidery (above), and silver jewellery with amber (below)

Folk art and design

Floral and nature-inspired, Polish folklore artwork comes in many distinctive styles and colours. The patterns differ depending on which specific area of Poland they come from. Nowadays, Polish art and design is experiencing a revival of folklore influences. Therefore, traditional patterns can be found on almost everything from clothing, bags and jewellery, to household items such as linen, tablecloths and rugs, and even on phone cases and stationery. Usually, the folk patterns are used in the form of embroidery and prints.

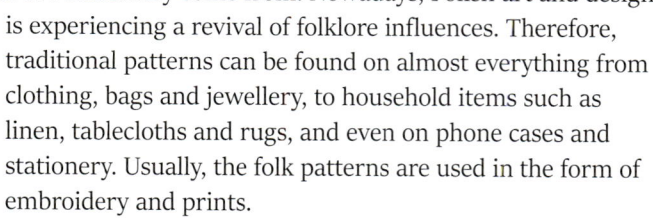

Amber, striped flint and artistic jewellery

Polish amber is a well-known gemstone, which comes in a variety of colours – the three key shades being golden, dark brown and green (▶ p. 41). It is commonly used in jewellery-making, including the highly creative artistic jewellery, as it is known in Poland. This usually refers to hand-crafted objects, often made from silver and unique in style and design. Polish amber retailers operate in Poland

IMAGES: Maria H. Żukowska

CHAPTER 2: The Geography of Poland

and worldwide, with physical and online stores in many European countries, including the UK.

Amber is, however, not the only gemstone that Poland exports. Another stone, the **striped flint** (or banded flint), is popular in the jewellery trade, and is endemic to the Świętokrzyskie Mountains. It is a striped, usually grey-, sand- or coffee-coloured stone of an uncommon, 'banded' appearance. Because of its rarity, striped flint is a valuable stone. Celebrity gossip has it that stars such as Victoria Beckham, Boy George, Madonna and Robbie Williams all found the charm of this striped gem irresistible, and ordered banded flint jewellery from Poland.

A striped flint ball, shaped and polished from an irregular piece of flint

Wood

In Poland, folk art often makes use of wood, as many contemporary artists specialise in wooden sculpture and craftwork. Wooden jewellery, household items, decorative pieces and furniture (including garden furniture) are also important areas of industry, and such items are often exported to other European countries. Poland is also one of the chief exporters of timber in Europe and, most notably, one of the key suppliers of wood to the major flat-packed furniture retailers.

Popular Polish crafts also include wooden jewellery. It comes in a range of colours and styles, from simple and traditional ones (like the necklace in the picture), to contemporary statement pieces

IMAGE: Maria H. Żukowska

73

Poland in the World

The shipyards of the port city of Szczecin are at the forefront of the Polish boat building industry

Boats and yachts

Polish shipyards, particularly the ones in Gdynia and Szczecin, are among the world leaders in boat production. They build all kinds of vessels, notably medium-sized luxury yachts (up to 82 feet or 25 metres in length), and they specialise particularly in building small motor boats (up to 29.5 feet or 9 metres in length). According to information published in 2015 by the Polish Ministry of Treasury, Poland is the world's second largest exporter of such boats, after the USA. Polish boats are popular in Europe, as well as further afield, and they sell mostly in the Bahamas, Liberia, Norway, Russia and Turkey. Polish boats are also highly regarded by British customers, and they can often be spotted on British waters, for example on Windermere Lake in the Lake District (Cumbria), and in other sailing and yachting spots across the country.

PART TWO
POLES IN THE UK

CHAPTER 3

World War II

This chapter explains the vital contribution of Polish people to the successful Allied campaign during World War II. It outlines the many reasons why British people today owe a debt of gratitude to the Polish men and women who fought alongside British forces, or made other essential contributions to the war effort, often at great personal sacrifice to themselves.

Poles in the UK

Polish people played such a significant part in the British war effort during World War II, often giving their lives to the Allied campaign as they did so, that this important story must be told in a chapter of its own.

The contribution of Poles in helping to defeat Nazi Germany was multi-faceted, and included work by mathematicians, dangerous espionage, resistance armies fighting bravely in Poland and more conventional military service alongside British navy, army and air force personnel.

Many of the tens of thousands of Polish servicemen who joined British forces had escaped the German invasion – and the terrible conflict that followed it – in their homeland. They had then made their way to safety in Britain, through many different means and across various countries. With around 35,500 air force personnel, soldiers and sailors, Poland had the largest overseas military force in the UK, after the French.

Taken together, it is now widely accepted that Polish forces made the fourth largest contribution to the Allied campaign during World War II, and many commentators have said that the war could never have been won without them.

Did you know?

Poland made the fourth biggest contribution to Allied forces during World War II (after the USA, the UK and the Soviets). Furthermore, the Home Army (Poland's resistance movement) is believed to have been Europe's largest resistance movement, with around 400,000 members.

Polish mathematicians played a key role in deciphering the German Enigma machine, which was used to send secret messages during World War II

IMAGE: Alessandro Nassiri

CODE-BREAKING

The pivotal role of Polish people in the decoding of the German **Enigma machines** has only recently become recognised, despite the fact that the first significant step in the work to unlock the secrets of the machines was actually taken in Poland.

The Polish code breakers realised that mathematics could be the key to decoding the Enigma machine, whereas previous British efforts had focussed on linguistics. The three important figures of this period were Jerzy Różycki,

CHAPTER 3: **World War II**

Did you know?

Polish civilians working at the Peenemünde missile research facility (northern Germany) provided microfilm and other secrets to the British, which helped the Allies mount the successful Operation Hydra bombing attacks in August 1943.

Information provided by the Polish 'spies' was considered at a special meeting of top British government and military personnel, held on 29 June 1943 in the Cabinet War Room, hidden beneath London.

The meeting, chaired by Prime Minister Winston Churchill, aimed to assess the threat of the German V-1 and V-2 missiles, the latter being the world's first long-range guided missiles. These were being developed 'in secret' at Peenemünde, and could easily reach British cities, with the Germans even having plans to launch them from submarines, bringing American cities such as New York within reach.

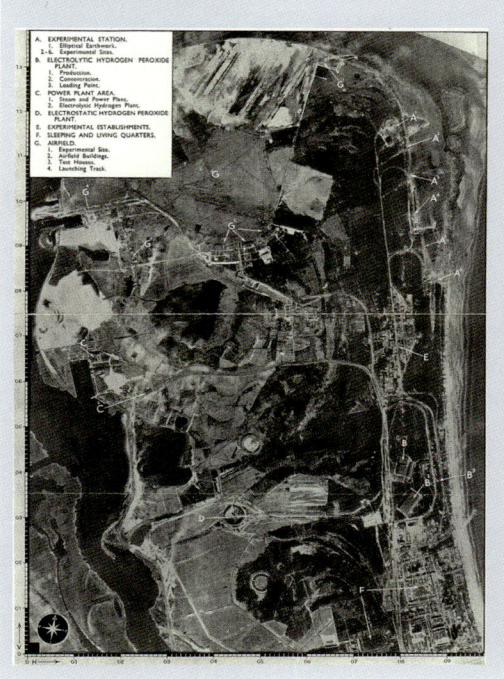

Following the meeting a major attack was planned for the night of 17/18 August 1943, in what would become known as Operation Hydra. The full firepower of Bomber Command was mobilised on the night of the attacks, which are generally thought to have delayed the development of the V-2 rocket programme by two months.

As well as causing extensive damage to the research facility, two German service personnel were killed during the bombing raids, including a senior engineer for the rocket programme. Sadly, over 700 (mostly Polish) civilians were also killed in the bombings.

A replica of a V-2 rocket at the Peenemünde museum, Germany

A British plan for the August 1943 Operation Hydra bombing raids at Peenemünde, Germany

Henryk Zygalski and Marian Rejewski, who studied mathematics at Poznań University and then joined the Cipher Bureau in Warsaw. Their knowledge was used to make electromechanical machines to search for solutions to the Enigma machine, which were called *bombas*.

This knowledge, which in turn was shared with British intelligence in 1939, eventually helped the British mathematical genius Alan Turing create his own version of the *bomba*. This, crucially, was capable of

Poles in the UK

Did you know?

One of the most extraordinary special agents of World War II was a Polish woman called **Krystyna Skarbek** [1908–1952], who later took the name of Christine Granville when she settled in Britain. Since her daring and adventurous work in Nazi-occupied Poland and France has become more widely known, Skarbek has become recognised across the world as one of the legendary figures of special operations.

Born in Warsaw in 1908, Skarbek was always ferociously independent. Known for her love of freedom – both for herself and for her beloved Poland – when war broke out in September 1939 she travelled to Britain to offer her services against the common enemy, Nazi Germany.

She soon became Britain's first female special agent, long before the Special Operations Executive was set up in 1940, and went on to become the longest-serving female special agent to work for Britain.

Skarbek took part in the kind of amazing missions that would normally only be associated with Hollywood movies. These included skiing through the freezing Tatra Mountains into Poland and being parachuted behind enemy lines in France, where the average life expectancy of a secret wireless operator was a mere six weeks.

She smuggled the first film evidence to the British of German preparations for Operation Barbarossa, the Nazi invasion of their former ally, the Soviet Union. Skarbek also made several other noteworthy contributions to the war effort, including:

- Making the first contact between the French resistance on one side of the Alps and the Italian partisans on the other
- Helping to secure the defection of an entire German garrison in the Alps
- Helping to prepare the way for the Allied liberationary forces in the south of France
- Saving the lives of three of her comrades, just hours before they were due to be executed by firing squad.

Among her many medals and awards were the George Cross and the OBE from the British, and the Croix de Guerre, awarded by the French.

The Polish special agent Krystyna Skarbek was one of the most celebrated 'spies' who worked for Britain during World War II

breaking the more complex codes that the Germans developed during the war.

The code-breaking work on the Enigma machine – pioneered by Poles and later by British mathematicians – is thought to have made a huge contribution to the war effort. Some commentators believe that it shortened the war by as much as two years, saving countless lives in the process.

CHAPTER 3: **World War II**

ESPIONAGE

Although much of the secret work carried out by Poles during the war will never be known, enough evidence exists in the public domain to show that Polish **spies** and **special agents** were very highly valued. A very successful Polish branch of the Special Operations Executive was established at Audley End House (near Saffron Waldon, Essex), in the early 1940s. Perhaps the most famous character from this 'theatre' of war was Krystyna Skarbek, who carried out daring missions to gather intelligence for the British and engage in other crucial acts which helped the war effort (▶ box).

Find out more
Krystyna Skarbek's amazing story is told in British author Clare Mulley's thrilling and moving biography, *The Spy Who Loved*, published in 2012 by Macmillan.

THE POLISH AIR FORCE IN THE UK

One of the most celebrated contributions of Polish people during the whole of World War II was the role they played in aerial warfare with Germany. This took place in the skies above Britain and mainland Europe, especially during the early years of the war.

Following an agreement in June 1940, the Polish Government in Exile formed a **Polish Air Force** in the UK, and approximately 8,500 Polish servicemen were deployed in Britain, working alongside their British and other Allied counterparts in the Royal Air Force (RAF) and Fleet Air Arm. They included Poles who flew fighter and bomber aeroplanes, and their associated ground crew.

One of the key sites of this period was RAF Northolt (west London). From 1940, it became the home of the 1st Polish Wing, which was under British command. This included what would become probably the most famous of all the 16 Polish squadrons in the RAF, 303 *Kościuszko* Squadron, whose pilots flew Spitfire and Hurricane fighter aircraft.

Many of the Poles who joined the Allied campaign had already fought against the *Luftwaffe* (the aerial warfare division of the German Air Force), earlier in their flying careers. This gave them a key advantage over their British counterparts.

The Polish War Memorial at RAF Northolt (west London) honours the vital contribution of Polish airmen to the Allied campaign during World War II

Poles in the UK

Royal Air Force Benevolent Fund

BATTLE OF BRITAIN
10 JULY – 31 OCTOBER 1940

Those who stood with us
A total of **2937** aircrew took part:

- Canada 112
- Ireland 10
- Great Britain 2342
- Poland 145
- Czechoslovakia 88
- USA 9
- Jamaica 1
- Barbados 1
- France 13
- Belgium 28
- South Africa 25
- South Rhodesia 3
- Australia 32
- New Zealand 127

Find out more

The full story of the extraordinary Polish Spitfire aces of World War II is told in the following highly-illustrated book: Matusiak, W. and Grudzień. R. (2015) *Polish Spitfire Aces*. Osprey Publishing

The insignia of the 303 Kościuszko Fighter Squadron, which played a vital role in the Battle of Britain

The Battle of Britain

Polish pilots played a particularly important role in the **Battle of Britain**, one of the most critical aerial battles of the whole of World War II. This took place from July to October 1940, as German aircraft tried to obtain air superiority over Britain, ahead of a planned invasion of the country by Hitler's troops.

The Poles were some of the most experienced pilots to fly in the Battle of Britain, with most having hundreds of hours flying experience from before the war, or gained in previous wartime battles. Polish pilots fought alongside those from Britain in the iconic Spitfire fighter aircraft, which are still admired to this day as the ultimate flying machines of their time.

Furthermore, the Polish fighter pilots shot down 201 German aircraft during the Battle of Britain, and 303 *Kościuszko* Squadron (with 126 aircraft shot down) was responsible for more enemy 'kills' than any

CHAPTER 3: World War II

QUALITIES OF POLISH FIGHTER PILOTS

In 1941 Group Captain Theodore McEvoy, the Station Commander at the RAF Northolt base, where squadrons of Polish fighter pilots were stationed, expressed his opinion on the quality of these pilots in an official report. Here are some of the highlights:

'They are very lovable.'

'Their pride is without vanity. It includes such attributes as courage, honour, patriotism, self-respect, good manners, skill, determination.'

'High courage seems inborn in Poles. Their escapes from Poland give astonishing evidence of their bravery.'

'Implacable in battle, they are yet gentle and considerate at other times.'

'The Polish fighter pilot shares the deep patriotism for which his race is famed.'

'All who meet Poles are impressed by their good manners. They are scrupulously polite to superior officers and to women, but at the same time natural and friendly without affectation.'

'The Polish officer has a keen sense of honour. Mess bills are usually paid on the day they are issued. They never draw a cheque that is not honoured.'

'Poles tell the truth, even if it be to their own hurt. They may offer a laughably inadequate excuse for a misdeed but never deny a wrong thing they have done.'

'They can enjoy thoroughly merry parties without alcoholic stimulants, but on the rare occasions when drink is taken they like the party to go on until dawn.'

'The Poles are a comradely community, and there seems no malice or envy amongst them.'

'The standard of self-respect and cleanliness is high.'

'They are artistic and appreciative of music. The Poles sing admirably in chorus and are seldom stumped for the words or music of a folk-song.'

'They spend much of their time diligently learning English and pick up our own language very quickly.'

'Their sense of humour is quick and akin to our own, and take leg pulling and ragging in excellent spirits.'

'There are no fellows more admirable and lovable than the Polish fighter pilots.'

Pilots of the 303 Kościuszko Polish Fighter Squadron, photographed in 1940

One of the legendary RAF Spitfires flown by Polish pilots in the Battle of Britain, complete with its distinctive tail markings

Members of the 303 Kościuszko Polish Fighter Squadron, which made a key contribution to the Battle of Britain, with a fighter aircraft behind

Three Polish fighter pilots who fought for the RAF during World War II

83

Poles in the UK

Wojtek the solider bear, who fought alongside Polish troops in the notorious Battle of Monte Cassino, which took place in Italy from January to May 1944. After four Allied assaults, the Axis forces were finally defeated on 18 May, allowing further advances on Rome

WOJTEK THE BEAR – A DIFFERENT KIND OF WAR HERO

As many brave Polish soldiers formed part of the Allied forces in World War II, so too did many working animals, such as horses and dogs.

A bear cub

Perhaps the most unusual of these was **Wojtek**, a Syrian brown bear, whose story starts in 1942. Originally born wild near Hamadan in Iran, a hunter shot his mother when he was only a cub. Unable to fend for himself in the wild, he was looked after by a local shepherd boy.

Not long after this, a group of Polish soldiers were travelling through the village, bringing released prisoners-of-war from the Soviet Union to a safe refugee camp in Tehran, Iran. They stopped for a break and spotted the bear cub at the side of the road. Irena, one of the young girls in the group, took a particular shine to the tiny bear and he was bought from the boy in the village.

As they continued their journey to the refugee camp in Tehran, Irena and the group looked after the bear cub, feeding him condensed milk, as he had problems swallowing anything else. He ended up spending three months in the Polish refugee camp before he was donated as a mascot to the Polish Army's 22nd Artillery Supply Company – the group of soldiers who had originally discovered him.

Wojtek the mascot

Mascots – more usually dogs, monkeys or similar creatures – served a great purpose in raising morale in war time. Many of the 22nd Company spent time playing with the bear when they were not on duty. They fed him treats such as fruit, marmalade, syrup, honey and beer, which became his favourite drink! They also taught him to salute when greeted. As he grew, he got stronger and several of the men enjoyed wrestling with him. The bear loved this form of play and thrived in the company of the men. They, in turn, grew very fond of him. They named him Wojtek, a nickname for the Slavic masculine name, Wojciech, meaning 'he who enjoys war'.

The Wojtek-themed badge of the Polish Army's 22nd Artillery Supply Company

Wojtek travelled around with the 22nd Company as they travelled across Iraq, Syria, Palestine and Egypt. When they were due to join the British Army fighting in Italy,

84

CHAPTER 3: **World War II**

however, he would have been stopped from boarding the boat from Egypt, as mascots were not allowed to accompany the soldiers. In the soldiers' minds Wojtek had become more than a mascot and they did not want to be separated from him. With this in mind, the Polish Army enlisted Wojtek as a soldier, and as an official member of the 22nd Company he was allowed to board the boat. The 22nd Company, together with Wojtek, continued their journey to fight in the battle of Monte Cassino.

The soldier bear

During the battle of Monte Cassino Wojtek was stationed at the firing line, and it was not long before he imitated his soldier friends by carrying crates of ammunition closer to the cannons. He was very strong, and the sound of gunfire did not bother him. He soon became a real asset to the Company, moving many ammunition crates during the battle, and was so admired by the 22nd Company that they put him on their official badge.

When World War II ended, the 22nd Company and Wojtek were sent to Winfield Camp at Berwick-upon-Tweed (Northumberland) to demobilise. As the soldiers eventually got sent to different places around Europe in 1947, Wojtek's home became Edinburgh Zoo, where he was well looked after and delighted many a child until he died in 1963. Many of his ex-servicemen colleagues visited him here, and he also gained much media interest, including appearing on BBC television's *Blue Peter*.

Even after his death Wojtek remains a hero, with statues erected in his memory in several cities including Kraków, Poland, and in Edinburgh, Scotland. A film was even made about him, which was broadcast by BBC2 Scotland.

Kathryn Needham

Find out more

Orr, A. (2010). *Wojtek the Bear: Polish War Hero*. Birlinn Ltd.
Film about Wojtek:
www.wojtekfilm.com/large/index.html

One of the authors at the magnificent memorial to Wojtek, which now stands in Princes Street Gardens, Edinburgh

IMAGE: Amanda Best

85

Poles in the UK

> **Did you know?**
> Following their outstanding success in the Battle of Britain, Polish fighter pilots became celebrities of their day across the UK, and even overseas. Journalists flocked from all over the world to their airfields to write about the Poles' heroic exploits; restaurant and bar owners refused to take payments from them; and bus drivers gave them free travel. They were even called 'the real Glamor Boys of England' by Quentin Reynolds, the well-known American war correspondent. There are reports that British RAF pilots even pretended to be Polish when off base, in order to attract the favourable attention of young women!

other squadron who fought in the Battle of Britain. Witold Urbanowicz, of 303 Squadron, was the most successful Polish pilot of all, shooting down 15 aircraft in the battle.

Tragically, 30 Polish airmen were killed during the Battle of Britain, but the death rate in 303 Squadron was lower than average for RAF squadrons, despite their success in battle. This is thought to have been due to the superior flying skills of the Polish pilots.

It is a sad fact that many British people today do not realise that the 145 Polish fighter pilots who flew in the Battle of Britain was the highest number from *any* overseas country to have fought in this key battle. Indeed, Polish pilots made up almost 25% of all overseas pilots in the battle, and 5% of ALL the pilots who fought in the Battle of Britain. They helped to defeat the German air force as they attempted to take control of the skies above Britain. This battle has been described as Nazi Germany's first major defeat of World War II, and was a key turning point in the war.

The names of the Polish airmen who fought in the Battle of Britain are inscribed on the Battle of Britain Monument, which was unveiled in central London in 2015

IMAGE: Beata May

CHAPTER 3: **World War II**

Tributes to Polish airmen

The Polish fighter pilots – or 'aces', as they became known – gained a reputation for being excellent airmen, with many positive characteristics being reported by their commanding officers (▶ p. 83). Thanks to these and other tributes, their close combat skills in shooting down enemy fighters and bombers became legendary.

Prime Minister **Winston Churchill**, who was the reigning Prime Minister of Britain during most of World War II, referred to the pilots who flew in the Battle of Britain in a very famous speech, made in August 1940. He said: 'Never, in the field of human conflict, was so much owed by so many to so few.'

As a result of this speech, all pilots who took part in the Battle of Britain would for evermore be known as 'The Few'. This included the 145 Polish pilots who defended Britain in that vital battle of 1940.

In 1948 a Polish War Memorial was erected at RAF Northolt to commemorate the contribution of Polish airmen to World War II. More recently, the names of the Polish pilots who fought in the Battle of Britain were inscribed on the Battle of Britain monument in London, which was unveiled in 2015.

Did you know?

Several **Polish ships** have sunk or run aground within UK waters over the years, particularly during World War II. Some, such as the SS Cieszyn, were sunk in action, with this particular ship sinking near Falmouth, Cornwall, in 1941. These shipwrecks are now proving popular with divers from the UK and Poland, who enjoy exploring the wreckage and looking for marine wildlife hidden in the nooks and crannies of the site.

Other Polish ships were salvaged from the sea. One example was the SS Kielce, which was lost in 1946 and whose salvage operation proved far more spectacular than its original sinking. It took over 20 years before the Folkestone Salvage Company was given the contract to clear the ammunition known to have been on board, and to salvage the wreckage. As the company decided to break the wreckage into smaller pieces to raise it they fired three charges, the third of which ignited some of the remaining ammunition and caused a huge explosion, which was felt in a nearby town. The blast measured 4 on the Richter Scale and left behind an underwater crater longer than four double decker buses, laid end to end!

Kathryn Needham

Poles in the UK

Barbara Domzal-Karpowicz's story (61)

IMAGE: Basia Domzal-Karpowicz

My name is Barbara Domzal-Karpowicz, or Basia for short, and I'm a second-generation Pole. I was born in the UK of first-generation Polish parents, who came here after World War II as refugees, or 'displaced persons', as they were then called.

I used to call myself an 'Anglo-Pole', as I always felt an affinity to both countries. This left me with a kind of dual identity complex – feeling very Polish in the UK and very English when visiting Poland!

I lived in Checkendon Camp for Polish refugees, now in Oxfordshire, for the first five years of my life. My husband, whose parents' wartime experiences were similar to those of mine, also lived at this camp. Both our fathers spent time in forced labour camps for a period during World War II (mine in a camp operated by the Germans; my husband's in one operated by the Russians) and later went on to serve in the Polish armed forces under British command. Both our mothers were deported to Siberia and were then evacuated to India via Iraq and Iran, before living at the Checkendon Camp between 1948 and 1960 and then in Reading for the rest of their lives.

Stalin's influence in Poland
Many people know about the Holocaust engineered against the Jewish people and other ethnic groups, like Gypsies, by the Nazis in German-occupied Poland.

However, the suffering of the Polish people during World War II was not only caused by the German invaders, but also by the Soviet Union, which also invaded Poland shortly after the Germans in 1939. This led to Poland being torn in two by both its eastern and western neighbours.

Many people do not know that Joseph Stalin, the then head of the Soviet Union, who was responsible for the killing of millions of his own people, also played a major role in Poland. He decided to deport between one and two million Poles from the eastern part of Poland, known as the Borderlands (*Kresy*), in 1940 and 1941. They were sent to the Siberian *gulags*, or labour camps, because he thought they posed a threat to his war effort.

Deportation to Siberia was a death sentence for many thousands of Poles who did not survive the harsh conditions of working in temperatures of -40°C during the Siberian winters. Many people also perished during the gruelling two to three

CHAPTER 3: **World War II**

week journey there in nothing more than cramped, unheated cattle wagon trains.

My mother's deportation to Siberia

My late mother, Czesia Domzal (born Naplocha) [1925–2014], and her family were unfortunately 'picked' by Stalin's henchmen to be deported to Siberia from her home town Luniniec, now in Belarus. This was simply because her father was a railway worker and an older brother a Polish Army officer. People in both these professions were considered enemies of the Soviet state. Additionally, the relatives of people in these positions were also regarded with suspicion because of the potential for them to provide support or important information to the enemies of the Soviets.

After the army unit of my mother's brother was disbanded, following its failed attempt to halt the German and Soviet invaders, he took to fighting in the forests around his home as a partisan in the Polish underground Home Army (*Armia Krajowa*). Following my mother's deportation her brother began fighting in the forests around Zamość (west of Luniniec), where he was caught and murdered by the *Gestapo* in 1943.

So my mother's family began their punishment for a 'crime' they had no knowledge of committing and an odyssey that my mother remembered all her life, which she sarcastically called her 'enforced wanderings'. Her life was just as traumatic as that of most of the survivors of the better-known Jewish Holocaust.

My mother said that they were woken at 3:00 am on the night of 18 June 1941 by a violent rapping on the door of their beautiful, beloved home. They were summoned by armed Soviet guards to pack their belongings in a few minutes and she described one of these men as a 'slit-eyed' Mongolian.

This was, typically, the way that all the deportees to Siberia were rounded up. It must have been

My mama in her younger years, wearing a sari in Valivade, India

IMAGE: Basia Domzal-Karpowicz

a frightening experience, especially for children like my mother, who was only 15 at the time. I can imagine how awful it was just from the photograph of my grandmother, which I still have, because it was crudely ripped from its frame that night by my grandfather, as one of the mementos he wanted to quickly pack. However, the terror of that dreadful night must have been encapsulated in this photograph, as my mother never wanted to look at it, let alone reframe it or hang it up in her new home in the UK, even though she loved her mother very much.

My mother was forced to work, although she was only a child, picking linen flax in the fields in the Altai Krai region of Siberia that they were sent to. It was tough work and it used to make her hands bleed. Later in life, my mother had a fear of forests, because of the ones around the camp, known as the taiga forests, as well as of small, confined spaces (claustrophobia), because of the cattle wagons they were transported there in.

89

Poles in the UK

Many Poles did not survive the cold, starvation or diseases that were rampant in these cattle trains and then the camps – especially the young, old and infirm. So in many ways my mother was one of the 'lucky ones', although she lost her childhood and the home she loved forever.

Evacuation to the Caspian Sea

When Hitler attacked the Soviet Union, Stalin decided to exploit the Poles he had enslaved by freeing them under an 'Amnesty' that he declared in 1942, so he could enlist them in the fight against the Germans. My mother, mother-in-law and father-in-law were therefore evacuated from their *gulags* and those who were old enough, like my father-in-law, Szymon Karpowicz [1915–1988], joined the newly formed Polish army led by General Władysław Anders, which became the so-called Anders' Army. He then fought with this army as a sapper in Palestine (now Israel), at Tobruk in Libya and Monte Cassino in Italy, before coming to the UK. My mother and mother-in-law, however, were too young to fight and so stayed with their ageing parents, making their way by train from Siberia, through Kazakhstan, down to the Caspian Sea to Iran, which was then called Persia.

None of my mother's family ever saw their beloved older brother again, as he was caught and murdered by the *Gestapo* in Poland in 1943, for refusing to reveal the whereabouts of his military unit in the forests.

Iraq, Iran and India

My mother and her parents continued their enforced wanderings through Iraq and Iran, ending up in a large 'transit' camp for Polish families in India, called Valivade. It was close to the city of Kolhapur near Bombay (now Mumbai), on the south-western coast of India, and they stayed there five years until 1948, making it a very long 'transit'!

It was here that my mother studied to be a school teacher, learnt English, sang soprano solos in the community choir, made friends and had what was almost a normal, happy life, be it living in tents in a tropical monsoon climate. She was once stung by a scorpion, which was, fortunately, not a poisonous one.

Arriving in England

My mother and her parents then sailed from Bombay to Tilbury Port in Essex in 1948, a journey which took three weeks on board the ship *SS Ormonde*. It appears that they were

IMAGE: Basia Domzal-Karpowicz

The Bug river in winter

CHAPTER 3: **World War II**

My mama with her parents, taken in India in c.1943

My mama, age 18, in Tehran (1943)

simply given the option of emigrating to a number of destinations, including the UK, Canada, the USA, Australia, New Zealand and even Argentina.

There is evidence to suggest that the Polish Government in Exile, based in London, tried to persuade displaced Poles not to go back to Soviet-controlled Poland at this time. This was because most of their property and homes had been requisitioned by the Soviet authorities, especially in the eastern part of the country, so there was very little to return to. People were also told that it would be dangerous to return to

IMAGES: Basia Domzal-Karpowicz

My mama and two friends in a tented transit camp, on the way to India

91

Poles in the UK

My mama (second right) and I (third right) at a Corpus Christi procession at Checkendon Camp (c.1958), with Nissen huts in the background

Poland if they had any links to the Allies or the Anders' Army, as they could be imprisoned or even executed for having these links.

She remembers seeing a whale in the Indian Ocean while en route. My family did not go back to Poland, as they knew that their home had been requisitioned by the Soviet government and that they would suffer repercussions for their involvement with the Anders' Army.

From 1948 to 1960 my mother and mother-in-law lived in the Checkendon Camp for Polish families, a former prisoner of war camp. This consisted of a large complex of corrugated iron Nissen huts with concrete floors (very hot in summer, cold and damp in winter). My mother's camp was near to the Nettlebed Camp for Polish soldiers, where my father and father-in-law were settled. They met, married and started their families, before moving to Reading, the nearest big town, when the camp finally closed in 1960. They bought our beautiful family home there, of which they were exceedingly proud, and which replaced the homes they had 'lost' almost 20 years before.

Growing up in the 1960s

As for me, I was born ten years after World War II ended and moved from Checkendon Camp to Reading with my family in 1960, and grew up listening to Bob Dylan and the Polish

My parents and I inside our Nissen hut at Checkendon Camp (c.1959). Note the corrugated steel walls of the hut

CHAPTER 3: **World War II**

blues rock band Dżem. I was so curious about my Polish heritage that I took a train to Poland with an English friend just after our A-level exams in 1973, met most of my parents' families for the first time and fell head over heels in love with the country, despite its austere communist conditions.

The sights, sounds and even the smells of Poland drew me in to what was my first 'epiphany' regarding the long-lost place where I felt I really belonged. My second 'epiphany' was while standing on the sandy bank of the Bug river in 1980. This river now separates post-World War II Poland from its pre-war eastern *Kresy* borderlands, where my parents lived. It was here that I promised myself that I would one day cross that border, to what's now Belarus, and visit their, and our, family homes, which I finally did with my husband and daughters in 2008 and 2012, but alas without my parents.

My college studies

I studied at the Chelsea School of Art for a year after my A-levels, as artistic ability was something I inherited from my mother and her family. I 'dropped out' to study for a BA in Polish and English Language and Literature at The University of London's School of Slavonic and East European Studies and University College London, where my lecturers included the late Professor Jerzy Peterkiewicz [1916–2007] and Professor Norman Davies [born 1939]. I attended the latter's inspiring Polish history lectures voluntarily to gain a crucial insight into the background to Poland's literary movements and traditions.

I travelled to Poland many times during and after my studies to buy books, and also attended a six-week language school at the Catholic University of Lublin (KUL). Lublin and Warsaw are the settings for many of Nobel laureate Isaac Bashevis Singer's novels about Polish Jewish life in pre-World War II Poland, which I wholeheartedly recommend.

IMAGE: Basia Domzal-Karpowicz

My parents, Czesia and Zygmunt Domzal, in the front garden of their beloved house in Reading in 1970

For those wanting to read other significant Polish literary works, I also recommend the nineteenth century novels of Henryk Sienkiewicz, many of which have (like Singer's works) been translated into English, particularly his historical trilogy, which is set in the seventeenth century. I'd also recommend any or all of Norman Davies's excellent histories of Poland, from his iconic *God's Playground* through *Rising '44: The Battle for Warsaw* to his latest *Anders' Army: Trail of Hope, An Odyssey Across Three Continents*. This last book is about the route my family took after being freed from their Siberian sufferings.

On a more contemporary note, I would recommend *The Books of Jacob (Księgi Jakubowe)*, the latest book by the novelist Olga Tokarczuk. However, if you'd like to explore the

Poles in the UK

dissident literary approach to what was going on during the time of the Polish People's Republic (the period from 1945–1989 when the country was under Communist rule), then any of Sławomir Mrożek's short stories about 1960s Poland are a joy to read.

Finally, the poetry of Adam Mickiewicz, who was Poland's most important nineteenth century poet, is also a must. And for children I'd recommend the verses of Julian Tuwim, another Jewish Pole, such as the classic *The Locomotive* (*Lokomotywa*) onomatopoeic poem, which was written so as to resemble the sounds of a train setting in motion.

Jobs and family life

I have, since my studies, worked as a translator for the Polish Airline LOT and the US Embassy in Vienna, and have also completed several freelance projects. I have also edited books for Collier MacMillan and Cambridge University Press, and spent a year at the Jagiellonian University's History of Art and Museum Studies Departments in Kraków. I am an avid member of the Kresy-Siberia Foundation on Facebook and enjoy researching my family's war-torn and pre-World War II past. I enjoy art and you can view a portfolio of my more recent artwork and illustrations on my Facebook page BD Art.

My third-generation daughters, Dominika (27) and Maja (21), are also bilingual in Polish and English and often visit Poland with us. Dominika works in marketing for the mental health charity Mind and is also a keen photographer and animal rights activist, which has inspired us all to become vegan. Maja is a patriotic Polish history buff and travel writer, who is currently studying for a BA in English with Creative Writing at Birmingham University, having completed an internship at the Warsaw Uprising Museum in 2014. Together with my husband (whose story appears elsewhere in this book) and daughters, I've been back to the towns where our parents lived in pre-World War II Poland (although they are now in Belarus). We actually found their houses, along with a few elderly people who remembered our families, which was a very emotional experience.

There are still many beautiful old wooden buildings and cobbled roads in Belarus, and I wish we could at least regain my mother's old houses (my father lived in the basement of the Inland Revenue building where his father worked, in Nowogródek). Sadly this is not currently possible as the government of Belarus has forbidden 'foreigners' like us to do this.

My younger daughter Maja in the traditional heavy, striped woollen folk costume of my father's native Łowicz region (c.2001)

IMAGE: Basia Domzal-Karpowicz

CHAPTER 3: World War II

My father's amazing life

My late Father, Zygmunt Domzal [1920–1985], was also subject to the same traumatic wartime experiences as my mother. As a 19-year-old boy living in the city of Nowogródek (now in Belarus), he was ordered by the invading Germans to inform on his schoolmates, so he decided to flee back to his native central Poland.

His mother gave him gold coins, which she sewed into the lining of his jacket. This was because, if the coins were found, he would have been robbed or shot. His mother also gave him identity documents that allowed him to safely cross the border to Lithuania, but his two friends were tragically shot by the Germans – for the simple 'crime' of not having the correct documents.

My father had to be liberated because soon after arriving back in Poland he was picked up in a street round-up by the Nazis and sent to a forced (slave) labour camp in the Alsace, eastern France. So, it was only in 1945 that he was able to join the war effort by enlisting in the Anders' Army in Edinburgh, although I don't know exactly how he got there.

However, my father never saw his dear mother or father again, as both unfortunately died soon after he fled. He did manage to invite two of his younger brothers to visit us in Reading in the 1970s, after more than 30 years apart, and returned to Poland to see his other brother in 1976, with my mother and myself. This was the one and only time he dared go back to a Communist Poland after World War II, as he was afraid of repercussions against his brothers and himself by the government.

My father never wished to talk to me about the terror of his wartime experiences, telling only my mother and his brother a little. I did not hold this against him as I can imagine what he went through and don't think I would have been able to talk to my daughters about anything so horrific.

I do know, however, that he managed to wend his way south from Edinburgh, via Wales, while working in the construction and mining industries. Only manual jobs were available to Polish ex-servicemen, despite their helping the British war effort and the fact that my father spoke good English.

My mother also spoke good English, but initially with a mixed Polish and Indian accent, as she was taught it by Indians during the British Raj (the period when Britain ruled India, which lasted from 1858 to 1947). This meant that she was often mocked because of her accent by the women she briefly worked with at Huntley & Palmer's biscuit factory in Reading. She never taught in a British school because of it, although she did gladly teach at the Polish Saturday School in Reading for many years.

Barbara Domzal-Karpowicz

My father, age 11, in his Boy Scout uniform (Nowogródek, May 1932)

My father in his 'Polish army under British command' uniform (c.1945)

IMAGES: Basia Domzal-Karpowicz

Poles in the UK

Jan Mokrzycki's story (83)

The remarkable story of Jan Mokrzycki and his inspirational mum Janina took place during one of the most terrible periods of Polish history, when the country was occupied by Germany and then Russia.

Janina the doctor
Jan's mum qualified as one of Poland's first ever women doctors in 1931, having studied medicine at the University of Warsaw. After graduating and marrying a fellow doctor, she worked as a general practitioner in the Polish capital, treating all types of illnesses in the period before many familiar modern medicines had been developed.

Jan himself was born in 1932 into a fairly typical middle-class family. He lived in a huge flat in central Warsaw, along with his grandfather who was a very successful dental surgeon and who ran his surgery from the flat. The flat was so large Jan was able to ride the bike he was given for his sixth birthday (his first two-wheeler) around it!

Family photographs from this period show the happy childhood that Jan enjoyed in the first ten years of his life. Life in Poland was great for people like him during this time, as the country began to modernise itself and became successful following independence in 1918.

The terrible war years
All that changed, however, when World War II broke out in 1939 and all the men in Jan's family were conscripted to fight. His mum stayed working in the hospital in Warsaw, which was now receiving soldiers who had been wounded in battle.

Soon, terror broke out across Warsaw, as German aircraft bombed and machine-gunned the Polish capital. This was a new type of warfare to anything seen before: everything and everyone was machine-gunned, including men, women, children and animals.

The Polish air force was very small compared to that of the Germans, meaning it was soon obliterated, leaving the Polish army and population with hardly any defence. Jan was moved from his childhood flat to the hospital where his mum worked, because she thought he would be safer there. The Germans then brought in the heavy guns, and although the city held out for a month, Warsaw eventually fell to the invading force and the occupation started.

CHAPTER 3: **World War II**

He moved back to his family's Warsaw flat, where he was joined by the men from his family, who had managed to escape from captivity in other parts of Europe. They were hungry and dirty, but not injured.

Ahead of Jan was a bitterly cold winter with no glass in the windows of his flat and no coal for the stoves that heated his home. Christmas 1939 was spent huddling in the dark, with the flat windows blocked up with cardboard, and with food in very short supply. There were no presents and no traditional feast on Christmas Eve; they just sang a few carols and swapped 'good' wishes.

It was a frightening time for young Jan. The sound of German boots on the pavements was never far away and he and his friends had to make way for the rows of marching soldiers by flattening themselves against walls or even walking into the road. As access to public areas, including seating on public transport, was restricted for Polish citizens, sometimes the only way to ride a tram was to hang from the outside. But at least that meant you got to go free!

The invading German forces brought devastating consequences for so many Polish people – including Jan's family. As had been the case throughout German-occupied Europe, Jewish people – and those who helped them – were targetted for especially brutal treatment in Poland.

One morning in June 1943, on returning from a walk near his family's weekend villa in the settlement of Sulejówek (about ten miles east of Warsaw), Jan noticed a German secret police car (the *Gestapo*) disappearing into the distance.

When the Germans discovered that several members of his family had belonged to a secret underground group supporting Jews (called Żegota), the consequences were truly terrible.

His father, uncle and grandfather had already been arrested in Warsaw and the *Gestapo* had been to pick up his mum at the villa. All of them were taken to the *Gestapo* headquarters in Warsaw where they were interrogated and tortured in the most terrible way. They were then sentenced to death for being members of the Polish resistance army.

His father, uncle and grandfather were all shot and dumped in the sewers, but his mum avoided death and instead was sent to the notorious concentration camp at Auschwitz in Poland (she was later transferred to Ravensbrück camp in Germany). This meant Jan was left behind at the villa with some other family members, while his family's flat in Warsaw and all their possessions were taken over by the Germans.

Jan as a child with his mother Janina, taken in 1933

IMAGE: Jan Mokrzycki

97

Poles in the UK

His mum survived one of the twentieth century's most shocking examples of human cruelty and evil, simply because she was as tough as nails, and because she had a slightly better life in the camp, as she was a doctor. She worked in the camp hospital at Auschwitz for just over a year.

Jan was thrown out of his family villa by incoming Russian soldiers in August 1944. He then witnessed the gunfire and devastating fires of the Warsaw Uprising, which lasted 63 days and resulted in the death of about 200,000 people (▶ p. 32). He watched this from the safety of a tomato farm outside the city, where he was working with his grandmother and some friends. Most of Poland's capital city was destroyed during this time.

He eventually returned to the original family flat in Warsaw, where he saw the efforts to rebuild the flattened city.

Two amazing rescues

Jan's mum somehow managed to survive the terrors of the concentration camps for over two years and in 1945 was finally rescued by the Americans, who arrived in their Jeeps to liberate Ravensbrück concentration camp.

Remarkably, one of the soldiers who first met his mum was a Polish-American serviceman who had actually specialised in surgery with her husband years earlier!

Neither Janina, nor her son – now separated by hundreds of miles – knew if each other had survived the war years. But Janina was determined to find her son, so she headed back from Germany to Poland (which was occupied by Russian forces) in the hope of finding her 12-year-old son.

The extraordinary story continued when Janina arrived just before Christmas 1945 at the flat in Warsaw, where Jan had been living with his grandmother. She rang the doorbell and Jan answered, but he didn't recognise the grey-haired, little woman who was shouting 'Jan' at him with tears in her eyes!

When he finally realised it was his mum, the joy was indescribable. And he had something special waiting for his mum: a silver cup, which he had been due to give her as a name day present the day after she was captured by the Germans, two years earlier.

It was still not safe for his mum to stay in Poland during this period, as she would have been sent to Siberia by the communists in charge of Poland. So she planned a daring escape from the country, whose borders were still strictly regulated.

The pair of them would travel by train to the border town of Cieszyn. From there, they would cross over the frozen Olza river to

The Olza river in winter

CHAPTER 3: **World War II**

The Austin Healey car that Jan's wife fell in love with

Czechoslovakia (now Czech Republic) at night on New Year's Eve 1945, when the border guards were drunk from celebrating the arrival of the new year!

An amazing walk to freedom took place that night and they took a bus to the occupied Czechoslovakia's capital Prague (now Czech Republic), where his mum had a friend from her Auschwitz days. From there, a passport and visa for travel further west in Europe could be arranged.

A new life in Britain

Jan and his mother's incredible escape from Poland eventually brought them to Austria, then to Germany (where she met her second husband and worked as a doctor for the Allied forces), and then finally to Britain in the autumn of 1947, where Janina's medical skills were much in demand two years after World War II ended.

Jan and his mum were first directed to a camp in Sherbourne, Dorset, that had been made in a clearing in a forest. His mum received additional training in her specialist subject, chest diseases, and then got her first 'proper' job in the UK at a hospital in Chepstow, Wales.

Jan (still 12) was sent to school in Bolton, Lancashire, where he boarded with a couple, Mr and Mrs Walker, whom he called 'mum and dad – much to his mum's annoyance! Mr Walker took him to his first football match (Bolton Wanderers), which started his lifelong love of the game. He went on to complete his secondary education in Bolton.

When Jan's mum and her husband came to join him in Bolton later, the family bought a house in the town. It was their first taste of 'normal' family life for many years.

He generally found people in his new home to be very welcoming in these years after World War II, despite speaking no English when he arrived. Although he was one of only three Poles in his school, he was able to focus on his studies, picked up English quickly and did well academically. He was eventually offered a place at Newcastle University to study dental surgery, which he started in 1955.

While at university, Jan became heavily involved in the student Rag Committee – a team that raised money for charity every year. His imaginative ideas led to record-breaking fundraising for local charities, and this spurred him on to further voluntary work.

He was eventually elected as President of the Student Representative Council at Newcastle, and in his final year at university he served on the executive committee of the National Union of Students.

He qualified in dental surgery in 1959 and headed first to London, as he wanted some Polish company. He met his future wife, Magdalena, at church and they married in that same church nine months later. Jan tells the amusing story that his wife claims she actually fell in love with his Austin Healey Sprite sports car, not himself!

The couple soon moved to Coventry in Warwickshire, where he set up the first of two

Poles in the UK

Jan and his wife Magdalena

dental practices. During his long and successful career as a dental surgeon he treated many thousands of patients and employed numerous people in his dental practices in England.

He and Magdalena went on to have two children (Jan and Wanda) who both speak fluent Polish, and they now have six grandchildren. One of his granddaughters is a high level gymnast, who has competed in international competitions.

With his wife he started a radio programme in 1991 on BBC Coventry & Warwickshire radio called 'Poles Apart'. The programme, which ended a few years ago, after being the station's longest-running series, celebrated Polish culture.

A very active retirement

Jan has always been very interested in voluntary work and politics, and he was able to channel this interest during his retirement by getting involved in various charitable and other organisations.

This included a period as the President of the Federation of Poles in Great Britain. One of the highlights of this role was being invited to a dinner hosted by Her Majesty the Queen, during an official visit to the UK by the then President of Poland, Aleksander Kwaśniewski. Jan is also currently the President of the Anglo Polish Society (Bristol and the South West).

His work with the Federation of Poles in Great Britain really gathered pace when Poland joined the European Union in 2004 and thousands of Polish people arrived in the UK. Jan took a very hands-on role during this period, helping these newcomers find somewhere to live and get work, as well as advising on the importance of joining a trade union. He was motivated during this period by the need to help Polish people integrate into British society.

He has received several awards for his work, including the Polish Order of Merit and the Cavalier's Cross of the Polonia Restituta Order (one of Poland's highest awards).

Jan continues to support work that helps promote Polish culture in the UK, and is a trustee of the Polonia Aid Foundation Trust — a charity that gives grants for projects focussing on Polish history and culture (including this book).

His remarkable mum Janina went on to give many more years service to the NHS as a specialist in diseases of the chest, before retiring in 1983. She finally passed away in Jan and Magdalena's home in February 1995.

CHAPTER 4

The Sciences

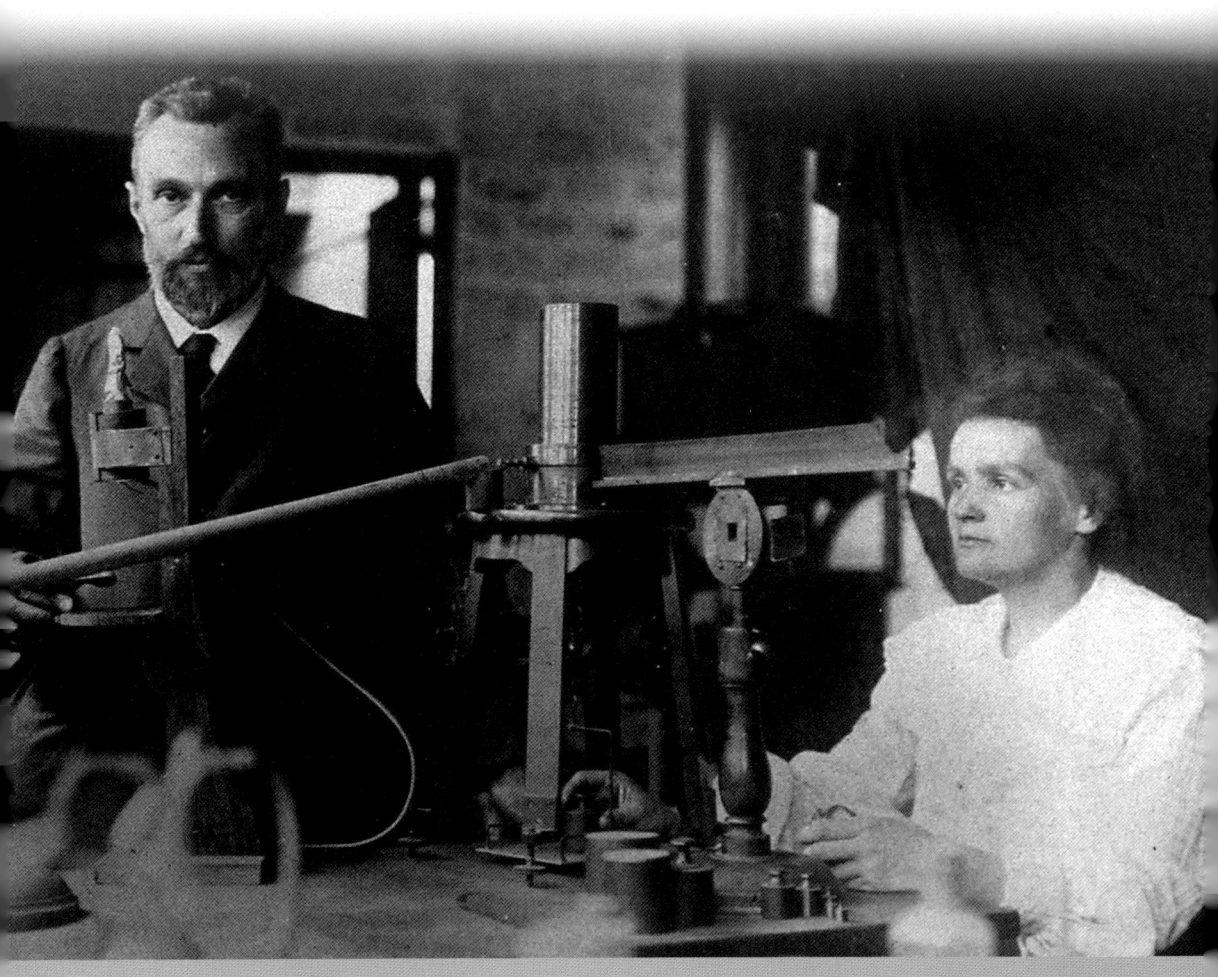

This chapter explores the many ways in which Polish people have made key contributions to science in the UK and worldwide, over the centuries. It includes the important sixteenth century astronomical breakthroughs of Nicolaus Copernicus, alongside many more recent contributions, which continue to impact on British society today.

Poles in the UK

The beautiful house where Nicolaus Copernicus is thought to have been born in 1473 is now a museum

Polish people, and those with Polish parents and grandparents, have made many important contributions to the sciences over the last six centuries. They include ground-breaking advances in mathematics, astronomy, physics and chemistry, together with pioneering work in applied sciences such as ecology and environmental management.

Many of these breakthroughs by Poles have had a worldwide influence, but there have also been many UK-specific contributions made by Polish scientists. Taken together, these scientific developments have created an important *Polish scientific legacy* in the UK.

This legacy is especially keenly felt in such areas as astronomy, where **Nicolaus Copernicus's** ideas provided a new blueprint for our understanding of the Solar System (▶ p. 103), and in physics and chemistry, where **Maria Skłodowska-Curie** discovered two new elements and pioneered the use of x-rays in medicine (▶ p. 106). This remarkable Polish woman's work lives on in the UK today through the highly respected national charity, Marie Curie Cancer Care.

Poland is a country with a very long history of formalised education and scholarly activity, which dates back to 1364 and the foundation of the country's first higher education institution – today's internationally renowned Jagiellonian University in Kraków. This has paved the way for hundreds of years of important

CHAPTER 4: **The Sciences**

SUCCESS STORY

The highly influential Renaissance mathematician and astronomer, **Nicolaus Copernicus**, was a Pole whose original name was Mikołaj Kopernik [1473–1543]. He revolutionised our understanding of the Earth's place in the solar system by placing the sun, not the Earth, at the centre of the solar system. He is considered to have made a major contribution to the history of science with this and other ideas. Copernicus's family home in the city of Toruń, northern Poland, is now a museum, dedicated to his life and his work (▶ p. 102).

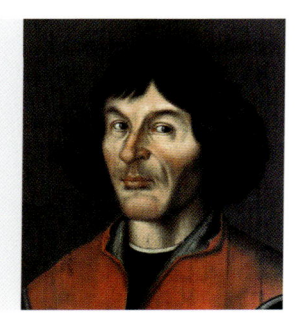

The influential Renaissance thinker Nicolaus Copernicus was born in the Polish city of Toruń (portrait painted 1580 by an unknown artist)

discoveries in science and other areas, many of which have had a direct impact on the UK, often helping to save lives or improve quality of life.

Furthermore, many British people do not realise that this tradition of pioneering science research has continued in Poland to this day, across numerous different scientific disciplines. One especially noteworthy example is the research into, and subsequent practical work carried out on, the management of ecosystems within Poland, for wildlife and people. This work, which has now been adopted much more widely across Europe, is being supported through a partnership with the Royal Society for the Protection of Birds, a leading British charity (▶ p. 110).

Did you know?

One of the world's most respected websites about the use of binoculars and other optical equipment is run by Polish brothers Arek and Richard Olech. The www.allbinos.com site contains hundreds of reviews of binoculars for use in nature observation, hunting and astronomy – together with background articles and the opinions of others.

A special feature of the website is the advanced process used by Arek and Richard to appraise models, which involves binoculars being tested on advanced machines which assess their technical aspects.

The Olech brothers have also reached out to binocular enthusiasts in the UK, including one of the authors of this book! A recent parcel to Brin, who is also the author of a popular book on the social history of binoculars, contained a lovely example of Polish military 'PZO' 6x30 binocular. It was the perfect gift to celebrate a shared passion for optics.

IMAGE: Brin Best

A very happy British binocular enthusiast tests out his Polish military binocular, during a break in his Polish language lesson in Leeds, West Yorkshire

103

Poles in the UK

The celebrated Polish explorer Marek Kamiński now also explores the world with his family. His first *Baby on Board* expedition (in 2006) involved travelling across Poland by car and boat, along the Vistula river. The expedition was 40 days long, starting at the Vistula's spring in the hills of the Silesian Beskids in southern Poland, and ending in the Kashubia, northern Poland. Kamiński was accompanied by his two-year-old daughter Pola, his wife Kasia and their dog, Aja

IMAGE: Marek Kamiński

'POLES TO THE POLE' – MAREK KAMIŃSKI AND JAN MELA

An inspirational explorer and travel writer

Marek Kamiński is a multilingual Polish explorer and writer. He is famous for his expeditions and for his books and journals documenting his adventures. Kamiński has travelled by a range of modes of transport, including boat, cargo ship, catamaran, hitch-hiking, skiing and walking.

He embarked on his first independent trip in 1977, when he was just 15. It was a short trip from the port city of Szczecin to Denmark, on a cargo ship. Although short, it was a difficult journey to arrange for a young adult in Communist Poland, where citizens needed special permission to be granted a passport. However, the teenage Kamiński was determined, so he organised and completed his trip successfully. He has since explored regions all around the globe, including the Baltic Sea, Scandinavia, the North and South Poles, the Amazon, the Bolivian Andes, North Africa, Mount Kilimanjaro, the Australian Gibson Desert and many more.

It is, however, his **Polar expeditions** that have brought him international acclaim. He has traversed the Arctic and the Antarctic numerous times. One of his first Polar expeditions, in which he set off with a Polish

CHAPTER 4: **The Sciences**

The importance of an expedition does not arise from whether we are going to the end of the world or to a nearby hill. We are not determined to do only spectacular things, but things that are really important. Let's remember that it is not the amount of arms and legs we have that makes us strong, but what we have in our mind and heart.

Jan Mela

companion, Wojciech Moskal, was aptly named 'Poles to the Pole'. He later became the first person to reach both the North Pole and the South Pole on foot, on his own and with no external assistance. He holds the Guinness World Record for this achievement.

Furthermore, Kamiński is known for his 2004 expedition, 'Together to the Pole'. This journey involved reaching both Poles within a year – this time with a young explorer, Jan Mela. Mela was 15 at the time, the same age Kamiński was when he began his travels. Mela lost his arm and a leg in an accident just two years prior to the expedition.

A courageous teenage explorer

Marek Kamiński met Jan Mela through his charity, *Fundacja Marka Kamińskiego*. The charity helps people with disabilities and those in need, among its other aims. The teenage Mela contacted the charity, because he wanted to embark on a Polar expedition. Kamiński took him on for extensive training, and soon they went on a daring expedition together – Mela's disability did not get in the way of making his dream come true.

Their 2004 adventure was a truly inspirational feat. As Kamiński explains on his website, organising and preparing for the journey was 'a big challenge, a huge responsibility, and a great success'. This was because Mela became the world's first person with a disability to reach both the North and the South Poles. At just 15 years of age, Mela was also the world's youngest ever explorer to achieve this.

Following his success under Marek Kamiński's guidance, Jan Mela set up his own foundation, **Beyond Horizons** (*Poza Horyzonty*). The charity reaches out to people who, like himself, have suffered life changing injuries following accidents. Mela and his foundation encourage and help countless people with disabilities to follow their dreams, by raising money for prosthetic limbs and organising expeditions.

Find out more

Marek Kamiński's website, featuring photographs from many of his expeditions:
www.marekkaminski.com

Jan Mela's charity website:
www.pozahoryzonty.org

105

Poles in the UK

A portrait of Maria Skłodowska-Curie from 1903

SUCCESS STORY

The famous Nobel Prize-winning scientist Marie Curie [1867–1934] was born in Warsaw, Poland, and is better known to her Polish compatriots by her original name, Maria Skłodowska-Curie.

Skłodowska-Curie was a highly distinguished physicist and chemist, who is best known for her pioneering work on radioactivity. She achieved several extraordinary 'firsts' in her lifetime, and is without doubt one of Poland's most important scientists.

A pioneering woman and scientist

Skłodowska-Curie was the first woman to win a Nobel Prize (awarded in 1903 for chemistry) and is still the only woman to have been awarded two (her second came in 1911, for physics). She was also the first woman to become a professor at the University of Paris, and in 1995 became the first woman to be entombed on her own merit in the Panthéon in Paris. This is the non-religious mausoleum which contains the remains of celebrated French citizens (Skłodowska-Curie became a naturalised French citizen after marrying the French scientist Pierre Curie in 1895).

While living in France, she adopted the name Marie Skłodowska-Curie and never lost sight of her Polish identity, teaching her two daughters Polish and taking them on visits to her country of birth.

Her achievements in the scientific field were many and included the theory of radioactivity, methods for isolating radioactive isotopes and the discovery of two brand new elements – polonium (which she named after her native country) and radium. Her work paved the way for many important discoveries in science and medicine after her death.

A person of high character

Despite Skłodowska-Curie's fame, she was notoriously modest in her lifestyle and approach, and often refused awards or returned money given to her. She is also known to have given much of the money from her Nobel Prizes to family, friends, students and research colleagues.

In a highly unusual move, Skłodowska-Curie did not take out a patent on the radium-isolation process (which could

The UK charity Marie Curie carries out vital work supporting terminally ill people and their relatives

Marie Curie
Care and support through terminal illness

106

CHAPTER 4: **The Sciences**

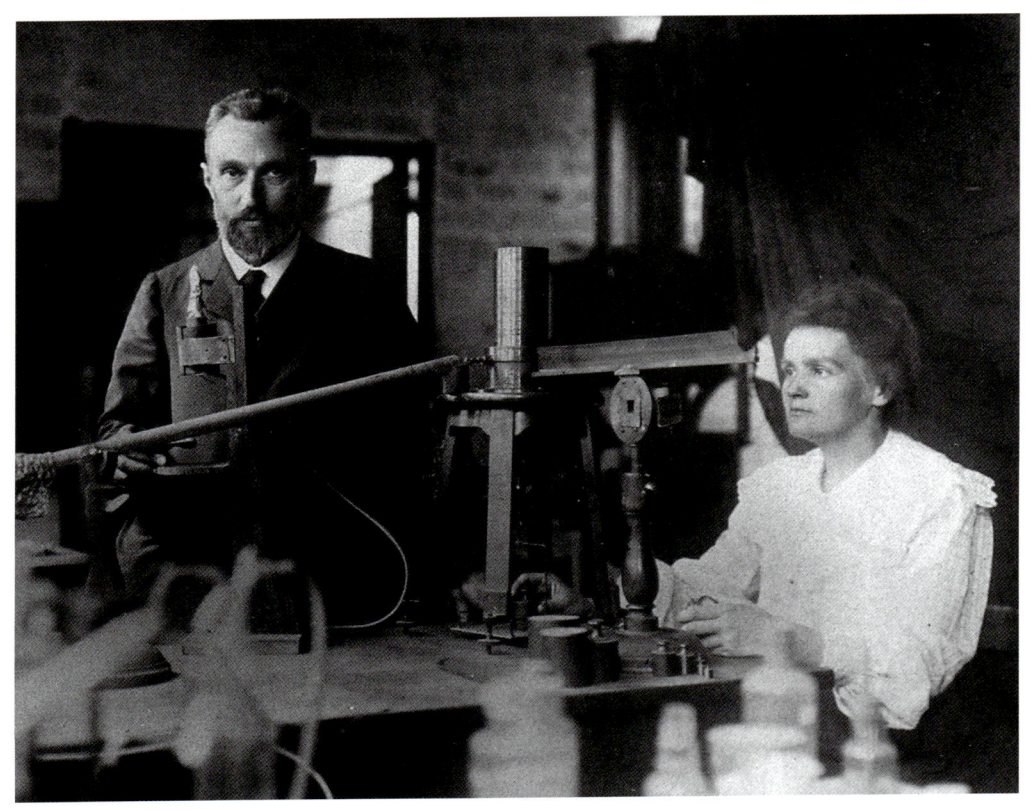

Maria Skłodowska-Curie at work in her laboratory (c.1904)

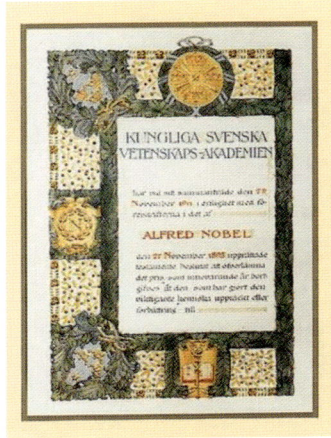

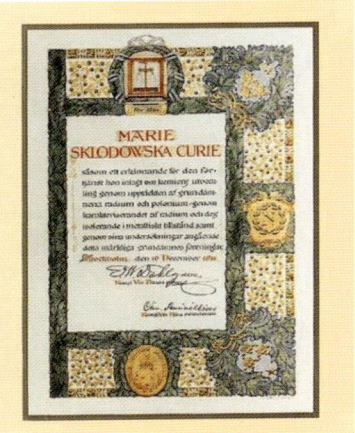

Maria Skłodowska-Curie's two Nobel Prize Diplomas

107

Poles in the UK

have earned her a fortune), so that the scientific community could freely carry on their research in this important new field.

A lasting legacy

Tragically, Skłodowska-Curie died at the age of 66 in France from aplastic anaemia, which is thought to have been caused by exposure to radiation during her important research and work.

Skłodowska-Curie's work has been recognised as contributing substantially to science and society in the twentieth and twenty-first centuries. She has become an iconic figure in science and was voted the 'most inspirational woman in science' in a vote organised by the British magazine *New Scientist* in 2009.

This remarkable woman's name lives on in many research institutes around the world, and in the UK through the charity Marie Curie, which provides care and support to people with terminal illnesses and their families. During 2014–2015 the charity provided care to some 40,000 terminally ill patients in its hospices and in the community.

The Maria Skłodowska-Curie statue near the Radium Institute in Warsaw, Poland

SUCCESS STORY

The BBC weather presenter **Tomasz Schafernaker** was born in Gdańsk, Poland, in 1979 and was educated both in his native Poland and in Britain. He took his A-levels in the UK and went on to gain a degree in meteorology at Reading University, before joining the Met Office. In 2000 he made his first broadcast for the BBC, making him (at 21) the youngest man to present the weather for the BBC. Schafernaker now has dual Polish-British nationality.

Did you know?

Many important inventions have been created in Poland, or by Polish inventors based in other countries. They include the following ten noteworthy innovations:
- The **bagel**
- The **holographic** technique (for creating a hologram, or a three-dimensional image of a subject)
- The **aeroscope** (an early type of compressed-air camera)
- The **bomba** code-breaking machine
- The **delta wing** (used for flight)
- The **ebulliometer** (a machine designed to measure the boiling point of liquids)
- The **K-202 computer** (an early mini computer)
- The **kerosene lamp**
- The **Mine detector Mark I** (developed for World War II)
- The **Gundlach Periscope** (used in tanks).

CHAPTER 4: **The Sciences**

KONIK POLSKI – THE POLISH 'NATURE PONIES'

Ponies called *koniks* are being increasingly used on nature reserves in Britain to help conserve some of our most precious wildlife.

A hardy breed

These ponies are called *konik* from the Polish word for 'little horse'. They are a small and stocky, dun-coloured breed, with a thick black mane and tail, and with black stripes down the back and legs.

Koniks are extremely hardy and are able to winter outside in severe weather, right down to temperatures as low as -40°C. They are adapted to foraging in the wild and will eat a wide range of vegetation including scrub, rushes and roots, as well as grass. They are known to be intelligent and adaptable, have been observed carefully exploring new sites, and will adjust their diet depending on season.

Polish ponies called *koniks* are used to help manage nature reserves in the UK

Polish ancestors

Koniks were originally believed to be descended from the tarpan, a pre-historic wild horse that continued to live in Central European forests up until the late nineteenth century, when it became extinct. However, recent genetic studies put this into doubt, and indicate that *koniks* are very closely related to many domestic horse breeds. This ties in with the view that the breed originates from farm draft horses, used on Polish farms in the summer months, but released and adapted to fend for themselves over the winter season when animal feed was in short supply.

Various breeding programmes in the nineteenth and early twentieth century aimed to add the features of the wild tarpan to the breed. In the 1920s a Polish biologist from Kraków, Tadeusz Vetulani, became interested in *koniks* and later set up a reserve for them in the Białowieża Forest (▶ p. 49). *Koniks* were then introduced to more nature reserves within Poland, and subsequently to the Netherlands and other European countries.

Koniks in the UK

In the 1990s *koniks* were brought to the UK to help manage a number of nature reserves where natural grazing from large herbivores was absent. Without grazing, grassland and marshland habitats will eventually cover over with scrub and ultimately develop into woodland.

Koniks will readily forage on a variety of vegetation, holding back scrub growth and preserving wildlife-rich grassland and fens. Their hardiness means they can thrive even in the poor quality grazing areas within a nature reserve, and do not require grass improved with fertilizer.

Some of the first UK nature reserves to introduce *koniks* were Redgrave and Lopham Fen (Suffolk Wildlife Trust), Hickling Broad (Broads Authority and Norfolk Wildlife Trust) and Wicken Fen (Cambridgeshire, National Trust). They have now been introduced widely across the UK, from Kent to Aberdeenshire, with great success in controlling rank vegetation to the benefit of threatened birds and other much-valued wildlife.

Amanda Best

Poles in the UK

Zbig Karpowicz's story (61)

IMAGE: Zbig Karpowicz

Zbig in the new RSPB offices inside the David Attenborough Building in Cambridge (Cambridgeshire)

Dr Zbigniew (Zbig) Karpowicz works as a European Country Programmes Officer for the Royal Society for the Protection of Birds (RSPB). This influential British charity is Europe's largest environmental organization, with an income of over £120 million every year.

I studied at the Centre for Russian and East European Studies at Birmingham University in the 1970s, and was awarded a doctorate (PhD) for my research there. My research focussed on environmental and land-use planning in Poland during the communist period. In the late 1980s, after the Soviet Union failed to hide the nuclear disaster that happened in 1986 at the Chernobyl Nuclear Power Plant in Ukraine, green issues became mainstream for both the public and politicians. Although this 'greening' was to some extent global, it was felt most strongly in Western Europe.

My environmental work across Europe
For the last 35 years I've worked on the conservation of ecosystems (habitats such as forests and wetlands) in Europe. I've also been involved in planning work for so-called 'protected areas', such as nature reserves and other areas that are set aside for wildlife. Another aspect of my work has been supporting non-governmental organisations (such as charities) in most of the countries in Central and Eastern Europe (including the Balkans), and the new independent countries in the Caucasus and Central Asia.

My day-to-day work is very varied and I don't have a typical day. I work directly with staff in non-governmental organisations in a variety of European countries, and this work can include:

- Advising on work programmes and helping to organise the implementation of strategies for environmental organizations
- Supporting organizational structures, including financial management issues

This major new publication on where to watch birds in Poland (published in 2015) indicates the importance of the country as a destination for nature lovers from the UK and other European countries. The bird featured on the cover (the aquatic warbler) has its European stronghold in Poland

110

CHAPTER 4: **The Sciences**

- Preparing projects for funding (mainly by the European Commission, but also a range of foundations).

Key tasks include attending meetings, providing training and communicating with others, especially via email. I also travel to the offices of each of our partners, at least once a year.

Poland's rich biodiversity

Poland was one of the first countries in the east of Europe that activated public support on environmental subjects (for example pollution, clean water and native forests) to protest against the Communist Government actions on censorship and freedom of expression.

Environmental issues therefore played an important part in the overthrow of central government control in these countries.

Poland did not take up the Soviet system of widespread land-use change and collectivised single-crop agriculture. This is where all the land (agriculture and forests) is owned by the government or state, and the only private land is the gardens around people's houses. The people in villages work in factory-style farms, with large amounts of machinery or large numbers of animals, and the fields tend to be huge, with no hedges for wildlife. Because this Soviet farming system was not taken up in

The Biebrza Marshes of north-east Poland are one of Europe's most important wetland areas

Poles in the UK

Poland, a diverse landscape, rich in flora and fauna, has survived.

Many of the small, privately owned farms still use traditional methods and do not use herbicides and fertilizers, which can be damaging to wildlife. This means that flowers and insects are abundant, with many types of farmland birds that are scarce or extinct in the UK still common in the Polish countryside. These include such species as the tree sparrow, skylark, corn bunting and red-backed shrike. The latter species is also called the 'butcher bird', because it often impales its prey on thorny bushes to be eaten later, in a natural larder!

Poland's protected areas
Poland has one of the oldest protected areas in Europe – the Białowieża Forest (▶ p. 49) – which helped to save the European bison from extinction, as well as being Europe's only primeval forest and an outstanding biodiversity site for many other species groups.

Poland also pioneered the 'ecological network' approach. This is a landscape management system with different zones of land being used for different purposes, but all interlinked and forming a network of key sites (the larger protected areas) and corridors (along river valleys, mountain chains, coastlines, lakes and forests). This model was revived by the European Commission nearly 30 years after being developed in Poland, and is now being introduced right across the continent.

The western half of Belarus, which before World War II was the eastern part of Poland (a region known as *Polesie*), remains to this day one of the wildest and most natural parts of Europe. Here you can find extensive marshes, vast forests and untamed rivers flowing in natural flood plains. These areas support major populations of European mammals such as wolf, lynx, elk and wild boar. These animals use the corridors of natural forest – and the rivers and undisturbed lands which cross Poland east to west – to migrate into Western Europe. This means that wolves can now again be found in countries as far west as the Netherlands.

Red-backed shrikes are still fairly common across much of Poland, thanks to farming practices sympathetic to wildlife

Polish science and research
Poland has a long tradition of science and research, and the Jagiellonian University in Kraków was one of the first to be established in Europe (in 1364). Throughout history Polish universities have carried out a lot of pioneering work, including many in the environmental sciences, such as the concept of 'ecosystem services'. This is where nature is viewed as having multiple benefits, including its intrinsic worth, its value to people's safety and well-being, and its ability to generate income.

A working example of the ecosystem services approach, which has been developed in Poland,

> *In a recent survey of travelling British birdwatchers, about one third had visited Poland, making it the fifth most-visited European country by them. Interestingly, all of them said that they would recommend their visit to a friend – which has to be the highest accolade in birding tourism.*
>
> Keith Betton

CHAPTER 4: **The Sciences**

> *Birds know no borders, and as the UK is an offshore archipelago, the RSPB has always benefited enormously from cooperating with our Partners across continental Europe in science, policy and practical conservation efforts. Having studied and worked extensively in Northern Europe, Zbig brings unique understanding, develops innovative approaches and exemplifies our inclusive approach to help conserve nature in the UK, Poland and elsewhere.*
>
> Dr Mike Clarke – Chief Executive, RSPB

is the harvesting of meadows in the Biebrza Marshes in the north-east of Poland – a national park and one of Europe's most important wetland areas. Here, the grasses and sedges (called the 'biomass') are converted into pellets of fibre, which are then used as fuel in power stations, for example at Ostrołęka, north-east of Warsaw. These fibre pellets are used in power stations instead of burning coal, thereby cutting down on a major source of air pollution. They are also used as litter and bedding for household pets.

More recently, universities in Warsaw and Poznań have measured how much greenhouse gasses (which are released into the air from dried peatlands and agricultural lands) are reduced when these areas are restored to their natural state, through the process of re-wetting. The owner of the land (which could be the government, an organization, or a private individual) can even benefit financially from this work, by selling the so-called international carbon credits, which are generated by not polluting the atmosphere with carbon dioxide. As just one part of my job, I played an important role in the application of this approach, which benefits both nature and the wider environment – while also bringing in much-needed income.

Polish attitudes to societies and clubs
One of the features of Polish culture (and that of other Central European countries) is that people do not readily join societies and clubs, in contrast to the situation here in the UK. This is a reaction to the time when, in Poland's communist past, all schoolchildren were forced to belong to governmental societies and organisations. In the UK, membership of bodies such as the National Trust and the RSPB (and doing voluntary work) is widespread and accepted. I think the UK can help Poland make the transition to a country where voluntary work – and engaging with charities – is considered more usual.

The fact that nearly a million Poles have now settled in the UK, while still maintaining their links with the fatherland, will probably mean that over time some of the nature-friendly aspects of British society will filter back into Poland.

Dr Zbig Karpowicz

Find out more
www.rspb.org.uk

Poles in the UK

Professor Jan Strelau

| Psychologist

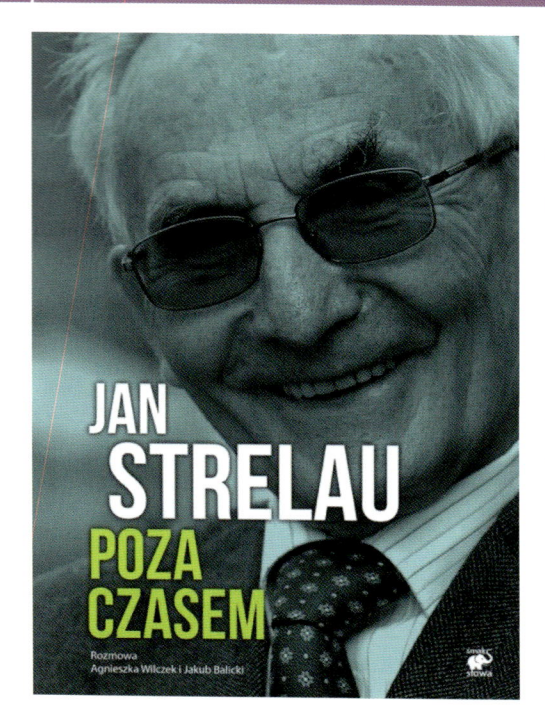

Professor Jan Strelau is one of the most acknowledged and recognised psychologists in Poland. He is now famous worldwide for his remarkable studies on temperament (an aspect of character).

His early life
Strelau was born in 1931 in Gdańsk, in the northern part of Poland. His biological mother asked his elder sister to look after her son after he was born, and then she moved to Germany. Despite having German roots, he decided to stay in Poland and chose to be a Polish citizen. This background could have been one of the reasons for the difficulties he experienced in later life.

Young Strelau's education was not easy in the interwar period. Later on, after World War II had finished, it was the new political and social regime he faced, while still a teenager, which caused serious problems. This all had a profound effect on his career as a psychologist.

The challenges begin
In post-World War II Poland many people were asked to inform for the Communist Party, providing information about what others (especially influential people) were doing. In his extra-curricular activity as an altar boy, Strelau was forced to inform on people in his parish, but later refused to do this. His reluctance to co-operate with the Security Service (Służba Bezpieczeństwa) resulted in his removal from college, and being blacklisted from applying to any public university.

Thanks to the priest who he was asked to inform on, he managed to complete his final secondary school exams (called the Matura) in a small clerical seminary in Słupsk. This helped him to get to the Catholic University in Lublin, the only university he was allowed to study at.

Unfortunately, in the early 1950s, psychology as a true science barely existed in Poland. Behind the Iron Curtain there was no access to foreign psychological books, and the ones that were available were very often soaked with political ideology. Strelau chose the subject which was the closest to his heart, namely the philosophy of Christianity, with a specialisation in psychology. In 1953 he was lucky to get an approval from the Ministry of National

Education to start his long-awaited studies at the University of Warsaw.

From prison to psychology
The rumours about his alleged participation in the Polish underground movement, which aimed to overthrow communism in the country, led to his imprisonment for three months. Inhumane conditions in prison did not stop him continuing his studies, moreover it only fuelled his appetite for learning more and strengthened his motivation.

That was the beginning of his passionate and successful career. In 1958 he completed his dream psychology course at Warsaw University and he then began working at the university as a research assistant of Professor Tomasz Tomaszewski, who would become his lifelong mentor. In 1963 he received a doctorate in psychology for his publication entitled *The Temperament and the Types of Nervous System*. Five years later he became professor of psychology at the University of Warsaw.

Academic success
As soon as he began working in an academic institution, his scientific ideas began to flourish. Between 1978 and 1981 Professor Strelau was the director of the Institute of Psychology at the University of Warsaw. His plan for creating a strong and internationally recognised scientific centre in Poland had been realised. He later (in 1984) established and led the first Polish Department of Psychology of Individual Differences, and in subsequent years, the Interdisciplinary Center for Behavior Genetic Research at the University of Warsaw.

Apart from his knowledge of the German language, he also learnt Russian. This enabled him to complete an internship in Moscow, where he met and cooperated with many influential people, such as Hans Jürgen Eysenck. Eysenck was a psychologist born in Germany, who spent his professional career in Great Britain, and is noted for the popular terms 'introversion' and 'extraversion'. They went on to write together the book *Personality Dimensions and Arousal*, published in 1987.

At the age of 40, Strelau taught himself the English language, while doing his annual stipendium in the USA. He understood quickly how this would help him to spread his ideas beyond Polish borders, and he subsequently made his mark on the international psychology scene.

The Regulative Theory of Temperament
He first encountered behavioural genetics, a science almost unknown in Poland, at the University of Illinois. He worked closely with the talented Jerry Hirsch, examining the locomotoric ability of common fruit flies. As a result of his research, he created the Regulative Theory of Temperament (RTT).

He based his theory on the idea that temperament regulates people's relations with the world, but its function is limited. Temperament modifies the strength of the stimulus which we perceive; so for example, if a person is oversensitive he or she will perceive a stimulus more strongly than a person who is emotionally stable. According to Strelau's theory, temperament traits are regulated by the reaction time and the energy level of each person, so even our speed of talking depends on temperament.

In 1983 he wrote perhaps his most important book, *Temperament, Personality, Activity*, which was written in the English language. The book was published in the USA first, and only after two years in Poland, because of the restrictions on foreign language publishing in Poland at the time.

The collaboration of Strelau and his colleagues resulted in the development of two tools used by psychologists: the Strelau Temperament Inventory (STI) and later, in 1999, the Pavlovian Temperament Survey (PTS). They have both since been adapted for use in dozens of languages.

During his career as a psychologist he wrote 22 books, a few handbooks for students of psychology and over 300 scientific papers. Among them there are very interesting reads such as *Temperament: A psychological perspective* (1998) and *Temperament as a Regulator of Behavior: after fifty years of research* (2008).

Further career progression and awards

After almost 50 years spent at the University of Warsaw, he took the position of vice-rector at the Warsaw School of Social Sciences and Humanities, where he is still working despite being retired. Strelau and his research team are looking for an answer (among victims of disasters and catastrophes) to whether the level of trauma depends on temperament traits, and if so, how the two things are related.

Jan Strelau is one of the most prominent psychologists working in his field. From 1984 to 1988 he was the first President of the prestigious European Association for Personality Psychology, and from 1993 till 1995 the first director of the International Society for the Study of Individual Differences. In Poland he was a member of the Polish Academy of Sciences (2002–2006) and an honorary member of the Polish Psychological Association, to name a few of his achievements in this country.

The list of achievements for Strelau, in Poland and further afield, is long. Amongst others, he has received honorary degrees from Gdańsk University, Adam Mickiewicz University of Poznań and the State University of Humanistic Science in Moscow. In 2000 he was honoured with the Prize of the Foundation for Polish Science (known as the 'Polish Nobel Prize'). Unquestionably, one of the most noteworthy awards for his outstanding work in education and research is the prestigious Commander's Cross of Polonia Restituta, presented to him by the former President of Poland, Bronisław Komorowski.

Strelau's unique personality

Jan Strelau has a fascinating personality. As a teenager he chose to be Polish. He was then brave enough to be unyielding under the repressions of the political system in Poland. There were also many social differences because of his German roots. He used the tough reality of the past as a challenge. He has admitted that he finds his meaning in life in being himself and following his own system of values. He trusts in people and treats others with equality and respect, and this has kept him optimistic throughout his life.

In his autobiographical book *Beyond Time* (*Poza czasem*) (published in 2015) Strelau reveals that passion, ambition and willpower are his keys to successful life and a brilliant career. He says: 'When I look at my professional and personal life from the perspective of all the years I have lived, I consider myself fulfilled'. He lives with his wife in Zalesie in the Mazovia district, Poland. He has two children and six grandchildren.

Joanna Ewa Bieniek

CHAPTER 5

The Arts

This chapter investigates the numerous ways in which Polish people – and those with Polish heritage – have made a significant contribution to the arts in Britain, including the fields of art, literature, music, new media and broadcasting. The chapter includes interviews with people who are highly respected in their fields, or whose work is well known in the UK.

Poles in the UK

The titans of the arts from Poland, such as **Fryderyk Chopin** and **Joseph Conrad**, are surely already part of the public consciousness in the UK, but there are many lesser-known Poles, or people with Polish heritage, who have also made important contributions to the arts in Britain.

Taken together, the contributions of these creative people to the arts in the UK can be seen as adding a distinctive and valuable *artistic legacy* to Britain. This embraces the past and looks forward to the future, while often celebrating the links between the two countries.

Building on the extraordinary foundations of Chopin, classical music of the highest order is still being composed by Polish composers, and people with close links to Poland, such as **Roxanna Panufnik** (▶ p. 138).

A particularly rich legacy of music from Poland has come in the media of film, where many internationally renowned Polish composers have won top awards for their work in big budget Hollywood movies or other productions.

Polish popular music is also proving increasingly more popular with international audiences and can be appreciated across the UK, with Britain now becoming a permanent fixture in Polish performers' tour diaries. Ranging in genre and style, contemporary Polish music has something to suit every musical taste.

Polish musicians and bands also contribute to the UK and global music

Stanisław Ignacy Witkiewicz (Witkacy), *Portrait of a Man (Portret męski)*, 1929

118

CHAPTER 5: **The Arts**

scene through their artistic collaborations with British artists. These include the many Anglo-Polish musical projects of English violinist, **Nigel Kennedy** (▶ p. 124). What is more, for over a decade the Polish coastal city of Gdynia has hosted one of Europe's largest and most exciting annual music festivals, which attracts music lovers from around the world, including many from the UK.

In the new media industry, Poland stays at the forefront of worldwide video game production. Polish animators, designers and producers have been celebrating international accolades as they provide cutting-edge gaming experiences to players around the world – with all key video games released internationally in English, as well as Polish, language versions (▶ p. 135).

Poland has a long and beautiful tradition of fine art, with numerous iconic pieces emerging from the country in the last eight centuries, across all of the major genres, periods and styles. The works by Poland's revered master painters can today be appreciated in art galleries across the world, including in the UK. Similarly, contemporary Polish artists are also celebrated in modern Britain.

Olga Boznańska, *A Girl with Chrysantemums (Dziewczynka z chryzantemami)*, 1894

SUCCESS STORY

One contemporary Polish painter, **Basia Hamilton**, has become popular with members of the British Royal Family, and is seen as a major contributor to the field of contemporary British art and culture. Born in Poland and based in the UK, where she works at her London studio, Hamilton is a highly successful portrait artist.

Her outstanding work, mostly in oil and pastels, has won her multiple international awards. Her paintings have been exhibited at world-famous galleries in the USA, Jamaica, Italy, Poland and the UK.

Her impressive portfolio features many prominent sitters, including Pope John Paul II (▶ p. 35), the Maharaja of Jodhpur, the Sultan of Brunei and Lech Wałęsa. She has also painted many British Royals, including the Queen Mother, Princess Alexandra of Kent, Prince Michael of Kent, the Duke of Kent, the Duchess of York and many more.

Poles in the UK

SUCCESS STORY

The composer and virtuoso pianist **Frédéric Chopin** [1810–1849] was born in Poland on 1 March 1810, where he is known as Fryderyk Chopin.

Chopin was a child prodigy, who had completed his musical education and composed his first musical works by the age of 20, when he left Poland and settled in Paris, France. There, he continued to compose music, all of it featuring the piano, and became a French citizen in 1835. Some of his many works are influenced by Polish folk music, and Chopin is recognised for his numerous innovations in musical style, form and harmony.

For the last few years of his life Chopin was supported by Jane Stirling (a Scottish amateur pianist), who also arranged for him to visit England and Scotland, in 1948, a year before his death.

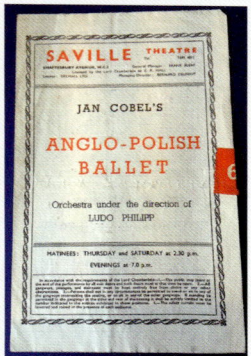

A 1835 portrait of Fryderyk Chopin by the Polish painter Maria Wodzińska

In the 1950s the Anglo-Polish Ballet performed classic dances from the repertoire in London's Saville Theatre, including *Les Sylphides*, with music by the Polish composer Chopin

SUCCESS STORY

The designer **Basia Zarzycka** sells the most amazing collection of bridal gowns and other stunning items from her boutique shop in Sloane Square, London.

The emporium has been described by *The Daily Telegraph* newspaper as 'the most romantic shop in London.' It is filled with many dazzling items inspired by fairy tales, nature and Polish folk history, including crystal lizard jewellery, gold-dusted butterfly brooches, pretty parasols and hand-embroidered shawls.

Zarzycka says that her Polish background has had a huge influence on both her and her work (she grew up in Birmingham, to Polish parents), with her parents always very supportive of what she wanted to do. The website **www.basia-zarzycka.com** provides some wonderful images of extraordinary and sought-after items created by Zarzycka.

CHAPTER 5: **The Arts**

Poland has given British lovers of literature some much-admired writers, many of whom were Nobel Prize laureates. This tradition continues through several noteworthy writers of novels and poetry active today, such as **B.E. Andre** (▶ p. 143) and **Maria Jastrzębska** (▶ p. 148). These writers have managed to connect with a British audience in a unique way.

CONTEMPORARY POLISH MUSIC

Every year, the Open'er Festival takes place in the Polish coastal city of Gdynia. It is fast becoming one of Europe's most exciting annual music events, alongside the UK's Glastonbury Festival or Hungary's Sziget. The Open'er has been on the European festival map since 2002 and has brought hundreds of international artists to Gdynia over the years, including Muse, Placebo, Björk, Massive Attack, Coldplay, Snoop Dogg, Nick Cave and the Bad Seeds, Rihanna, Arctic Monkeys, Jack White, Kings of Leon and many, many more.

However, every year hundreds of home-grown artists also attract large crowds at the Open'er. Ranging hugely in genre and style, some of Poland's most interesting musical exports are on show at the festival (in addition to British artists closely associated with Poland). The

Did you know?
The celebrated British playright **William Shakespeare** is thought to have alluded to early Polish links to Britain in his play *Hamlet* (first published 1603).

Tadeusz Makowski, *Three Children By a Roadsign* (*Troje dzieci pod drogowskazem*), 1930

121

contemporary Polish music scene has never been more electrifying, and many Polish musicians and bands are recognisable and successful internationally.

Warsaw Village Band

The music by this band, known in Poland as *Kapela ze Wsi Warszawa*, is as intriguing as their name. Just as Warsaw is hardly a village, this band is not a typical folk group. Although their style is predominantly world music influenced by Polish folk, with many traditional instruments, Warsaw Village Band weave contemporary elements and techniques into their music. Their lyrics focus on modern social issues and the band participates in social initiatives such as the Music Against Racism (*Muzyka Przeciwko Rasizmowi*) movement.

As the band quote on their website, they are 'living proof that Eastern Europe can (bring) good and unique elements to the global village'. And it seems they are right – the band has performed at many international festivals and they continue touring the world. Having won the BBC Radio 3 Award for World Music ('Newcomer' category) in 2004, they have performed in the UK in such prestigious venues as the Howard Assembly Room in Leeds, West Yorkshire.

For a flavour of Warsaw Village Band's music, the 'Chassidic Dance' ('*Taniec Chasydzki*') off their 2002 *People's Spring* LP (*Wiosna Ludu*) is a perfect introduction. This enchanting Jewish melody is a whirl of fiddles and traditional drums. Their most notable works also include 'In the Forest', with its distinct hip-hop influences, and the hypnotic 'Fishie' from their award-winning album *Uprooting* (*Wykorzenienie*), from 2004.

Finally, 'Hey You, Yokel's Son' ('*Ej Ty, Gburski Synie*') from one of their more recent albums, *Nord* (2012), is an example of what the band do best – fusing a folk tune and vocals with a mix of traditional and modern instrumentation, all produced with a contemporary feel and topped off with a modern music video.

IMAGE: Uli Blass

The 2004 album *Uprooting* by Warsaw Village Band has been praised by critics the world over

Find out more

Warsaw Village Band website:
www.warsawvillage-band.net

CHAPTER 5: **The Arts**

POLISH MUSIC IN INTERNATIONAL FILM

Jan A.P. Kaczmarek [born 1953] is a Polish composer whose film scores have brought him international acclaim. He won the Academy Award (the 'Oscar') for Best Original Score for *Finding Neverland* (2004). Some of his other work includes the score for *The Visitor* (2007), an award-winning and Oscar-nominated drama, and the music for the British-American drama *Hachi: A Dog's Tale* (2008).

Wojciech Kilar [1932–2013] was a prominent Polish composer of classical and film music, known internationally for his remarkable film scores. He often collaborated with Polish film-makers such as Andrzej Wajda, Krzysztof Kieślowski and Krzysztof Zanussi. Some of his most famous and critically acclaimed film scores include *Bram Stoker's Dracula* (1992), *The Pianist* (2002), *Death and the Maiden* (1994), *The Ninth Gate* (1999); and the more recent *We Own the Night* (2007). One of his compositions was also used as part of the score for *The Truman Show* (1998). He has won or been nominated for numerous prestigious awards throughout his career, including a BAFTA nomination and a César Award for his music for *The Pianist*.

Krzysztof Penderecki [born 1933] is considered one of Poland's most distinguished modern composers. He has written operas, choral music, concertos and symphonies, and is also a conductor. He is a three-time Grammy Award winner, and has received many other accolades over the years. Some of his most notable pieces are *Polymorphia*, *Threnody for the Victims of Hiroshima*, *St. Luke Passion* and the *Polish Requiem*. He also composed the score for the Oscar-nominated feature film *Katyń* (2007). His atmospheric, gripping works have also been used in the soundtracks of several well-known films, including *The Exorcist* (1973), *The Shining* (1980), *Wild at Heart* (1990), *Inland Empire* (2006), *Children of Men* (2006), and *Shutter Island* (2010).

Katy Carr

Katy Carr is a Polish-British alternative pop and folk singer-songwriter, multi-instrumentalist and aviator. She draws much inspiration from Polish culture, language and history (particularly the 1940s and the World War II period). Having received praise and awards both in Poland and in the UK, Carr is one of the most interesting musicians of her generation.

Her songs usually tell stories inspired by real-life characters, such as Polish soldiers, complemented by her timeless sound. She often takes

123

part in and performs at various World War II commemoration and memorial events, including performing for veterans. She also promotes British-Polish cultural links and the countries' shared history.

Carr has also produced a documentary film, *Kazik and the Kommander's Car* (2012), which was devoted to the remarkable story of Kazimierz (Kazik) Piechowski [born 1919]. The film focusses on this retired Polish Home Army soldier and his spectacular escape from the Auschwitz concentration camp. Carr also released a song based on Piechowski's story.

Carr's most significant songs on the British-Polish theme include 'Kommander's Car', 'Mała, Little Flower' and 'Wojtek (The Soldier Bear)' from her bilingual *Paszport* album, from 2012.

Nigel Kennedy

Find out more
Nigel Kennedy's website: **www.nigelkennedy.co.uk**

Nigel Kennedy's work is an example of a fruitful Anglo-Polish artistic collaboration, as well as a Polish contribution to the British music scene. He is an internationally renowned British violinist, who frequently works with Polish musicians. Kennedy's wife, Agnieszka, is Polish and he divides his time between his homes in England and Kraków, Poland. He has best-selling albums to his name, as well as awards – he received a BRIT Award for his Outstanding Contribution to British Music in 1997, and was voted Male Artist of the Year in 2001.

Kennedy takes an unconventional approach to classical music, as he often explores other genres such as jazz and fusion. For example, he has reworked rock classics by The Doors and Jimi Hendrix for the violin.

East Meets East (2003), by Nigel Kennedy and the Polish band Kroke, was highly successful in Poland and in the UK

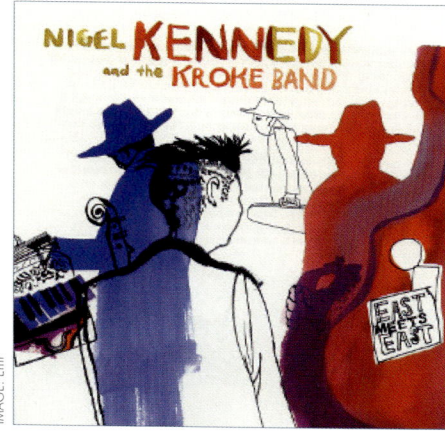

Furthermore, he does not think that having a conductor is crucial for an orchestra, so he leads his Orchestra of Life (consisting mostly of young Polish musicians) with just his virtuoso violin.

The Orchestra of Life is one of Kennedy's many regular collaborations with Polish musicians. He has also recorded three studio albums with the Polish Chamber Orchestra, of which he is also Artistic Director. Together with four Polish jazz musicians, he has recorded three other albums as the Nigel Kennedy Quintet. Finally, he has recorded a critically acclaimed album *East Meets East* (2003) with the Polish jazz band Kroke (Yiddish

CHAPTER 5: **The Arts**

for Kraków, the band's home city). The record explores traditional Jewish klezmer music and free jazz elements, as well as Polish and Eastern European folk melodies.

An ideal introduction, for those wishing to begin listening to Kennedy's collaborations with Polish artists, would be 'Kazimierz', 'Lullaby for Kamila' or 'One Voice' from the *East Meets East* album (2003). Sometimes delicate and sentimental; sometimes vibrant and lively, these pieces will stay with the listener for a long time.

KARI

Kari Amirian, known under her stage name KARI, is a Polish singer-songwriter and producer. She currently lives and writes her music in Leeds, and she also plays live shows across the UK. Her unique brand of indie pop has won over the hearts of many.

KARI's angelic voice is complemented by, as stated on her Bandcamp page, 'tribal-sounding drums and experimental, electronic soundscapes'. She is definitely a Polish artist to watch.

Her more recent singles, such as the alternative 'Hurry Up' (from her 2013 album, *Wounds and Bruises*), provide the best introduction to her sound. A truly mesmerising vocal melody from KARI comes in the form of 'The Winter is Back', a single off KARI's 2011 debut album, *Daddy Says I'm Special*.

Pati Yang

Pati Yang is a Polish singer-songwriter, visual artist, DJ and yoga therapist who has lived and worked in the UK for a number of years. Her music is a blend of trip hop, electronica, post-punk and alternative pop.

She has performed in venues across the UK and has earned well-deserved acclaim from the radio stations XFM, BBC Radio 1 and BBC Radio 6 Music. She has recently released new singles and announced that her new album will be out in late

Find out more
KARI's Bandcamp page:
www.karimusic.
bandcamp.com

KARI's music is best appreciated live – her gigs are atmospheric, as well as contagiously energetic

IMAGE: Nextpop/Parlophone

UK-based Pati Yang is one of Poland's most successful electronica and alternative pop artists

IMAGE: Mikołaj Długosz

125

Poles in the UK

Find out more
Pati Yang's Soundcloud page:
www.soundcloud.com/yangcloud

2016. In the meantime, Pati Yang runs inspiring yoga workshops for people of all ages.

Some of Pati Yang's most interesting singles are the cool and melodic 'All That is Thirst' (2005), the deliciously moody 'Invisible Tears' and post-punk 'Anonymous Face' (2016), the up-tempo pop treat 'Hold Your Horses' (2012), and the boldly electronic and catchy 'Near to God' (2011).

Riverside

Riverside are undoubtedly Poland's most significant contribution to the international progressive rock and metal scene. Lyrical and atmospheric, then energetic and powerful, with masterful guitar solos – Riverside have created a unique sound, appreciated by fans all around the world. Riverside's guitarist, Piotr Grudziński, tragically passed away in early 2016, but he will be remembered by fans worldwide for his soulful guitar skills as 'the Polish David Gilmour'.

The band have toured the world extensively, putting on superb live shows. They mostly draw a British audience at their gigs in the UK, although there are always groups of dedicated Polish fans in attendance.

IMAGE: Mystic Production

Riverside's unmistakeable sound and heartfelt lyrics have won the band countless fans worldwide, and a particularly strong fanbase in the UK

CHAPTER 5: **The Arts**

The songs 'I Believe' and 'In Two Minds', from their stirring debut album *Out of Myself* (2003), make a good introduction to Riverside's unique sound. Another example of the band at their musical best is 'The Depth of Self-Delusion', from *Shrine of New Generation Slaves* (2013). Finally, the single '#Addicted', from their latest album *Love, Fear and the Time Machine* (2015) is also noteworthy. With its 1980s-influenced, infectious melody, '#Addicted' addresses the issue of loneliness in the age of social networking.

Tides From Nebula often gig in the UK, and are increasingly popular with British audiences. The band have three studio albums to their name, with the fourth LP to be released in 2016

Tides From Nebula

Tides From Nebula is a four-piece band which formed in Warsaw in 2008. Their music belongs to the post-rock genre, or how the band describe it, 'catching the sound of the universe'. They skilfully create dreamy and cosmic musical soundscapes, with a rock kick and catchy guitar riffs.

The band have performed across the UK, including at music events such as the Damnation Festival in Leeds. They will be releasing their fourth studio album *Safe Haven* in 2016 and will also play five gigs in the UK.

A flavour of Tides From Nebula's take on post-rock can be found in the dark 'We Are the Mirror' (2016) from their upcoming album, or the uplifting 'Only With Presence', a single from their *Eternal Movement* LP (2013).

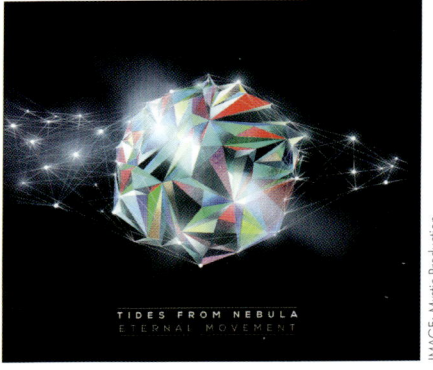

IMAGE: Mystic Production

Find out more
Tides From Nebula Facebook page:
www.facebook.com/tidesfromnebulaofficial

POLISH ART

Many **Polish artists** have made important contributions to art over the centuries, across all the main movements. The history of painting in Poland dates all the way back to the thirteenth century, and the following are among the most significant of the artists who worked over this long period. Their work is likely to be seen in art galleries in the UK, or be known to those who have a keen appreciation of the key figures in European art.

Piotr Michałowski [1800–1855] – romantic artist best known for his battle scene paintings and portraits.

127

Poles in the UK

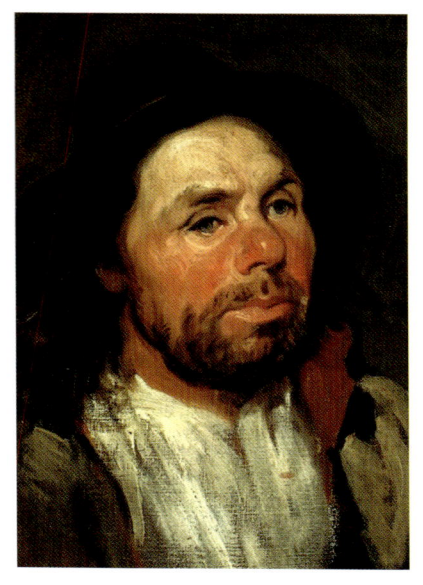

Piotr Michałowski, *Portrait of a Peasant in a Hat* (*Portret chłopa w kapeluszu*), c.1846

Jacek Malczewski, *Death* (*Śmierć*), 1917

Juliusz Kossak [1824–1899] – illustrator and history painter, famous for his masterful depictions of horses.

Aleksander Kotsis [1836–1877] – an artist celebrated for his romantic and realist paintings, mostly depicting rural life.

Artur Grottger [1837–1867] – romantic painter and illustrator, celebrated for his works devoted to the January Uprising of 1863.

Jan Matejko [1838–1893] – a revered realist artist. He is famous for his depictions of Polish monarchs, as well as for his distinguished, large-scale works devoted to the most significant battles and events in the history of Poland. The internationally renowned Academy of Fine Arts in Kraków is named after Matejko, as he was a student and then the principal there. At the time when Matejko was directing the Academy, many other prominent artists studied there, including Jacek Malczewski and Stanisław Wyspiański. See p. 21 for Matejko's *The Battle of Grunwald* painting.

Józef Chełmoński [1849–1914] – realist painter specialising in depicting the rural way of life and natural landscapes. See this chapter's title page for Chełmoński's iconic 1875 paining, *Gossamer* (*Babie lato*).

Aleksander Gierymski [1850–1901] – realist and impressionist painter and illustrator.

Jacek Malczewski [1854–1929] – symbolist painter and one of Poland's key artists, associated with the modernist Young Poland movement.

Wojciech Kossak [1856–1942] – son of Juliusz Kossak, also specialising in history and military scene painting; author of large-scale panoramic works. His most famous panorama, a cycloramic oil painting, is *The Racławice Panorama*, painted between 1893 and 1894. It is on permanent display in Wrocław, Poland. The impressive dimensions of the canvas are 15 metres high by 114 metres wide (49 feet by 374 feet).

CHAPTER 5: **The Arts**

Aleksander Gierymski,
Jewess with Oranges
(*Żydówka
z pomarańczami*),
1880–1881

Aleksander Gierymski,
In a Gazebo
(*W altanie*), 1882

Poles in the UK

Aleksander Kotsis, *The Last Belongings* (*Ostatnia chudoba*), 1870

Aleksander Kotsis, *Children in Front of a Mountain Cottage* (*Dzieci przed chatą*), 1872

CHAPTER 5: **The Arts**

Juliusz Kossak,
St George Killing a Dragon (Święty Jerzy zabijający smoka)

Wojciech Kossak,
Artillery in Retreat (Artyleria w odwrocie), 1812

131

Poles in the UK

SIX IMPORTANT POLISH WRITERS

Joseph Conrad [1857–1924] Born Józef Teodor Konrad Korzeniowski. Joseph Conrad was Polish, but became one of the most famous British writers of all time. He is best known for his *Heart of Darkness* novella, on which the film *Apocalypse Now* was based. His work is extensively studied in UK universities, as part of English literature courses.

Władysław Stanisław Reymont [1867–1925] Polish writer and Nobel Prize in Literature laureate (in 1924) for his four-volume novel *The Peasants*, which depicts rural life in Poland at the end of the nineteenth century. It has been extensively translated into other languages.

Henryk Sienkiewicz [1846–1916] Polish novelist and journalist, awarded the Nobel Prize in Literature in 1904. Much of his international success is attributed to his historical novels. Some of his works became bestsellers in his lifetime in Poland, Western Europe and the USA. Many of his works contain patriotic messages and subplots, which were intended to give hope to Polish readers, as he was writing at a time when Poland was still partitioned and not an independent country.

Czesław Miłosz [1911–2004] Polish poet, writer, diplomat and Nobel Prize in Literature laureate (in 1980). His work has been extensively translated, including into English. His poetry books can often be found in major bookstores across the UK.

Stanisław Lem [1921–2006] Poland's most successful and internationally celebrated science fiction writer. His work also includes philosophical texts. He is probably best known for being the author of *Solaris*, published in 1961. It has been adapted for the screen a few times, with one of its adaptations being the 2002 film of the same title, starring George Clooney.

Wisława Szymborska [1923–2012] One of the most internationally acclaimed Polish poets and Nobel Prize in Literature laureate (in 1996). Her work has been translated into English and many other languages.

132

CHAPTER 5: **The Arts**

Olga Boznańska [1865–1940] – modernist portrait artist, author of many famous paintings of women and children.

Władysław Podkowiński [1866–1895] – impressionist and symbolist artist, renowned for his *Frenzy of Exultations* painting. The work was highly controversial at the time of its first exhibition, and today it is regarded as one of Poland's most iconic works of art.

Stanisław Wyspiański [1869–1907] – a celebrated modernist and symbolist artist, associated with Young Poland, whose classical works span many areas of the arts, including painting, literature, architecture and design.

Tadeusz Makowski [1882–1932] – creator of unique paintings and woodcut illustrations, inspired partly by the cubist movement and partly by Polish folklore.

Władysław Podkowiński, *Frenzy of Exultations (Szał uniesień)*, 1894

Władysław Podkowiński, *Village by the Water (Mokra Wieś)*, 1892

133

Poles in the UK

Jan Matejko, *Christianisation of Poland A.D. 966* (Zaprowadzenie chrześcijaństwa), 1889

Jan Matejko, *The Jester* (Stańczyk), 1862

THE WITCHER (WIEDŹMIN) – THE CULT POLISH FANTASY NOVEL AND VIDEO GAME SERIES

The award-winning 1994 fantasy novel *Blood of Elves* (*Krew Elfów*), by **Andrzej Sapkowski**, was translated into numerous languages and gained a strong worldwide following among fans of fantasy fiction. The novel was the first in a series. It introduces the character of *Wiedźmin*, the Witcher, the monster-hunting main character. The saga builds on the stories and the fantastical world first developed by Sapkowski in his earlier short stories.

The Witcher novels were so successful that they were chosen as the foundation for a series of multi award-winning video games for adults – *The Witcher* (2007) for Microsoft Windows, *The Witcher 2: Assassins of Kings* (2011) for Windows and Xbox 360, as well as *The Witcher 3: Wild Hunt* (2015) for Windows, PlayStation 4 and Xbox One.

Developed by Polish animators and directors in the Warsaw-based CD Projekt Red studio, the Witcher series are fantasy action role-playing games. They received wide international acclaim and were a huge commercial success. *The Witcher 3* won two prestigious Game Developers Choice Awards in 2015, in the 'Game of the Year' and 'Best Technology' categories. Its exceptional design and storytelling also won the game other prizes at international gaming award shows, including The Game Awards and The Golden Joystick Awards.

Sapkowski's novel is soon to be adapted for the screen for the second time (the first being a low-key Polish adaptation from 2001). It has been announced that work is currently under way for a new Witcher film, which is going to be an international co-production, with a premiere date planned for 2017. The film is much anticipated by fans around the world.

The film will be directed by **Tomasz (or Tomek) Bagiński**, an award-winning Polish animator and director. Among Bagiński's greatest successes are a nomination for the Academy Award in 2003 for his acclaimed short animation *Cathedral* (2002), and a BAFTA Award for Best Short Animation in 2005, which he won for the darkly humorous *Fallen Art* (2005).

It will be Bagiński's first time working on the *Wiedźmin* story, though he has previously created and directed animations and trailers for the Witcher video games. British viewers might remember his work, too, as he directed the epic, atmospheric trailer for the 2014 Winter Olympics in Sochi for the BBC television – which was developed with a Polish production crew.

More Polish gaming successes
Poland's latest successes in the gaming industry also include the following two creations:

- *Dying Light* (2015). A first-person zombie apocalypse horror game. This survival role-playing game is available for Microsoft Windows, PlayStation 4 and Xbox One. It received positive reviews from gaming critics worldwide, including a 4 star (out of 5) rating from *The Guardian* newspaper, which called it a 'scarily immersive experience'
- *This War of Mine* (2014). A unique, war-themed game. This strategy-based, civilian survival game focusses not on military combat, but on the terrifying war experience of ordinary people. The game conveys a decisively anti-war message. It was initially released for Microsoft Windows and OS X, followed by Android, iOS, PlayStation 4 and Xbox One versions. The game received much international acclaim.

Poles in the UK

Stanisław Wyspiański, *Planty Park at Dawn (Planty o świcie)*, 1894

Stanisław Ignacy Witkiewicz (Witkacy) [1885-1939] – a highly acclaimed painter, photographer, thinker and writer. His unique personality and the sense of myth surrounding much of his life story, together with his unconventional style, make him one of Poland's most interesting artists.

Tamara Łempicka, also known as Tamara de Lempicka [1898-1980] – Poland's revered art deco painter, famous for her portraits of women.

Stanisław Ignacy Witkiewicz (Witkacy), *Australian Landscape (Pejzaż australijski)*, 1918

CHAPTER 5: **The Arts**

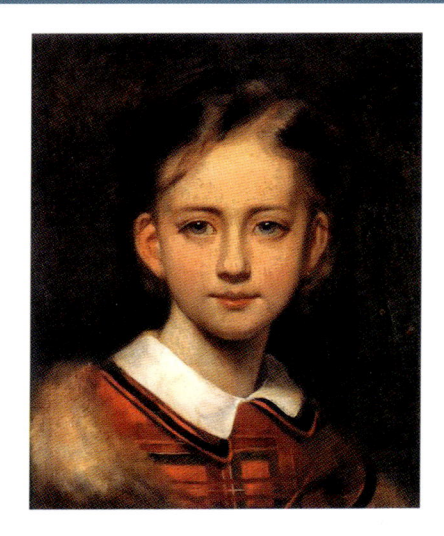

Artur Grottger, *Portrait of a Girl (Portret dziewczynki)*, 1860

Artur Grottger, *Reconnaissance (Rekonesans)*, 1862

Poles in the UK

Roxanna Panufnik (48)
| Classical Composer

IMAGE: Paul Marc Mitchell Studios Ltd

Roxanna Panufnik, born in the UK in 1968 to a Polish father and English mother, has been described as 'one of the UK's most popular and loved composers'. She is the daughter of the composer and conductor Sir Andrzej Panufnik [1914–1991], who left Poland to settle in the UK in 1954. Her works, mainly in the classical field, have an ability to make a deep emotional connection with audiences all over the world.

Roxanna studied music composition at the Royal Academy of Music in London and has subsequently written a wide variety of different music. This has included opera and ballet works, music theatre pieces, choral works, chamber compositions and music for film and television. Roxanna's music is regularly performed right across the world.

Her critically acclaimed overture *Three Paths to Peace* was commissioned by the World Orchestra for Peace and premiered in Jerusalem, Israel, in 2008, under the baton of celebrated Russian conductor Valery Gergiev, who was until 2015 the principal conductor of the London Symphony Orchestra – one of the world's leading professional orchestras. The same orchestra and conductor performed the European premiere of the work at the 2014 BBC Proms season, which was broadcast live on BBC Radio 3 and later released in DVD form.

Other notable works by Roxanna include her oratorio *Dance of Life: Tallinn Mass*, the violin concerto *Four World Seasons* (composed for British violinist Tasmin Little) and *Memories of my Father*, a composition for string quartet which was commissioned and premiered in the UK and Poland by the Brodsky Quartet, a leading British ensemble.

She is currently writing an opera, *Silver Birch*, for Garsington Opera (UK). This follows *The Music Programme*, which was commissioned by the Polish National Opera for their millennium season, and received its UK premiere at the BOC Covent Garden Festival in 2000.

Roxanna's compositions are published by Peter's Edition Ltd and recorded on many labels including Warner Classics, Chandos, Signum and EMI Classics.

You can learn much more about Roxanna's music, and listen to excerpts from her works, by visiting: www.roxannapanufnik.com

CHAPTER 5: **The Arts**

🎙 We interviewed Roxanna for this book, and particularly wanted to know how her Polish heritage has influenced her work as a composer.

The way my Polish heritage has influenced my music is all to do with personal and genetic factors, rather than cultural ones.

It's fascinating to me that whenever I attend a performance of my music in Poland people come up to me afterwards and say they can't believe I was born and brought up in the UK, as my music sounds so Polish.

I've never managed to get them to define what they mean by that (partly because my Polish is atrocious!) but I would hazard a guess. One of the things I love about Poles is our ability to 'wear our hearts on our sleeves'. We are very spontaneous and often say what we feel, which is not always a good thing! And that's what happens when I compose. I'm expressing my innermost feelings and emotions – no holds barred.

I've also worked on numerous occasions with Polish folk music. I love its sense of joy and quirkiness.

Faith also plays a massively important part in my work. Being a devout Catholic, I'm very comfortable, even 'at home' with the religious music I write. One day, I'd love to set the Catholic Mass in Polish.

I'm very chuffed that BBC Radio 3 refer to me as an 'Anglo-Polish composer' because I'm very proud of my dual identity.

For young people wanting a good introduction to my music I would recommend 'Zen Love Song' and 'Love is Master', which are both available with animations on YouTube and are accessible both musically and visually.

Reviewers' comments on Roxanna's music

Roxanna Panufnik is one of the finest contemporary vocal composers around. No matter how demanding the subject matter, she always seems to find a way to set words that sit hand-in-glove with the text.

Julian Haylock,
International Record Review

A gifted young composer with a fast-growing reputation for heart, spunk and individuality... distinctive in voice, serious, bold and appealing.

Fiona Maddocks,
The Observer

Panufnik's art is something special, putting her among the elite composers in the world today.

Stephen Ritter,
Audiophile Audition

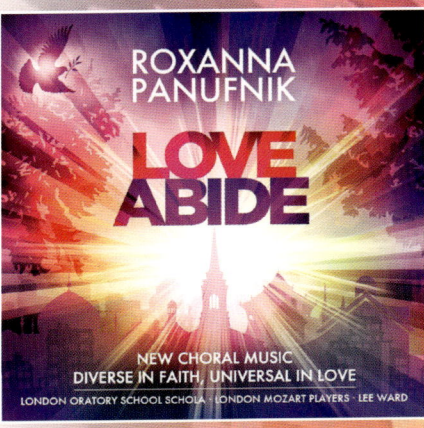

ROXANNA PANUFNIK
LOVE ABIDE
NEW CHORAL MUSIC
DIVERSE IN FAITH, UNIVERSAL IN LOVE
LONDON ORATORY SCHOOL SCHOLA · LONDON MOZART PLAYERS · LEE WARD

139

Poles in the UK

Kinga Kreffta (30)

Singer-songwriter,
Singing Teacher

What brought you to England?
I first came to London just for the summer, after completing my studies in Poland. My plan was to earn some money and I worked as a waitress. Because I'm a singer, I also wanted to make some music contacts and start my career here in England. I'm a classically trained opera singer, but I did not want to do opera at the time. So I started researching jazz and pop music courses in the UK. I found Leeds College of Music very interesting, the pop course in particular – it's the best and one of the most popular courses in the country. So after I earned some money in London, I came to Leeds – and here I am! I'm now a student at the Leeds College of Music.

When you first moved to England, did you encounter any problems?
The beginnings are difficult everywhere. I moved here on my own, without any family or friends, so I was a little bit lonely and making friends was a problem. Also, I found that my English was rubbish! [*laugh*]. So I had to learn the language. I'm still learning it, actually. I've only lived here for two years, and all my life I was learning German, not English. But now I no longer have these moments when I cannot express myself; I can communicate easily now.

CHAPTER 5: **The Arts**

How have you managed to overcome these difficulties?
Everything came with time – I made new friends, I found a place to sing and perform. My friends helped me a lot during this period. Leeds College of Music enabled me to make many new contacts.

How did you find learning the English language? Was it difficult?
English is not very difficult compared to other languages. It was new to me, but I knew some English because I've been singing in English. I've been translating song lyrics from English into Polish for years, because it's important to me to understand what it is that I'm singing about. People comment on how much I've improved my English, but it came really naturally to me, mostly by talking to people – I didn't do any serious studying. I had three-hour English and Polish language-exchange lessons with Brin (the co-author of *Poles in the UK*) each week, so that also helped a lot, because he's a fantastic teacher!

How does it feel to live in England now?
It's getting better, it's good! I really enjoy my course. It's my priority at the moment and I concentrate on my studies and my music – I'm aiming to release my first album this year. Having learnt the language is a major advantage. Living in England is an adventure for me. It is a challenge – and I like challenges! What would I do in Poland? Probably get married and have kids. But instead, I'm now launching my career and doing all these interesting things, which people my age in Poland often don't get to do. I'm happy here.

What do you think about British people? Have you had positive interactions with them? Have you come across any prejudice?
I have never come across any prejudice from British people. I think they're very sweet and helpful. Once when I got lost in the city centre I walked into an office to ask for directions, and the staff even printed some maps off for me! People are very friendly, especially here in the

141

North. I found that London can feel quite cold, probably because it is a busy capital. But here in Leeds people are warmer. The only thing which I find strange about English people – it's not that I don't like it, it's just different – is that Polish people are very open and frank, and English people sometimes seem too nice, too polite! [laugh]. Sometimes I'd like to know if anything is wrong – but an English person will not tell me, because they don't want to make me feel bad! But of course it's better to be like this than to be rude – so I still prefer it this way.

What do you think is your contribution to Leeds, or Yorkshire?
Over the last few years I've performed many gigs in Yorkshire, in pubs, restaurants and wine bars, especially in the Leeds area. In a duo with a keyboard player, I perform my original songs and cover versions of songs in the charts, for example by Adele and Paloma Faith. You can watch videos and listen to my music on my YouTube channel, Kinga K.

I also teach singing to both children and adults from the Leeds area. For example, I have worked with Bobby (an eight-year-old) and Grace (also eight), helping them improve their music skills, teaching them to sing songs which they like and helping to build their confidence. On Christmas Eve 2015, I launched a special video on YouTube of me and Bobby performing a bilingual version of 'Silent Night', which we filmed in the amazing interior of Leeds Minster. I also teach adults singing too, including those who want to prepare for competitions, improve their confidence or people who always wanted to sing, but were never able to afford lessons.

I'm very passionate about cooking, especially recipes from my home country, and I love to introduce my British friends to traditional dishes from Poland. And I've had some wonderful comments back, in particular for my 'signature' dish, żurek (a sour, sausage soup).

What's your plan for the future?
I still have one year of my studies left. For now, I'm staying in England, but no-one can tell what the future holds! I would prefer to go somewhere else, maybe the United States, but probably not back to Poland – unless I'm a celebrity by then! [laugh]. I also plan to develop my cooking skills, as I think cooking is a very creative pursuit, much like my making music. I'm hoping to launch a cooking blog in the next few months.

IMAGE: Kinga Kreffta

CHAPTER 5: **The Arts**

B.E. Andre (58)

| Author

The author B.E. Andre has had considerable success in recent years with her novel *With Blood and Scars*, which delves deeply into the life of a post-war Polish community in Manchester.

What is your Polish heritage?

My father and my maternal grandparents, along with my mother, came to England after World War II. Dad was wounded and in a German prisoner of war camp when the war ended. Unfortunately for him, he was in the zone that was 'liberated' by the Russians. My dad didn't trust the Russians. Even though they were supposed to be allies and should have helped, they had stood by and watched the destruction of Warsaw by the Germans while the Polish Home Army (to which my father belonged as a scout in the Grey Ranks) fought on valiantly.

With a group of friends who helped him, my dad escaped from the Russian sector to the American sector. The Americans handed him over to the British, who transported him to the UK to recover from his wounds. The British military doctors managed to save his leg from having to be amputated.

Meanwhile, my mum's family had been deported from eastern Poland to the Russian *gulags*. The Russians told the people to pack some bags, and then basically kidnapped them, putting them on cattle trains going to various parts of the Soviet Union, where they then had to work in the slave labour camps.

My mum's family ended up in Archangelsk Oblast in the extreme north of the Soviet Union. When the Soviet leader Joseph Stalin changed sides because Germany attacked the Soviet Union, he declared an 'amnesty' for the Poles in the Soviet Union. They were suddenly needed to fight in the war, so he tried to get the Poles to join the Soviet army, but it didn't work. For obvious reasons they preferred to join the Polish army. Hundreds of thousands of Poles from all over the Soviet Union had to find their own way to where their army was being formed, initially in Kazakhstan and then Pahlevi in Persia (now Iran).

By this time many of those fleeing the Soviet Union were starving and diseased. Many of them, seeing proper food for the first time in years, overate and died – their bodies simply couldn't take it. My maternal grandfather joined the Polish army. My mother and grandmother were transported to a refugee camp called Koja near Kampala in Uganda, where they stayed for six years.

When the war was over, the family reunited in the UK. Having been subjected to the *gulag* experience, they didn't want to return to their country which was now run by communists under Soviet control. The memories were too painful to bear.

143

Poles in the UK

In what ways do you feel Polish? And in what ways do you feel British?
I've always enjoyed being a 'hybrid.' In my mind I got the best of both worlds. The Polish side is important to me: Christmas Eve – *wigilia* – with the family, saints' days, the Polish language and culture, Polish cuisine, my extended family in Poland. Whenever I land on Polish soil, I feel as if I've come home.

And yet, I'm very British, too! I was born in England, spent many childhood holidays in Wales and studied there, and often visited Scotland as a child. Unfortunately, I haven't been to Northern Ireland yet.

I love the UK and all it has to offer. When you've lived in the same country all your life, you often take it for granted. Not me! Whether it's the craggy, romantic coasts of Devon or Cornwall, the forests and lochs in Scotland, the looming majesty of the Cambrian Mountains, or the tranquillity of the Norfolk Broads – I love it all. We're so lucky here.

In what ways does your Polish heritage influence your work?
My novel *With Blood and Scars* is, for the most part, about my Polish roots. In it the protagonist, Ania, finally learns to value all that has been given to her – her Polish heritage. I don't feel that I ever had to learn that the hard way as Ania does in my novel. For me, having an English and a Polish side has always been a benefit. Indeed, when it came to learning other European languages at school, I had the advantage because speaking a different language didn't feel alien in any way. If you're brought up bilingual, other languages aren't so hard to master.

What are the main themes in your writing?
The themes that emerged in *With Blood and Scars* were loss, longing, homeland, friendship and also the importance of welcoming and trying to understand immigrants – whether they be refugees or economic migrants. As Harper Lee put it in *To Kill a Mockingbird*, 'You never really know a man until you understand things from his point of view, until you climb into his skin and walk around in it'. Many actions and reactions to a given situation will be different when the person experiencing them has survived a war, starvation or extreme financial hardship.

Have you been inspired by any specific writers to pursue a career in literature?
I always loved reading. As a child I read children's books that are no longer fashionable today. The first proper 'story for adults' I read was by American author John Steinbeck, a novella called *The Pearl*. I think I was about 12 when I read it and it moved me in a way no other book had done.

Many other writers have influenced me: Harper Lee, J.D. Salinger, Franz Kafka, Andrea Levy, Isaac Bashevis Singer, Monica Ali, Jane Austen, Arundhati Roy, William Golding – in fact, there are too many to mention! One of my favourite Polish novels is *The Doll* (*Lalka*) by Bolesław Prus, because it combines the history of nineteenth century Poland with a tale of tragic, unrequited love. It's probably one of my favourites of all time.

Do you have a sense of the breakdown of readers for your work? (i.e. the proportion of people with and without Polish heritage who read it)
So far, from what I can gather, it's about 50/50. English readers find *With Blood and Scars* interesting because it's so far removed from their own experiences. Many of them knew Polish people – maybe just as neighbours – who came to the UK after the war, but they had no idea how they got here or what they had been through. It never ceased to amaze me that my granny had seen so much of the world – first as an economic migrant to South America and

CHAPTER 5: **The Arts**

THEN

Ten a penny we were, us Anias – me and Ania Tarczak, Ania Skokowska, Ania Kubek, et-cet-era, et-cet-era. Except I was the only one who was ten. The others were all younger or older. I only ever met them down there in Polska Land which was to the left of our gate on Upper Chorlton Road. But first, next door, Mr. and Mrs. Nasmith from Ghana, who were usually nice apart from when I played two-a-ball right next to their window. Then, the 81 and 82 bus stops. After that, Kombo's, Brooks's Bar and the Polski deli. Then, the number 53 bus, the stinky Hyde's Anvil brewery, Alexandra Road, Polski church and Polska School.

The right side was miles better. First, in the house attached to ours, Ossie, which was dead good because his bedroom was right next to mine. Then Granny and Grandad further up, and down the road the doctor's surgery and Chorlton library. It was the best library in the whole universe because a very rich man called Mr. Andrew Carnegie said it had to have a domey thingy built on top of it, like a cathedral. It was probably his favourite library too, even though the lady who stamped our books told me he'd built hundreds of them. When you went past the library and turned left, Quarmby's was on the other side of the road – another good thing about to the right because they sold the best pens and pencils and everything.

Round the corner of Ossie's house on the avenue was the rest of my gang – Dermot, Gianni and Manuela, plus those other boring kids. Then, spreading out, the Candy Box, Ayres Road and Seymour Park Junior and Infants School.

Across from our road there was nothing interesting, just more houses with people I didn't know and the Territorial Army base. So that was that.

But our back garden was great because it had a swing, a pear tree, a fab place to hide behind the garage and an escape route. My best thing was hanging by the backs of my knees on the top of our swing, even after Granny made me tuck my skirt into my knickers because I was a shameless heathen communist. Sometimes when I was upside down counting Groucho's poos on the grass, I heard the cheer from the Stretford End, when Georgie Best scored a goal for United. Not always, just if the wind was in the right direction and if it wasn't raining. Mum wouldn't let me go that far though. And Maine Road was also off the map, not that I cared, somewhere beyond the frontiers of Polska Land. I never did hear a peep from over there because Manchester City were rubbish. It was a well-known fact.

Granny and Grandad's back garden was another brilliant place. A bit like a farm except smaller. Well, exactly the same size as our garden probably. But they grew loads of vegetables and fruit, because of "in Siberia when we were slaves and only ate water soup" blah-blah. And Granny had her three fat chickens who talked to her when Grandad didn't feel like it. Which was nearly always.

From Chapter One of *With Blood and Scars* (2014) by B.E. Andre, published by PebbleStone.
© B.E. Andre

Poles in the UK

later, having returned to Poland in the 1930s and been deported, as a stateless refugee.

People from all around the world who were born to the post-war Polish refugees have been in touch with me to tell me how similar their upbringings were to Ania's in *With Blood and Scars*. The same daily events happened in New Zealand, Australia, South Africa, the United States, Canada, Argentina, Mexico etc. Polish refugees found homes all over the globe, yet what went on inside their communities repeated itself everywhere, as they maintained their traditions and culture.

In your novel, you tell the post-war story of what some people call the Polish expat community in Manchester. Why is it important to talk about such stories today? What can one learn from exploring one's family history and heritage?
Strictly speaking, I don't think we can call it an 'expat' community: it implies *choice*. Most of these refugees had no choice because their homes no longer existed. In fact, their country no longer existed. The Polish territories where they came from were given to communist Russia after the war, then known as USSR, the Union of Soviet Socialist Republics. These days those territories are called Lithuania, Belarus and Ukraine.

I believe it's very important to talk about stories which *should* have an effect on how society behaves now. We must learn from the mistakes of the past, learn compassion for our fellow human beings, no matter where they come from. If we explore our family histories, Polish and English, we can perhaps see the situations that influence the people we become, see what has been passed down through the generations.

What place do you think Polish communities hold in British cities like Manchester? Do they introduce something positive to these British spaces?
Manchester has been a melting pot of nationalities as far back as the Industrial Revolution. The mid-nineteenth century saw an influx of immigrants from Ireland, who came to escape the Potato Famine, which began in 1845. Not much later, large numbers of Jewish people came from Central and Eastern Europe.

Manchester's Polish community, although it existed before World War II, really began to flourish when the post-war refugees arrived. Many set up their own businesses, employing people from a variety of backgrounds. I tried to reflect this in *With Blood and Scars*. These days Manchester continues to be a very cosmopolitan city.

Whereas in the past the Polish refugees might have kept themselves to themselves due to a lack of confidence and maybe also as a result of fear, the Poles who have arrived in the UK since 2004 have nothing to be afraid of. Whether they come just for the experience of living and working abroad, or as economic migrants, they contribute to our economy and are happy to make friends with their English neighbours and participate in English culture.

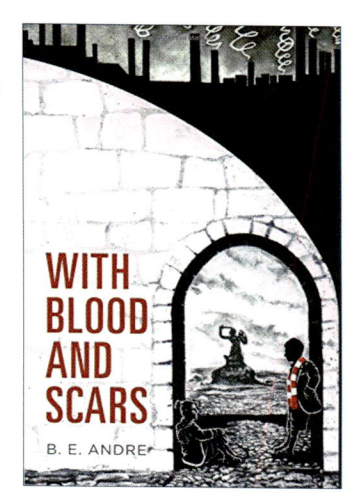

CHAPTER 5: **The Arts**

The protagonist of your novel is a young Mancunian, yet she goes to Polish Saturday School. Do you think it's important that Polish-British children learn the Polish language and culture?
Most definitely! I know quite a few older second-generation Poles who didn't go to Polish school and didn't take part in Polish activities. Now they regret it with all their heart. Learning the language and culture of another country makes you a more tolerant person, someone who isn't scared to travel and learn about other nationalities.

What do you think the future of Poles in the UK will be? Will more continue to move over here? Will they become fully integrated into the community?
It depends on what you mean by fully integrated. I sincerely hope they keep their traditions and culture in the home, whilst being open to and sharing in all the positives the UK offers.

I doubt whether more Polish people will continue to move here, but that's all about politics. Although communism fell in 1989, the real freedom to travel and work came when Poland joined the EU. Polish people wanted to work hard and achieve their personal goals.

In all honesty, I hope more won't move here – not for any sinister reasons, just because I'd like to see the Polish economy flourishing and for better opportunities to be available to all who want to stay in their homeland.

Ironically, while many Poles have moved to England, second generation Poles like myself are emigrating or retiring to Poland! The landscapes are beautiful and, despite what many people who haven't been to Poland think, the weather can be glorious. The hospitality and welcome you receive in Poland, especially when on a personal level, is second to none.

Do you plan to write another novel soon? Will you continue to work with the Polish-British theme in your future books?
I'm writing another novel which has no historical aspect; it's very much 'of the moment.' So far I haven't included a Polish-British strand, but I'm sorely tempted to do so. There are so many aspects of the Polish psyche and culture that seem 'exotic' to an English reader, whilst simultaneously being vaguely familiar. Nowadays, I think there's more that English readers could relate to, so I'm considering ways to incorporate 'Polishness.' It could be a challenge I'll enjoy!

Poles in the UK

Maria Jastrzębska (63)
| Poet

What is your Polish heritage?
I was born in Warsaw and came to England with my family as small child in the late 1950s.

In what ways do you feel Polish? In what ways do you feel British?
I feel I'm totally Polish, but I'd describe myself as 'British-Polish' as compared to 'Poland Polish'.

Does your Polish heritage influence your work?
Yes, I think it has had a massive influence. There is for starters another language sitting on my shoulder as I speak. Right from when I was growing up I was aware of being different from the children around me – on account of my family's customs, food, songs, books and preoccupations, as well as the language. And I knew that I had more than one way of looking at the world.

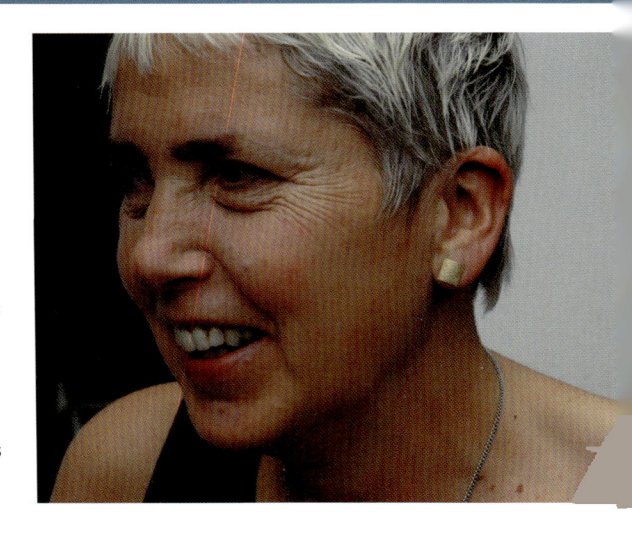

IMAGES: Maria Jastrzębska

What are the main themes in your poetry?
Love and war. By love I mean all kinds of relationships, but especially family and romantic love. As for war, I have written things about World War II which my parents lived through, but this has made me think about wars all over the world too. I always think I'm done with writing about my family for instance, but then writers tend to return to the same themes, maybe from different angles.

Have you been inspired by any specific writers to pursue a career in literature?
I've been inspired by countless writers, whose work thrills and nourishes me as a poet. But I don't think anyone suggested it would be a career! I think poetry is very much the poor relation in the arts. This makes it a very tough life choice, though at the same time it gives poets a certain freedom.

Do you have a sense of the breakdown of readers for your work?
Since I write in English and have been published mainly in the UK, I'd say the majority of my readers are English speakers, or from

English-speaking communities. British audiences have surprised me by enjoying bits of Polish, which I throw in to readings sometimes.

Polish people living here have responded warmly too when they've come across my work, so they're certainly in my mind. Though for non-native speakers, who have arrived more recently in the UK, there is a language barrier.

Some of my work has appeared in Finnish, Slovenian and French journals or anthologies, and I've read at some festivals in Europe. However, very recently my selected poems have been translated into Polish and published in Poland in a dual-language collection, *Cedry z Walpole Park/The Cedars of Walpole Park* from K.I.T Stowarzyszenie Żwych Poetów. I hope this will make my work more widely accessible now to those who read predominantly in Polish.

Would you recommend any other Polish-British poets for our readers?
I'm most aware of poets who came to the UK as adults and continue to write in Polish. One

IMAGE: Maria Jastrzębska

OLDER GENERATION

In fur coats
Fur caps or grey wool, brown macs
With the occasional brightly flowered
Peasant-style scarf, a flash
Of rainbow plumage
Against soft charcoal.

In their best –
Medals buffed up,
Jewellery sparkling, they meet
On the church steps
After mass
Or just before the cabaret
At the Polish club, kissing
Each other on both cheeks
Counting the dead
And the survivors.

Bohdan's had a by-pass
Irka might not last
Mind, she's always been a goer
Who does that leave
For the committee?

Death tries to slip in
Among them, to mingle
And eavesdrop on their conversations
Ingratiating itself with condescending
Smiles. But they're not easily fooled.
They've lived with informers before.
When it turns its back, they wink
At one another, carry on talking as if
It wasn't there, kissing and shaking hands

Looking out for each other
As they once did
When they were terribly young
And death ran amok
Among them, jeering.

This poem first appeared in *Syrena* (2004) by Maria Jastrzębska, published by RedBeck Press.
© Maria Jastrzębska

Poles in the UK

IMAGE: Maria Jastrzębska

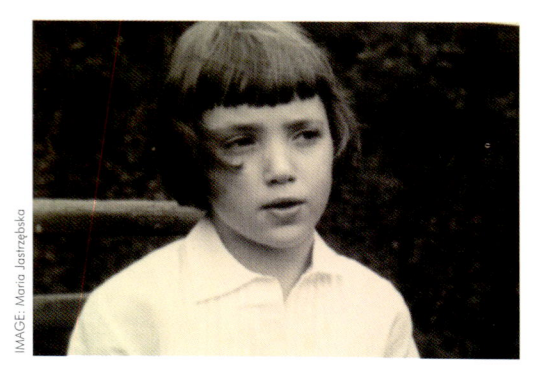

obvious and inspiring such poet is Wioletta Grzegorzewska, who's been living here for a decade now and whose Polish work has been translated into English (*Finite Formulae & Theories of Chance*, published by Arc Publications). She also has a new prose book, *Swallowing Mercury*, coming out in 2017 with Portobello Press.

Other voices include Iza Smolarek, Anna-Maria Mickiewicz and Tomasz Mielcarek. There are many Polish organisations promoting Polish writing in the UK, such as KAMPe (led by Aleksy Wróbel) and Off_Press (led by Marek Kazmierski and the long-standing Union of Polish Writers in Exile).

What place do you think Polish communities hold in the UK? Do they introduce something positive here?
Of course. I've always believed that what makes Britain an exciting and good place to live is the diversity of its various communities – Afro-Caribbean, Asian, European etc. Poland has such a rich culture. I'm thinking of its artists, poets, thinkers, film and music makers, as well as the fact that we make scrumptious *pierogi* and proper cheesecake! (▶ p. 208 and 205 for recipes). Polish people have much to contribute, given their experiences and given Poland's history within Europe, and within the world.

What do you think the future of Poles in the UK will be? Will more continue to move over here? Will they become fully integrated into the community?
I can tell you what I hope for. I'd like to see Poles preserving the wealth of our heritage, with Polish children growing up in Britain retaining their Polish – it's an amazing and beautiful language.

At the same time I'd like to see Poles opening out to the other cultures in Britain, rather than closing in on themselves or trying to secure a foothold in the pecking order by looking down on other races or cultures. When this happens, exciting fusions and cross-pollinations are possible!

And finally I'd like to see the dominant, mainstream culture here – in turn – fully embracing, enjoying and truly appreciating Poles and other migrants, instead of fear-mongering and complaining about too many foreigners. That would be my understanding of integration.

CHAPTER 5: **The Arts**

Kasia Madera (40)

BBC World News Anchor and Journalist

IMAGE: Milton Boyne

When I was little, every summer holiday my mum would pack our car with clothes, food and toys and we would leave London and drive to visit my family in Poland.

At that time Poland was a communist country which had rationing, so there were shortages of nearly everything. One of my earliest memories is my grandfather getting up at 3:00 am to queue for bread. So the things we brought with us from the UK were essential.

When I look back at those summer holidays I appreciate how important they were, not just in letting me practise and perfect my Polish language skills, but in giving me an insight into the country. That insight and my bilingual Polish

skills have proved invaluable in my professional life as a journalist and presenter at BBC World News.

My first-hand experience of the impact of the Soviet Union on Eastern Europe gives me an understanding of how important it was for Poland to regain its independence, and the troubled relationship it has with Russia. As the daughter of migrants my own background means I have strong links with the UK's large Polish community. It also enables me to understand why so many Poles came to the UK when Poland joined the European Union.

Working at the BBC
At work I'm regularly called upon to cover a wide range of Polish stories, from reporting on the European Union elections to filming a theatre in Gdańsk dedicated to Shakespeare. Whether it is interviewing Polish political leaders, including the former Prime Minister Donald Tusk (currently President of the European Union), the former President Bronisław Komorowski and the current President Andrzej Duda, or the Polish baritone singer Mariusz Kwiecień about performing a Polish opera for the first time at the Royal Opera House in London's Covent Garden, the very nature of working on an international rolling news channel means that I have to be ready for anything.

Although fascinating the interviews with politicians and celebrities are rarely as memorable as those with ordinary people who find themselves in extraordinary circumstances. Those who have experienced the greatest

151

hardships are the most stoic and humbling to interview.

I had the honour of speaking to Halina Birenbaum, who survived Auschwitz. On the 70th anniversary of the liberation of the Nazi death camp I asked her how she could face coming back. She simply said because she came back as a free person. Her dignity and strength has left a lasting impression on me.

Polish heritage

My Polish heritage has greatly enriched my life, both personally and professionally. As a journalist the personal and professional frequently overlap. As a child I heard Lech Wałęsa, the Solidarity leader, address parishioners at the Our Lady Mother of the Church Polish church in Ealing, west London, before going on to be elected as the first post-communist President of Poland in 1990.

Years later, when I interviewed Mr Wałęsa and told him about how most of those gathered in Ealing, including myself, cried during his speech, he laughed and jokingly said he did not realise he was such a bad public speaker. I'm always touched by how modest and self-deprecating some of history's most influential figures are.

Tragic reports

After the Smoleńsk air crash in 2010 in which nearly a hundred Polish dignitaries, including the then President and First Lady, were killed, I ended up reporting outside the St Andrzej Bobola Polish Church in Shepherd's Bush, London. I was interviewing people I knew about an unspeakable tragedy, made even more poignant because the much-loved parish priest, Monsignor Bronisław Gostomski, was also on the plane.

A week later I was at Trafalgar Square reporting on and hosting a vigil being held for the victims of the air crash. I will never forget the moment the whole square fell silent as thousands of people kneeled in prayer.

My parents' gift

None of these experiences would have been possible if it were not for my Polish background. I owe that to my parents who left their country in difficult circumstances to start a new life in a free world.

Kasia Madera

CHAPTER 6

Public Services

This chapter presents an overview of the profound influence that Polish people – and those with Polish heritage – have had, and continue to have, on Britain's public service industries. It includes a special section showcasing the work of children from one of the many Polish Saturday Schools in the UK.

Poles in the UK

Britain is renowned all over the world for the quality of its public services, especially its National Health Service and its many excellent schools, colleges and universities. Yet British people sometimes overlook the fact that Poles, and those with Polish heritage, make an increasingly significant contribution to the UK's public services.

Polish people work in a range of roles in most large hospitals in the UK (▶ p. 173), as well as in the health and social care sector, where they carry out an invaluable role helping people to stay healthy and safe (▶ p. 176). Many of these Polish people work in roles that are difficult to recruit for.

Within the education sector, it is now increasingly common to find Poles employed in nursery, primary and secondary schools, working with Polish and British children, plus those from many other nationalities. And in the higher education sector Poles, and people with Polish heritage, carry out a wide range of roles, from those engaged in cleaning duties, to support staff (▶ p. 166), academic researchers (▶ p. 170) and even the top management role of university Vice-Chancellor.

As well as the education taking place in British state schools, learning of a different kind is a feature of the wide network of Polish Saturday

Did you know?

The current Vice-Chancellor of Cambridge University is the Polish-British immunologist **Sir Leszek Borysiewicz** (a Vice-Chancellor is the chief administrative and academic officer of a university). Borysiewicz was born in 1951 in Cardiff, Wales, to Polish World War II refugees from what is present day Belarus. He was elected to the highest paid position at Cambridge University in October 2010, and is the 345th Vice-Chancellor of the university. Before this, he was the Chief Executive of the British Medical Research Council (2007–2010).

CHAPTER 6: **Public Services**

> **Did you know?**
> Since the 1940s many **churches** in the UK have been rescued by Polish congregations, who have breathed new life into buildings that would otherwise have fallen into disrepair, or even been abandoned. The continued interest in Catholicism among Polish communities across Britain has occurred against a backdrop of declining church attendances in the wider population.
>
> Churches such as **St. Andrew Bobola**, in London, have been given a new lease of life after being gifted to the Polish Catholic community. This former Presbyterian church, which has been described as one of London's hidden gems, has been restored as a memorial to the Poles who died in World War II. Among its many beautiful features are ten wonderful stained glass windows by the Polish architect Alexander Klecki [1928–2014].
>
> *Kathryn Needham*

Schools now established across the UK. These important institutions, which are run as charities, experienced much growth and are more vibrant than ever after Poland joined the European Union in 2004. As well as focussing on the teaching of the Polish language, its culture and traditions, these schools are often part of wider Polish Centres which reach out to their communities in a wide variety of ways.

THE LEEDS POLISH CATHOLIC CENTRE AND SATURDAY SCHOOL

The Polish Catholic Centre in Leeds is a community centre established, built and run entirely by volunteers. Its history dates back to 1951, and today the Centre is more vibrant than ever.

Members of the The Leeds Polish School in 1954

The heart of the community

The Centre is the cultural and social heart of the Polish diaspora in Leeds, and surrounding areas. Many events take place throughout the year, including Polish national celebrations and the joint Anglo-Polish annual commemoration of Remembrance Sunday (which is also Polish Independence Day).

Poles in the UK

The Polish Catholic church in Leeds

The Centre organises various events, such as Easter and Christmas fairs, the Harvest Festival, seasonal music and drama performances, the New Year's Eve and Valentine's Day balls, the Bonfire Night party, community barbecues, charity events, guest lectures and more.

The Centre also offers fitness and dance classes, a regular social gathering for the senior Polish community members, UK-wide excursions and day trips, as well as English language courses.

There is also a Polish Catholic Church on site, built in 1976. It offers services and worship in the Polish language. The Polish Church also participates in the annual cycle of 'Ecumenical Masses' – services bringing together different Christian movements, such as Evangelicalism.

The Polish Catholic Community Centre is an integral part of its local community in Leeds

IMAGES: Maria H. Żukowska

CHAPTER 6: Public Services

POLISH FOLKLORE AND LEGENDS

Poland's history is full of **folklore** and **legends**, as shown by these stamps designed by children's book illustrator Elżbieta Gaudasińska, and launched in 1986. Some of the characters and their tales are well known and widely accepted, but the stories of others are less clear.

One of the best-known figures is **Golden Duck**, an enchanted princess. She lives under the Ostrogski Castle in Warsaw, only to be set free if a man can spend 100 ducts for three consecutive days, without sharing the money with anyone else. This is harder than it may seem, as various potential rescuers have given the last coin away to a beggar, when they are running out of time to spend it.

The story of **Boruta**, a spirit from Slavic mythology, is less clear. He appears in countless Polish myths and stories. He is known as a devil and a nobleman, but also to some as the man of extraordinary strength who rescued a king's carriage from getting stuck in the mud – and for his kindness was presented with Łęczyca Castle.

Some Polish legends have similarities to English folklore, such as **Juraj Jánošík** (commonly referred to simply as Janosik in Poland), a Slovakian folklore character with tales very similar to Robin Hood. In Polish versions of the legends, he is associated with the Polish Tatra Mountains. Others are legends that cross borders, like the **Basilisk**, a reptile known about since Roman times and said to kill any man or woman with a glance. It is so evil that even its breath can destroy surrounding vegetation – and if a man on horseback stabs one with a spear, its poison will travel back up the spear and kill both rider and horse!

A further stamp in Gaudasińska's series shows the **Lajkonik**, a character who may have its origin in a real event, when the city of Kraków was invaded by the Tatars (people who were part of the Mongolian invasion of the thirteenth century). Thanks to the Lajkonik, the legend goes, the city remained unconquered and an annual celebration was declared by the mayor. To this day, every year, there is festival in Kraków which involves a great procession – led by the Lajkonik – with much singing and dancing. The character is also one of the city's official symbols.

The final stamp in the series shows **Duke Popiel**, a ruler who was reported to have not been very good at the job. In fact, legend has it that Duke Popiel did such a bad job that his 12 uncles all wanted to get rid of him; however, he found out about the plot, and retaliated by poisoning them at a banquet he and his wife held for them. His subjects were angry with what the Duke had done and drove him and his wife into hiding in a tower where, the story says, hordes of mice and rats ate them alive!

Kathryn Needham

Polish folklore and legends are kept alive in Polish Saturday Schools across Britain. This stamp series from 1986 shows Basilisk and Duke Popiel (5 zł), Devil Boruta and Golden Duck (10 zł), Juraj Jánošík (20 zł) and Lajkonik (50 zł)

157

Poles in the UK

Children from the Leeds Polish Saturday School at work

Food and drink

Each Sunday, the Centre runs a 'coffee and cake club', aimed predominantly at those coming for the Sunday service, but open to all. Anyone can drop by and have a hot drink with a slice of delicious cake – traditional Polish cake, of course! The cakes are usually home-made and donated by the Centre's volunteers. The prices are very reasonable, and each week the money collected from the sales contributes towards a different charitable cause, as well as the Centre's maintenance costs.

If coffee and cake is not enough, upstairs there is also a Polish Restaurant serving the best of Polish cuisine. This includes comforting soups, hearty main courses with refreshing side salads and scrumptious desserts, such as traditional Polish pancakes with sweet cheese. The dishes here are sure to satisfy both a demanding and a very hungry guest. Senior citizens can enjoy special rates.

The restaurant within the Polish Catholic Centre in Leeds provides the chance for people from across the city to sample authentic Polish cuisine at very reasonable prices. The menu includes many of the classic specialities from Poland

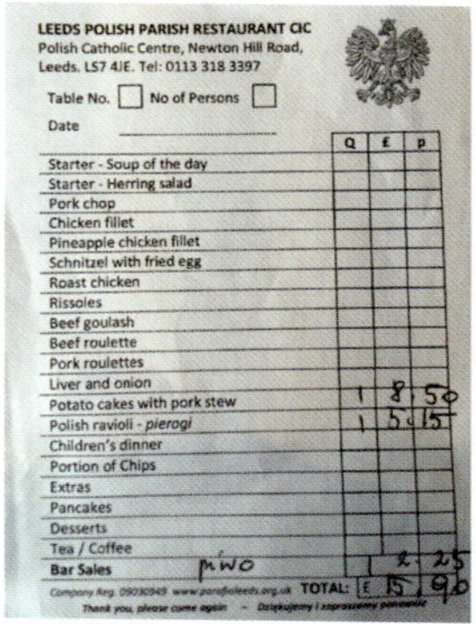

For those who wish to relax after a delicious meal, there is even a bar at the Centre, popular with the Polish community, as well as the non-Polish locals. It gets busy on football nights (particularly those

158

THE LEEDS POLISH SATURDAY SCHOOL

The Leeds Polish Saturday School is run by volunteers. It provides education for students of all ages, from preschool right through to the youngsters studying A-level Polish.

I work with the preschool group. I currently take care of a group of 15 four- and five-year olds (together with Miss Bożenka, who helps me). Classes are held on Saturdays during term time, starting at 9:15 am with an assembly and prayer (we are a Catholic Community Centre) and finishing at 1:00 pm.

We plan each lesson diligently and we prepare all our teaching resources ourselves (based on specialist teaching materials dedicated to children who study abroad). We focus on giving the children an opportunity to develop and reach their full potential in their mother tongue.

Among other topics, we teach the children about the country they come from. We read and discuss poems and stories to help them develop their Polish language skills. We also try to encourage their imagination, through creative games and manual, crafty tasks, which are a part of each class.

For example, one lesson we recently had was entitled 'We help the birds survive winter'. After we discussed a poem and worked on colourful drawings of birds such as the bullfinch, each child built their own bird feeder! We did this by covering the cardboard tube from a loo roll with peanut butter and then rolling it around in various seeds, so they stuck. The next step was for the whole group to go for a walk together and place our feeders on tree branches.

Our philosophy is to organise fun, hands-on learning and not just teach the dry theory. We try to develop this practical element of our teaching as much as possible during our one weekly class. But the most important thing for us is that the children come back to us eagerly and they are willing to learn. This our great success!

Kasia Dejewska

Poles in the UK

involving Polish teams), when regulars gather to watch the games. The bar also proudly hosts a monthly live music night.

Moreover, the Centre boasts a library (with books in Polish, as well as English-language publications on subjects relating to Poland) and a Polish shop, selling all the traditional delicacies and fresh bread.

Finally, the Centre is home to some other important social initiatives – the Polish Girl Guides, Scouts, Brownies and Beavers make it an especially lively place, as does the Polish Saturday School.

An inclusive space

Its rich cultural programme and a vibrant atmosphere make the Leeds Polish Catholic Centre an integral part of the wider Chapeltown community in Leeds. With its main hall regularly hired for various purposes, such as arts and craft workshops, Sikh community classes and Caribbean weddings, it is a truly inclusive space.

THE LEEDS POLISH SATURDAY SCHOOL'S SUCCESSES

In 2002, our children and young adults performed for the Queen and Prince Philip at Harewood House, near Leeds. It was during the year of the Queen's Golden Jubilee (the 50th anniversary of her accession to the British throne), when she travelled around the whole of England. At the time, I worked with a lady who was the Queen's representative for the Yorkshire region, and she asked our students to take part in the celebrations. We prepared a fantastic programme for the occasion. Prince Philip even came up to us at the end to congratulate us – he said our traditional dress and dance were beautiful!

Teresa Hough, Head of Polish Saturday School

IMAGE: Leeds Polish Saturday School

CHAPTER 6: Public Services

MY POLISH HERITAGE

Oak trees are a sign of strength and my picture of an oak tree represents the strength of my links with my Polish heritage, from the roots to it being something I hold dear to my heart. The Union Jack represents the land that has now become home – the UK. Each leaf represents different feelings, all of which are as important as the next and represent my love for my Polish heritage.

Text and artwork by Adrianna Green

161

Poles in the UK

THOUGHTS ON THEIR POLISH HERITAGE FROM CHILDREN AT THE LEEDS POLISH SATURDAY SCHOOL

Poland is a beautiful country. Poland is worth a visit, because one can find many historical monuments here. The most significant chapter in Polish immigration started in 1940, when the Polish government came to London to continue working for the Polish cause in exile. After World War II, it is estimated that 50,000 Poles remained in the UK and settled here permanently, started families, set up Catholic community centres, built churches and maintained national traditions. The next wave of emigration was in 2004, when Poland joined the European Union and we were enabled to come and work here. Many people took up this opportunity and came here in hope of a better life, because in many regions of Poland it was not possible to find employment. Most children in our Saturday School were born in England and do not know much about Poland. This is why we go to Polish School, to learn to speak and write in Polish, to maintain our national traditions and so that we never forget who we are.

Wiktoria Szykuła, age 8

Jan Łaski came to England to organise protestant communities here. He is seen by the British as one of their originators. British business also has some Polish roots. We all know Tesco, but few of us know that the creator and owner of this chain was Jack Cohen, son of Polish immigrants. It is similar in the case of Marks and Spencer supermarkets. Michael Marks was born in the Polish-Lithuanian Commonwealth, in an area that belongs to Belarus today.

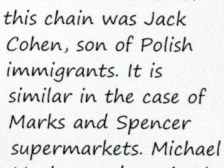

Michalina Kulikjan, age 9

IMAGES: Roman Paszel

162

CHAPTER 6: Public Services

THOUGHTS ON THEIR POLISH HERITAGE FROM CHILDREN AT THE LEEDS POLISH SATURDAY SCHOOL

Polish people come to the UK to earn a better wage and to get new experiences, personal and professional. Living abroad gives people a chance to learn the English language. British people invite the Poles to work with them and to develop their talents. Polish people help the British to build houses, make clothes, teach in schools and they also help in other jobs. Some Polish people are afraid of coming to the UK, and some British people are afraid of coming to Poland.

Laura Tubacka, age 5

In all areas of life in the UK, one can find examples of Poles who have made a contribution, and one can find many Polish traces. Over 10 centuries ago there ruled a king who had some Polish blood. King Canute, ruler of England and Denmark, is thought to have been a grandson of Mieszko and Dobrawa [a Polish monarch and his wife]. One cannot overlook Ignacy Jan Paderewski, a Polish pianist and composer. As an acclaimed musician, he performed for Queen Victoria. In 1919 he was the Prime Minister of Poland, and the country's foreign secretary. After World War II broke out, Paderewski joined the Polish Government in Exile. Although Polish football does not usually see any particular triumphs, other clubs are keen to hire or buy our players, such as Marek Saganowski. Grzegorz Rasiak and Tomasz Kuszczak also spent a few years in the UK playing in Manchester. The most well known Polish players are probably Maciej Żurawski and goalkeepers: Artur Boruc and Jerzy Dudek. I could write about many more Poles – but what is important is that they all show that one's Polish heritage is rooted deeply in a person, and emigration cannot change this.

Emilka Solny, age 9

IMAGES: Roman Paszel

163

Poles in the UK

THOUGHTS ON THEIR POLISH HERITAGE FROM CHILDREN AT THE LEEDS POLISH SATURDAY SCHOOL

A famous scientist, Maria Skłodowska-Curie, wasn't French as some think, but in fact Polish. She was the woman who pioneered the use of the x-rays and found two elements which now have their place in the periodic table [Polonium and Radium]. Did you know that a golf cart, a paraffin lamp, a bulletproof vest, the walkie-talkie and a mine detector were all invented by Poles?

Anna Cieśluk, age 10

Polish people come to the UK to find employment and in hope of a better life. Us children learn a new language and meet friends of different nationalities and learn about their cultures and traditions. Poles have contributed to the UK through our shared history, and by working and developing the economy and industry. Although life is better in England, us Poles often feel lonely and we miss our families and close ones. Poles open Polish Centres and schools, to learn our language, history and culture, and therefore they feel more united.

Radosław Kolator, age 10

My family has been living in Leeds for almost eight years. Dad has worked at the same company all the time, and mum has been changing her job a lot but now she works in an office, in a Polish lettings agency. We also have some family here and we have a black and white kitten. My auntie works in an English shop. We always spend holidays together with the family, and my granddad visits us for Christmas.

Dominika Szymańska, age 9

IMAGES: Roman Paszel

CHAPTER 6: Public Services

THOUGHTS ON THEIR POLISH HERITAGE FROM CHILDREN AT THE LEEDS POLISH SATURDAY SCHOOL

Polish people came to the UK to help. They came here to help in World War II, and then they opened shops and restaurants. Many Poles came to the UK after 2004 because the borders opened – Poland joined the European Union. A large proportion of the Polish community in the UK start by working in factories to make a dignified living. Those who have a skill, such as bakers, mechanics, hairdressers or doctors, start their own companies. This way they create workplaces so that they can employ other people.

Zuzanna Malka, age 8

Poles in the UK can be of a few different backgrounds. Firstly, the post-war immigration, or the people who fought in the war and started their families here. They can teach us the history. Secondly, those who were victims of the Communist regime in Poland and had to leave the country, or they did not want to live in a country that was not free. They can also teach us about the difficult Polish history. Thirdly, the economic migration, or the people coming to the UK in search of a better work and dignified living. They want a better life but they can also enrich this environment with their culture and values. Lastly, the young people, such as students and those who want to make an international career. They learn and develop, they gain excellent experience in some of the best colleges and universities.

Marek Bucholc, age 8

Poles came to the UK for education or to work. They brought with them foods that are not known here in the UK, for example **pierogi** [dumplings], **barszcz** [beetroot soup], **żurek** [another special soup] and **twaróg** [white, crumbly cheese made from cow's milk]. Poles also built churches so that religious people can come and pray. John Paul II was a Polish pope.

Idalia Maria Cruz, age 8

IMAGES: Roman Poszel

Poles in the UK

Maria Helena Żukowska (24)

Education Service Officer at the University of Leeds, Writer and Singer-songwriter

IMAGE: Michał Bryś

What brought you to England?
Well, my mum and I share a love of adventure. We wanted to see a bit more of the world. We've also always enjoyed the English language, British music, shows and the sense of humour – there are bits of Monty Python's Flying Circus and 'Allo, 'Allo! that I know by heart. Another, much more practical reason, was the economic situation in our home country. Unfortunately, life wasn't easy.

When Poland joined the European Union, suddenly there was the opportunity for us to come to England. It was the natural choice. We decided to see what life was like in England. We wanted a challenge and couldn't resist the opportunity. My mum arrived first, in 2007, and I joined her three months later. At first we lived with some friends in Wakefield, and a few weeks later we moved to Leeds.

What was it like for you at the beginning?
The beginning was, of course, difficult, but also exciting. I was allocated a place at a secondary school not long after we arrived, so I had to find my feet quickly. Although I had just completed my *egzamin gimnazjalny* (the Polish equivalent of GCSEs), it was not recognised here, so in November 2007 I jumped straight into Year 11 to complete my GCSEs. I was almost 16 at the time.

The school I went to was not doing great academically, or in terms of student behaviour. But the teachers were amazing, especially at working with challenging children, but also at spotting talent. I remember that my English teacher somehow saw and encouraged my literary flair after just one class, even though my English was hardly fluent at the time!

In the seven or so months I spent there my English improved massively, and I made friends with kids from all over the world – England, Mauritius, Pakistan, Lithuania, Egypt, Slovakia, China and other countries. We would compare our languages, customs and traditions – fascinating stuff. I'm grateful for this wonderful experience.

Apart from that, some of the most exciting things for me at the beginning were my discovery of Madeira cake, a realisation that British people love their tea with milk as much as I do (I knew it from home, as it's typical for some regions of Poland), the massive daffodil flowerbeds everywhere in spring, and seeing that people smile so much.

How did you find learning and studying English?

I studied English at school in Poland, but much of it was just 'textbook knowledge'. The real, 'live' language in day-to-day use is so much different. Back in Poland, I would also learn English independently by listening to a lot of British music and doing my own translations of the lyrics. I learnt much of my best vocabulary from the lyrics of oldies such as Pink Floyd, Jethro Tull or Marillion – the old soul that I am!

But most of the language skills I have today I learnt by just living, studying and working in the UK. Also, my friends at school, college and then university really helped me with things like dialect and slang words that you wouldn't learn from textbooks. No, not just swear words, we were good kids after all! [laugh].

I then went on to do my A-levels at Leeds City College (then Park Lane College), including English Language and Literature, which I loved. It improved my written and spoken English further. I was over the moon when I found out I got an A*. With this as an encouragement, I decided to do my BA in English Literature at Leeds Beckett (then Metropolitan) University. This was a good decision. I made wonderful friends and developed so much in those three years. The course was very intellectually stimulating.

I completed my studies with a prize for best dissertation in 2013, which I couldn't quite believe, but was extremely happy about! So, because I couldn't get enough of all the critical thinking, thought-provoking discussions and fascinating reads, I continued with an MA in Contemporary English Literature at the same university. I just loved my studies and the English language, so it was the right thing for me to do.

I read tonnes of books and articles, and I must have written tens of thousands of words of essays during the four years of my studies! The tutors were incredibly supportive, and I had an amazing supervisor who helped me enormously to really refine my written English.

IMAGE: Michał Bryś

Generally speaking, though, it all comes with time. I had no idea that there were so many accents in the UK before I arrived here, so sometimes it felt like learning a completely new language! I listened to English people as intently as I could and I picked up different elements of pronunciation from different people. This resulted in me developing a mixture of vaguely northern-sounding accents, and people often cannot guess where I'm from. They say there's

Poles in the UK

some Yorkshire there, some Welsh and some Geordie, and even an odd Scouse sound here and there!

My English keeps gradually getting better with time. This is the amazing thing about language – every week, every month, I learn another new word, phrase or saying. It's fascinating.

What do you do now?
My current role at the University of Leeds was my first 'proper job' after graduation. I work as an Education Service Officer in an area called Programme Support, at the School of Languages, and I absolutely love it!

> *I work at the University of Leeds with Maria Żukowska. She's always smiling and it's a pleasure to have a chat with her in the kitchen! She takes a lively interest in everything around her, and enjoys travelling and learning about all sorts of people and things. She works hard and is reliable and level-headed. She's a truly pleasant colleague to have and is always enthusiastic about life! I think Maria is a gentle and kind soul. I've never heard her say a bad thing about anyone.*
>
> Tamsin Wragg, University of Leeds

The students and staff there come from all over the world. My work involves supporting lecturers and students throughout the entire academic process, from enrolment to graduation. My responsibilities range from timetabling to arranging exams, and everything in between. It's a varied and dynamic role which involves a lot of communication with academics and learners – and I love working with people! Also, I think I am incredibly fortunate, because my team is the best ever.

Maria with her mama at her Masters graduation ceremony in 2014

Outside of work, I sometimes do short academic translations from Polish into English, but that's more of a hobby, really.

How are things for you now, here in the UK?
Things are good. I've made many wonderful friends, I have a fantastic job. Leeds feels like home to me now. I have 'discovered' all those exciting cultural things that Leeds has to offer, like music venues, festivals and independent cinemas. Of course I miss my Polish friends and loved ones, and my beautiful home country. But I like it here a lot, too.

What are your plans for the future?
I haven't decided yet. I'm quite happy here at the moment. I don't really want to plan anything, apart from what my next travel destination is going to be. You never know what the future holds.

What do you think about British people?
I really like British people and I've been lucky in that I've never come across any racism or prejudice towards me or my nationality. The

CHAPTER 6: Public Services

people here have always been very open and friendly to me. What I like most about England is actually the people. I love that they smile such a lot here, that they often engage in casual conversations with others, that they love a good laugh and have this brilliant sense of humour. It gives me plenty of positive energy for every day.

What do you think your contribution to the UK is?
By doing my Bachelor and Masters degrees at an English institution and paying my course fees I contributed to the UK higher education sector. I worked part-time throughout my studies, too. Today, I still support higher education here in Leeds. In my line of work, I interact with students a lot. I love to see them succeed. It's nice to know that, through my work, I support them in their exciting university adventure.

I also volunteer at the Polish Catholic Centre here in Leeds. I assist with the teaching and I organise events and school plays. The Centre is the heart of a vibrant community and the festivals are fun and open to everyone. For example, our Independence Day festival coincides with Remembrance Sunday, and it's a truly Anglo-Polish commemoration. The Centre plays an important part in our local community.

My other contribution, while still at university, was writing a study guide on John Milton's *Paradise Lost* for A-level students. It was an exciting project and the book was later used as a teaching resource in Welsh colleges and sixth forms.

I'm also a singer-songwriter in my spare time – when I have any time left to spare! This is just for fun, a creative outlet. My music is, I suppose, mostly acoustic, slightly folksy, alternative. I take inspiration from many artists, including Tom Waits, Coldplay, Pink Floyd, Leonard Cohen, Enya and Lana del Rey, but also from the Eastern European genre of 'sung poetry'. You can sometimes see me perform at open mic nights in Leeds.

And finally, of course, I'm the co-author of *Poles in the UK*. I got involved in this project because it was an opportunity to tell the readers about my beautiful country and its links with *this* beautiful country. The story of Anglo-Polish cooperation over the ages is rich and fascinating, but often overlooked. As a Polish and a British citizen, I hope that this book introduces something new and positive, and helps to build bridges and deepen Polish-British ties.

Interviewed by Kinga Kreffta

IMAGE: Michał Bryś

Poles in the UK

Agnieszka and Rafał Kulmaczewscy (36 and 35)

Soon to be Trainee Teacher and Postdoctoral Fellow at the University of Leeds

IMAGES: Agnieszka Kulmaczewska

When did you first come to England and what brought you here?
The first time we came here was in June 2005, but only for three months (2006 was our graduation year). We were hosted by one of my closest friends — our friendship began in secondary school, over 20 years ago. The aim was to put together as much money as we could from simple, temporary, physical jobs. The money we saved helped us a lot (I mean, *a lot*!) in surviving the last year of our studies.

In July 2006, straight after graduating from Gdańsk University of Technology with our MSc degrees, we came back to the UK. We lived in Leeds for six years. Rafał obtained his PhD from Loughborough University in 2011. The following year, we moved to New Zealand where he did a postdoctoral fellowship at Otago University in Dunedin.

When Rafał's postdoctoral contract ended our decision was to come back to Europe, or to be as close as possible to our families in Poland. Rafał's mum got seriously ill at the beginning of 2012. Rafał applied for just *one* position (at Leeds University) and, believe it or not, he was appointed! So, luckily for us, and maybe with some help from the Holy God, we came back to Leeds.

What were things like at the beginning?
In general, people were very kind and helpful. Sorting out all the formalities (National Insurance, Home Office registration etc.) was a bit of hassle. Our verbal communication skills were limited, and our knowledge of the laws and our rights was also narrow. We both ended up with emergency tax codes (but getting a tax rebate at the end of the year was like a cherry on the top of the cake!). Waiting times and the meetings associated with National Insurance were a big concern. Opening a bank account was the easiest thing — no proof of address was required, just a passport.

The biggest limitation for us was the language. We thought we had a basic knowledge of English — what a mistake! The Yorkshire accent, the way of speaking, expressions, the speed with which people talked; they were all problems. Most of our first conversations included the same phrase – that is, 'Could you please repeat, slowly?'. Moreover, telephone conversations were something we hopelessly tried to avoid for as long as possible. The simplest of chats was stressful. There was this fear that you might say something grammatically incorrect, or you wouldn't find a word accurately expressing what you had in mind. Looking back at it now, it was hilarious.

How did you overcome this language barrier?

That was actually our second aim when coming to the UK – to test our English skills (and to learn the language by living among the English). We were both at beginner level back then.

I think time was the crucial factor which helped us improve our English (and we're still improving it, every day is a school day!). By this I mean the time we spent in an English-speaking environment. It's hard to tell exactly how much it improved, but after a year of living here there was no comparison to what our English was like at the beginning of our journey. In terms of our vocabulary and phrases, we understand much more. I mean much, *much* more.

How are things now for your family?

In terms of what? Size? [*laugh*]. All of us, all four of us, currently live in Leeds. Our family grew a little bit over the past few years. To cut a long story short, in 2008 we got married. In 2010 our daughter, Zuzanna, was born – what a bundle of joy?! In 2014, our son Jan was born to join our family. Rafał is a postdoctoral fellow at the University of Leeds, in the Chemistry Department. I, his lovely wife, am currently a housewife (personally, I hate that term).

Were both your children born in the UK? Do they, or will they, go to Polish school? How do they find English school?

Our kids were born in Leeds. Zuzanna started English school in 2014 and she joined Polish Saturday School the same year. We spent one and a half years in New Zealand and Zuzanna was two at the time. She attended the local nursery, therefore I suppose English for her was not a problem at all. I cannot say for certain if she is bilingual, but I can say she speaks both languages. She understands both. She is just starting to read and write in English, but she cannot do it in Polish yet. We've decided that we will introduce the 'complicated' Polish once she gains that skill in English first. Jan, our son, is 19 months old and he spends most of his time

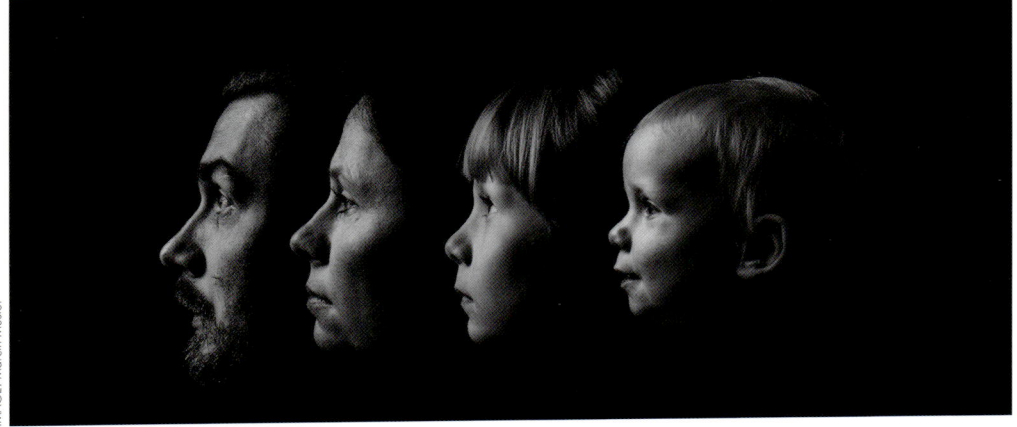

IMAGE: Marcin Musioł

with his mum, so he understands Polish, but his replies are limited – he doesn't speak much yet, just a few words. I hope that Jan will start nursery this year, and when he's four, he'll start attending both schools, like his sister.

What are your plans for the future?
Future – what a dilemma! I would rather say what our dreams are. Rafał is currently limited by his contract, which ends in 2018. He is very keen on developing his career in academia. At the moment, he is on his second postdoctoral position, at Leeds University. His aim is to become a lecturer. Where he ends up and when – this is one big unknown.

There's no country limitation for us, I mean English-speaking country. As for myself, I'm about to apply for a PGCE course – secondary school chemistry. Quite a challenge, however most of us find that we're able to do unexpected things in order to pursue our dreams.

What do you think of English people? Have you come across any prejudice?
I would say that we've come across a wide range of people, from shop assistants to those at the university. They all have the same attitude – they're very kind, helpful and nice, with a smile on their face when they greet you. However, after a few pints some of them become more perky and cheeky, and they can then truly say what they think. They are very tolerant people. Prejudice – no, I don't think so. We've never heard any racist comments against us.

What's your contribution to the UK?
That's a really 'difficult' question. Mainly, we're part of society. By our work and by being taxpayers, we contribute to the UK economy in a big way. By travelling around the country, we support the British railways. By renting a flat, we support our landlord.

Through his work at the university, Rafał significantly contributes to the higher education sector and supports Masters and PhD students. Living here and buying things like groceries and clothes at local shops is another way in which we support the British economy. Personally, I support local charity shops because I love them. I think they are one of the best things here in Leeds and generally in the UK.

Finally, we're a family and we didn't come here to live on benefits. Our opinion is simple. When you're an immigrant, of a minority group, just blend in – out of respect for the country that accepted you. 'Give something to receive anything'.

Finally – any interesting or funny stories you'd like to share?
Well, there's one off the top of my head. Rafał's first job was a shop assistant in a Kwik Save shop. The situation took place almost at the end of his shift, and it was one of his first days there. Seeing his staff badge, a customer approached him and asked, 'Where is the loo?'. Rafał didn't think much and didn't want to be embarrassed by not quite understanding what the guy was looking for. So he told him to follow on and showed him an aisle full of toilet paper!

CHAPTER 6: **Public Services**

Zuzanna Sawicka (36)

| Consultant Physician

What's your job title?
Consultant Physician in Elderly Medicine at Pinderfields Hospital, Mid Yorkshire NHS Trust.

Could you describe a typical day at work?
During my average week, I have a ward round on the acute admissions unit (mainly a morning), during which I assess older people who come to hospital with medical problems such as falls or infections. Other mornings, I have sessions where I go and visit residents in care homes, assess their medical problems and ensure their medication prescriptions are up-to-date and decisions are made to promote their ongoing health. My afternoons are spent in meetings about how we can develop our service, or in keeping up-to-date with administration (looking at results, writing letters or speaking to patients' relatives).

Does your Polish heritage influence your work in any way?
My involvement in Polish Girl Guides has helped me in my work a great deal. I first became a Girl Guide when I was 11 years old, having been a Brownie from the age of six. From early on I made friends with other girls and boys from different backgrounds. One thing that was common to all of us was our Polish heritage. I learnt from an early age to be respectful to others and their opinions and to be tolerant, but most of all the importance of teamwork.

Teamwork is fundamental in insuring the best care for people who are unwell. Underpinning a team there has to be a mutual respect of others' opinions and skills. Working with the Girl Guides, I've learnt these skills in abundance.

You might think that they could have been obtained from joining the English Girl Guides, but I'm not certain that this would have been the case.

Now I'm the District Commissioner for Lancashire and Yorkshire (*Hufiec Kaszuby* in Polish) I'm continuing to improve my management skills, including those needed to get the most out of people, which I can use in my work. It is such 'transferable skills' which have influenced the way I work and made me even more passionate about my Polish heritage.

Over the last few years, I've used my Polish language to translate for patients who speak very little English, or to understand test results that have been brought back from Poland. For example, I recently translated some investigation results to work out somebody's allergy status, so they could have further tests to work out what was wrong with them.

On other occasions I have translated patients' histories and helped other consultants to make a diagnosis. It is not only very fulfilling to be able to use my Polish language skills, but also a great comfort to individuals.

As a very junior doctor I was asked to translate for a man who had been shot and was at risk of having his leg amputated. He explained that a translator had been called, but that person became very emotional when they were telling the man he may lose his leg. He was grateful that someone more objective had been found. By translating a number of times I learnt all about individuals and this helped me understand more about the effects of trauma on a person, especially when they are so far away from home. It's extremely gratifying to be able to help those in need in such difficult situations when they are

IMAGE: Zuzanna Sawicka

Poles in the UK

Zuzanna and Zygmunt's wedding in 2003

feeling so vulnerable – especially if they are new in the United Kingdom.

In my current job my employer has four 'core values' and these are very similar to the values that I grew up with within a Polish home. For example, I've always had a respect for my elders. I was taught at an early age the role that individual members of my family played in World War II and what hardships my grandparents experienced, both back in Poland and when they arrived here in the UK. I have huge respect for people who lived through the war, and it helps me to understand how my patients' lives have been affected by this conflict.

On arrival in England, other than the initial help to set up a home life and find jobs, all other funding for the formation of Polish communities and Polish schools was raised by Poles themselves. For example, my grandfather Leon rode his bicycle around the streets of Coventry to get donations from other Polish families to support a parish priest in that city. For these early 'immigrants' the Polish communities were very important because they were built to ensure that they maintained their Polish heritage, so someday they could return to Poland.

Polish people tend to be very family-orientated, and this has been especially so after World War II, when many families lost loved ones. I was always exposed to a caring and loving family, which again helps me with my work.

When my grandparents arrived in England they had nothing and my parents were therefore encouraged to make a positive impact on society through their careers. My mother is a headteacher and my father an engineer. My brother and I were always encouraged to do our best and be pleased with our achievements. From an early age I was encouraged to do well and continue to improve, and this is part of my work ethos to this day.

Having to go to Polish Saturday School, as well as mainstream school, I always had to manage my work for school in an effective manner, but I was also encouraged to do my best to the highest standard. Working to a high standard has for me become the norm and continues to influence the way I approach the challenges I face in medicine.

Through the years I've also been part of the Polish Medical Association. This has been an important part of my professional development. It has allowed me to attend lectures organised specifically for Polish doctors and medical professionals, and often given by those who have links with Poland. The most memorable lecture I attended was given by Dame Cicely Saunders, the founder of the hospice movement, in the Sikorski Museum in London. She fell in love with a number of Poles over the years, most notably her husband, the painter Marian Bohusz-Szyszko.

I've also had the opportunity to be able to read Polish literature on subjects which interest me and have been able to help translate articles into English for use by other medical professionals. Additionally, I've used my language skills to write articles related to health in a Polish newsletter, which was published in Leeds for many years.

CHAPTER 6: **Public Services**

Could you describe your links to the Polish community outside your work?
I moved to Leeds in 1997 to study medicine and took over running the Polish Girl Guides group in the city. I'm now District Commissioner for Yorkshire and Lancashire for the Polish Girl Guide movement. I'm also a qualified instructor and regularly take groups of children away for activities.

In 2003 my husband Zygmunt became chairman of the Polish Catholic Parish Council in Leeds (▶ p. 178), and we have continued to be part of this community to this day. Most recently I've been the vice-chairperson of the committee, but have also held the position of social secretary.

Maintaining our Polish heritage is important to me and my husband and we've therefore been eager to ensure our daughters attend the Polish Saturday School in Leeds. They have attended since they were four years old and both manage to keep up with children who have just arrived from Poland, despite being fourth generation Poles, which is remarkable.

Nine years ago I began *Iskierka*, a weekly bulletin to help children in the parish learn about the Catholic faith. It is now sent electronically to other parishes in England, such as in Huddersfield and Stratford-on-Avon, and is even sent as far afield as Hungary.

Why do you still feel your Polish heritage is important, given that your immediate family have not lived in Poland for over 50 years?
Your roots are who you are. If I turned away now from my Polish heritage I would see it as very disrespectful to my great-grandparents and grandparents. They went through so much in World War II and afterwards to ensure we had a brighter future. For me my Polish heritage is the norm and without it I would feel its loss.

I have cousins who do not speak Polish and see the effect that this has had on their lives, and I pity them that they have lost their Polish links. I remember my mother always having to persuade my brother to go into Polish school. He now, having spent time in Poland during his studies, has a doctorate in philosophy which investigated the economic links between the West Midlands and the Lower Silesia region in Poland. Furthermore, this summer he is to marry in Poland and I'm therefore certain my great-grandparents' and grandparents' legacy will continue. It is to them and to my parents that I owe the greatest debt.

Polish communities in the UK are devoted to keeping Polish traditions alive. This includes celebrating Polish national dress at special events

Poles in the UK

Jacek Wandzel (42)
| Head Care Assistant

What was your early life in Poland like?
I grew up in a traditional family in the Polish southern highlands in the 1970s. My home town was Żywiec – it's located in an area that's famous for its beautiful scenery and its beer. I have great memories of my childhood. We had snow every winter and we always used to go skiing and sledging, and I was very close to my family.

What did you study at university?
At university in Cieszyn I specialised in social work and its management. However, after graduating I found it difficult to get a job in this area of work, even when I moved to Poland's capital city Warsaw. I tried many different jobs and for a while was even a mountain guide for foreign tourists in southern Poland.

Why did you move to the UK?
I realised that if I couldn't find a job in social work in my home country I would have to be prepared to travel overseas. I then found an advert for work opportunities in the UK in a newspaper. After thinking carefully about this opportunity, even though it wasn't in my profession, I decided to make the big move to the UK. This was in October 2005.

How did you get on in the UK when you arrived here?
I got a few jobs in a warehouse to begin with. My basic English was holding me back, so I took some one-to-one lessons and was able to get a higher level qualification in English, which helped me progress into better paid jobs. A former girlfriend also helped me develop my English.

What was the next step?
With my improved English skills I was then able to get a job in care work with a company called Helping Hands, which is based in Harrogate (North Yorkshire). My job was to act as a one-to-one carer, helping people carry out their day-to-day life: eating, washing, going to appointments and that sort of thing. I worked with some lovely people and it was great being able to help them. For many years I worked with a young boy who was deaf and I even managed to learn some sign language, which was so much fun.

What is your job now?
I'm still employed in the care industry, helping people to be independent or live their lives to a higher standard. My job title is now Head Care Assistant. I really enjoy it – I get a real sense of achievement helping people and I'm lucky that I have really supportive managers.

What do you do in your spare time?
I like to do charity work and have carried out this sort of work in Yorkshire, mainly supporting elderly people. I also enjoy going to the Polish church in Leeds, sharing my Catholic faith with other people from my home country.

How do you think you have made a contribution to the UK?
I realise that I've made a contribution to the UK in lots of different ways. I've worked in many different professions and all these have helped British people in some way – some directly, others indirectly. I know I've made a difference as I've received some really good feedback from the people I have worked with. I've never claimed a penny of benefits during my time in the UK, and overall I feel Polish people have contributed so much more to the UK than they have taken.

What is your ultimate career aim?
Ideally, I would like to become a social worker, as this is what my university training was in. I'm starting to feel more and more British as I live here for longer, and am thinking of applying for British citizenship. I have lots of British friends, enjoy British food and even enjoy the British sense of humour!

Poles in the UK

Zygmunt Green (43)
Volunteer in the Polish community

How do you contribute to the Polish community in the UK?

On moving to Leeds permanently in 2003, I was asked to become chairman of the local Polish Catholic Parish Council and continued in this role until 2012, when I became its treasurer.

As chairman of the Parish Council, I was part of the team which oversees the day-to-day running of the parish. This includes our own church, the parish buildings and surrounding land, which were bought and built by the post-war Polish immigrants with their hard-earned money. It is an honour to continue this legacy.

The parish offers a centre to bring together those of Polish decent or origin (and people with Polish interests), not only to fulfil their spiritual but also their social needs. This has become much more necessary since Poland joined the European Union and the numbers in the parish have increased significantly. This can be seen in the Polish Saturday School, where the total number of children has steadily increased from 50 to over 250 in recent years.

Currently as treasurer, I'm responsible for the financial administration of the parish so it continues to thrive. I'm inspired to continue working for the community by my beautiful daughters, so that they can benefit from their Polish heritage. I was always taught the value of my dual heritage and in particular to be proud of my Polish background. Even though my father is English (▶ p. 232) and my mother was not born in Poland (but had Polish parents), I do have a strong Polish identity — for example, I was and still am in the Polish Scouts rather than the English equivalent.

From birth my brother and I attended Polish church services with both my parents. We were both altar boys and at the age of ten I started playing the church organ for Polish masses. I still play the organ on a Sunday in Leeds and for special occasions.

It is important for my wife and I that our children have the opportunity to benefit from being bilingual and be proud of their Polish heritage. This is why my wife and I support the Leeds Polish Saturday School by helping run the school, of which I'm treasurer.

I believe strongly that children with Polish heritage should be taught to speak Polish, and it saddens me when they do not have this opportunity. At school, children are taught German, French or Spanish, so why shouldn't they be taught their mother tongue? When living within a Polish family, children who speak Polish at home often have the advantage that their spoken Polish is far superior to those who are taught a foreign tongue as a second language. So why are such children not supported to achieve a relevant qualification in school? Those who speak Polish at home are often not taught to write and read in the language, and so are disadvantaged if they do not attend the Polish Saturday School.

CHAPTER 6:   Public Services

I'm also a trustee of the Polish Catholic Mission in England and Wales. This role involves responsibility for the administration and governance of the Polish Catholic Mission, which is the overseeing administration for all Polish parishes in England and Wales.

Finally, I'm a Scout leader and help run summer camps for Brownies and Beavers where Polish is the language spoken. These camps have a variety of themes, which in recent years have included 'The History of Poland', 'The Olympics' and 'Under the Sea'. Such camps are important because they bring children together and allow them to learn through play.

> I provide support to a range of patients in a health centre in Leeds. My role is to help patients have the best possible experience, especially during meetings with doctors, consultants and nurses, and during all their treatment. I reassure patients about the procedures, help with routine examinations and provide additional information when patients ask for this. I really enjoy my job.
>
> Agnieszka Paszkowska, NHS support worker

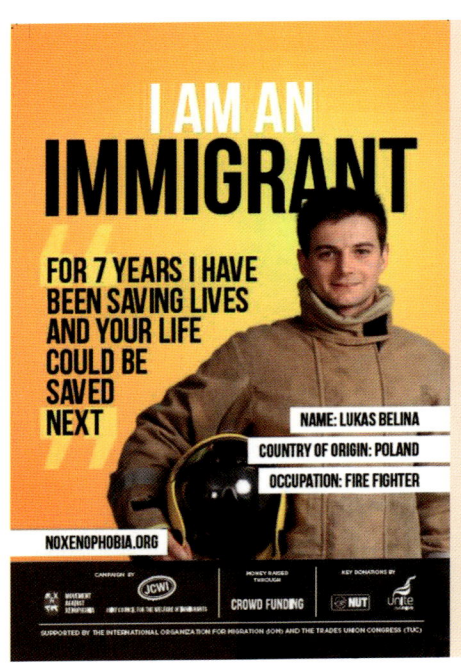

Did you know?

Several British health authorities have looked overseas in order to recruit trained **Polish paramedics**, because of the lack of suitably qualified candidates in the UK. The first authority to do this, in 2015, was the South Central Ambulance Service, which covers Oxfordshire, Buckinghamshire, Berkshire and Hampshire. A spokesman for the service said: 'It has been well publicised that all UK ambulance services are currently experiencing a shortage of qualified paramedics within their workforce.' As well as beginning training programmes in the UK, the service has already employed four paramedics from Poland with the help of an international recruitment firm.

In a separate development, a **Polish firefighter** has featured in a poster programme to challenge stereotypes about workers from overseas. He is one of many firefighters from Poland who are now working alongside their British counterparts to save lives and protect people from injury, on a daily basis.

Poles in the UK

Matt Małecki (25)
Accountancy student

🎙 **What was your childhood like in Poland?**
I was born and brought up in the southern city of Wrocław. I grew up with a strong interest in history, partly because my dad used to watch lots of History Channel documentaries. Later, at secondary school, I got really interested in the history of Poland and in particular what happened to Polish people during the Holocaust (▶ p. 30). I organised lots of activities in my school and the local community, which included a visit from an elderly lady who had helped Jewish people escape persecution. I was eventually given a national award in Poland for my work, which I was really proud of.

When and why did you come to the UK?
I travelled here in 2008 when I was 18, mainly because myself and my partner felt that we could not live freely in Poland together. We came to Yorkshire because my partner's dad was already living here and he put us up in his house for the first few months. Like many newly-arrived Poles, I got lots of different jobs to begin with, including fruit-picking and factory work. I then found a job in a Subway sandwich shop in Leeds.

What do your studies involve?
I'm training to be a Chartered Accountant at the moment. I'm currently studying two days a week at Leeds City College for a Level 3 qualification in accountancy. I've always been good with numbers and I find the studies very interesting. The accountancy qualification will give me more career options in future, as well as the chance of a good salary in the end.

Do you have any hobbies or interests?
I love walking and I have a dog, a two-year-old beagle called Bella. We gave her an Italian name to remind us of the amazing times we spend in that country every year, as my family lives there. So at the weekend myself, Bella and my husband head out into the Yorkshire Dales from Leeds to stretch our legs and get some fresh air. I really like the local town of Otley, with its vibrant market, and we're considering doing the Otley to Leeds walk, which stretches over 10 miles of pretty countryside.

How do you contribute to the UK?
I volunteer at church in Leeds, helping with the music. Later this year there will be a special event taking place, where groups are invited to perform for charity.

I'm also a member of the local residents' association where I live. This role involves working with fellow residents, from the UK and around the world, to make sure that we get the

180

CHAPTER 6: Public Services

best services and the area if kept clean and tidy. There's a brilliant community feel to my neighbourhood, and residents often socialise with each other, including having barbecues in summer.

And of course I pay may taxes, helping to maintain Britain's services, and I also support the economy by purchasing goods and services here.

What have the been the benefits of moving to the UK for you?
There have been lots of benefits and the UK feels very much like my home now. I have worked with some great work colleagues, and I have also received a first-time buyer grant from the government, which has allowed me and my husband to buy our own town house close to the centre of Leeds. This would never have been possible for me in Poland at this stage in my life.

In 2014 my partner and I were able to fulfil our dream of getting married. In fact, we were the first same-sex couple to get married in the whole of Yorkshire! It was a fantastic day, with our families flying in from Poland to join us and our friends also helping us celebrate this very special day in our lives – both at the Register Office and afterwards at the reception!

I am very grateful for what the UK has given me. I'm accepted here for who I am and have never had any negative comments from people here about my sexuality.

Do you think of yourself as Polish or British now (or both)?
First and foremost I feel European. I was born and brought up in Poland, but have now lived in Yorkshire for eight years. I think I share a lot of values with British people and am planning to gain British citizenship in the near future.

IMAGE: Matt Małecki

What will the next few years hold in store for you?
My husband and I want to adopt a British child (or two children from the same family) to start our own family and to give a loving home to a child who's currently in care. It's a very long process that requires lots of interviews, intense discussions and the preparation of detailed documents. The process will hopefully end with us being matched with a British child (or children), some time within the next year or so. We feel strongly that we want to adopt a British child, because the UK has done so much for us.

I love working with Matt because he really makes me laugh and always brightens up my day.

Jade Jones

What are your plans for the future at work?
As soon as I've passed my accountancy exams I'll have a whole new career area available to me, which is very exciting. But I also like keeping my options open, so who knows where I'll end up?

Poles in the UK

Teresa Hough (60)

Head of the Polish Saturday School in Leeds

When did you first come to the UK and what brought you here?
I first came to the UK in 1978 as an English Studies student. This is when I met my future husband, who's English. After I returned to Poland, I finished my studies and I got married in 1979. After I received my passport, for which I had to wait six months, I came back to the UK – this time permanently.

What were things like for you at the beginning?
Very interesting, although a little lonely. Far from the family, in a small town in Hampshire, in the south of England, with no Polish people around. But I met lots of very friendly people, from whom I learnt about the British customs and way of life. I already knew the English language, as I studied it in Poland, at university.

What is your life in the UK like today?
After 37 years of living in the UK, I feel completely at home here. I've worked at a variety of schools and colleges – from primary to further education, including 20 years at the Thomas Danby College in Leeds, working with international students (teaching English as a foreign language). I've always enjoyed my work, and have met many people; not just from the UK, but from lots of different countries.

Apart from this, I've been working at the Polish Saturday School in Leeds for 30 years now. I'm also often at the Polish Community Centre on Sundays, when we run a coffee and cake club and collect money for our Polish School in this way.

You dedicate plenty of time and heart to the Polish School mission. Why do you do that?
Yes, the Polish School is an important place for me. I began working there when my children were young. They used to go every Saturday, starting in the preschool group, up until passing their A-levels in Polish language. I believe it's important that children of Polish heritage know the language of their parents and grandparents, their country and its customs.

How do you envisage the future of Poles in the UK? Looking at the bilingual (and even some trilingual!) students at Polish School, do you think Polish people will become fully integrated into British society?
From my observation, more Poles continue to come to the UK. Student numbers at the Polish School seem to prove this. When my children began at the school in 1986, there were only 50 children there. Now there are around 250. Children from a Polish background go to various English schools and they do great. They have Polish as well as British friends, and they integrate well with British society.

CHAPTER 6: **Public Services**

To what extent do you feel British? To what extent do you feel Polish?
I do feel British to an extent, because I've lived in the UK now for longer than I've lived in Poland. My children were also born here. And, although they like Poland very much (my son actually worked in Kraków, Poland, for some time), the UK is their country.

I also feel that I'm Polish. My parents, my sister and the whole family live in Poland. Therefore, we go to Poland for every holiday, so that we can spend some time together, at least those few weeks each year. We also maintain and celebrate Polish traditions in our household during Christmas and Easter.

What's your contribution to the UK?
I worked in the British education sector for over 30 years, which included time helping children with learning difficulties, teaching English as a foreign language and even teaching the Polish language to British people. This was at the University of Bradford and on evening college courses in Leeds. My former British students work in Poland now. Some of them are employees of the Poundstretcher chain – a company which launched operations in Poland recently.

I was also an interpreter, working for the police and in hospitals, often in a voluntary capacity. Finally, I always participated actively in the community at my children's English schools.

Any funny stories you would like to share?
Although I had a degree in English, there were still a lot of words and expressions I didn't know when I first came here. When I worked in a bar, customers would ask me for 'a whisky on the rocks' or 'a rock in a glass?'. Or how about 'a chip butty' – what on earth is a chip butty?!

I also once got lost while travelling on a train, which 'split'. As I didn't understand what 'split' meant and sat in the wrong part of the train, I went in the opposite direction to my destination and got completely lost. I was helped by a very kind conductor, who put me on the right train and let me use the same ticket to get back to my station.

The Polish Catholic Centre and School in Leeds often organises events promoting Poland's culture, history and religious traditions. Its students have performed across Yorkshire, including at the Leeds City Museum and Harewood House

IMAGES: Leeds Polish Saturday School

183

Poles in the UK

Mariam (15), Fatima (16) and Sara (13)

Were you all born in the UK?
No, Sara and I were born in England and Fatima was born in Poland.

You go to English school, you used to go to Polish school, now you also go to Arabic school. What is it like, as British teenagers, to keep all this rich family heritage alive?
It's hard because we're always busy and have to keep up with our school work and with all our friends, whilst having our family days and our community meetings (for example Eid celebrations, Polish national days and events).

How do things work linguistically in your household?
All three languages are used. We speak English between ourselves, we speak Polish with our mother and Arabic (mixed with a bit of Polish) with our father.

When you travel to Poland, do people pick up that you are from the UK by your accent?
Sometimes they pick up that we aren't from Poland because we may pronounce some words wrong.

In what way do you feel Polish? In what way do you feel British?
I feel Polish in the sense that I can speak and understand the language, and I take part in some traditional and cultural habits. I feel British because I was born and raised here.

The trilingual sisters: Sara, Mariam and Fatima

What are your ambitions or career plans for the future? Do you plan to continue living in the UK, or maybe to travel to work in Poland? Or somewhere else?
My ambition is to help others, to work with old and young people that need help (as a therapist, psychologist). I don't know if I want to continue living in the UK. I would like to live in the best country available for me where I will be able to communicate well with others. Being trilingual helps increase the number of areas I could live in.

Do you think it's important that Polish-British children attend the Polish Saturday School? Is it important for such children to learn the Polish language and culture?
Yes, I think it's important because then the Polish children will understand their culture and traditions, which will help them understand and know about who they are and where they come from. Also, when they have their own children, they can pass on the traditions.

CHAPTER 6: **Public Services**

What do you think of Polish traditions?
I love the Polish traditions. I find them interesting. Everything has a reason, and they all just look good!

Do you sometimes teach your friends about Polish traditions, foods or the language?
I try teaching my friends the language. They are always intrigued and try, but sometimes they find it difficult to pronounce some words. I offer my friends a lot of Polish food, which I love. They then become fond of it.

What do you think the future of Poles in the UK will be? Will more continue to move over here?
I think that the Poles will start their own companies in the UK, and more Poles will continue moving here. They will join the community and social groups that are already settled in the UK.

Mariam and Fatima during an Anglo-Polish themed workshop at the Polish Saturday School in Leeds

Any funny stories?
Once we were in Poland and we were shopping. We forgot where we were and we started talking in English. Suddenly, we noticed that people started looking at us, so we thought, 'why don't we speak in Arabic?'. And so we did! Everyone that we walked past turned to look at us!

Answers by Mariam Al-Janabi

Did you know?
Well over a thousand Polish people **gave blood** in the UK during August 2015, as a way of demonstrating their contribution to British society.

The blood donation campaign, which aimed to help people and save lives, was organised in part as a counter measure against a call from the *Polish Express* newspaper for Poles to go on strike, to protest against discrimination. George Byczyński, of the British Poles initiative, stressed that Poles wanted to be seen to be contributing to British society by donating blood.

One donor, Kasia Paterek (25) from Bristol, said she found giving blood an emotional experience, as it was to show the UK is now her home. 'I wanted to do something for the society here,' she said.

The NHS said that it was grateful that members of the Polish community had donated blood, as there is always a need for this vital resource. Every year over 200,000 blood donors are needed in the UK.

Save a life give blood
0300 123 23 23

Poles in the UK

Kasia Dejewska (37)

Polish School Teacher and Teaching Assistant

it?! We then also decided that I would join Michał in December. My good friend lived in Leeds at the time, so my decision was that I would try a new life in a different country, but here in Leeds, where I have at least one close friend near me. So, as part of our compromise, my husband relocated to Leeds, and I joined him!

When did you first come to the UK and what brought you here?

I first came here in December 2006, just for a month, to research job opportunities, schools for my daughter Natalka (who was seven at the time) and the formalities of renting a flat. I relocated properly in March 2007.

And what brought me here? Well, it was my husband! In Poland I was a single, working mum. Everything changed when I met my future husband, Michał, in July 2006. My whole life suddenly turned upside down, and so did Natalka's!

Michał told me at the very beginning that he had already bought tickets to go to the south of England, for work purposes. After a few weeks he sort of proposed to me. It was as we were talking about our situation. We thought we needed to do something about it, because otherwise our relationship might not have stood the test of distance.

So, in a very short time, we decided to get married – we went to the Register Office on 30 September 2006. That was quick, wasn't

What was the beginning like for you? Did you come across any problems, here in the UK?

The beginning was very difficult. Fortunately, however, we met many good people along the way (we are still close to some of them today) and so everything somehow worked out fine. After a few months of living with my friend, we went on to rent our own little house.

Only my husband worked at the time, as it was hard for me to find a job which I could fit around my daughter's school hours. And, of course, our family could not lend a hand, because we were here, and they were all in Poland. Sometimes, when necessary, my friend and I would swap and share our childcare responsibilities. We tried to help each other as much as we could. It wasn't easy, but somehow we managed.

Could you speak English before you arrived here? How did you find learning the language?

Although I thought I knew the basics of English, in practice it turned out that I couldn't really speak it properly. This caused a lot of apprehension in me and a fear of living here. So when my daughter Natalka went to school I decided not to waste my time and enrolled on an English language course at a college (free at the time, thanks to the government's support).

At college, I met some more wonderful people. One of them continued to support me later on, when I was going through a small crisis, thought I'd had enough and wanted to go back to Poland. I owe a lot to her, and to the other people I met at the college. I don't know if it was luck, or whether something else was at work, but I've had many well-meaning people around me (and fortunately just a tiny number of less well-meaning people). Thanks to this I gradually learned the language, in small steps (and I'm still learning it). So today, I no longer have these language barriers or moments of doubt about whether I'm going to manage.

What's your life in the UK like today?
I would give my life in the UK an A now! I have two wonderful, healthy children, enough to eat and a roof over my head. Both my husband and I are healthy and able to work. We earn enough to make a living. We have lovely people around us. The only thing that I miss are my family and friends from Poland, but I focus on the positives – there is a direct flight from Leeds Bradford Airport to my home city of Gdańsk!

I've volunteered at the Polish Saturday School since 2008. For the first few years I gained experience while helping with the preschool class. Now I teach my own preschool group and I dedicate my whole heart to it.

I'm passionate about teaching the children and I love to play with them. This is why, after I was made redundant while pregnant with my son, that I decided that I needed to take some steps towards a teaching career. After he was born, I enrolled on all sorts of courses, including equality and diversity, music therapy and even business and administration!

However, the most important one for me was the teaching assistant course, because it's thanks to this one that I can now work at an English school. Although it's not a full-time role yet, I know a time will come for that, too. The most important thing for me is that I like what I do, and I'm gradually getting closer to achieving my aim – while at the same time keeping things interesting. I recently started another teaching course, one level up from the one I completed previously.

How do your children find their English school?
My daughter was born in Poland and her adventure with English school started in 2007. She didn't know the language at all, but the Catholic school she went to provided plenty of support with that. Thankfully, a child's brain is incredibly receptive, so she got it in a blink of an eye, complete with the Yorkshire accent!

Today, Natalka is almost 17 and she goes to college. She's my linguistic guide and I can always count on her when it comes to making corrections in written work. She also went to Polish School, up until she passed her GCSEs.

My son Oliver is almost 5. He was born here and he started going to nursery in 2014. He didn't know the language either; the only thing we taught him at the start was how to say in English that he needs to go to the toilet. The beginning was tough, because he was nervous and cried – it was probably the separation from me, but I think it was also partly to do with the language difference. Fortunately, that phase did not last long. His teacher told me recently that Oliver is making great progress and the language barrier seems to be gone. He plays with the other children and speaks English as if it was his first language. It's amazing to see how Oliver can easily switch between Polish and English, as if by a click of a button – it looks so natural and easy!

Poles in the UK

What are your plans for the future?
We don't have any specific plans. We're not thinking of going back to Poland, because our children feel at home here, they have a space of their own here – and so have we. But maybe some time, when we retire? And who knows, maybe we'll be lucky enough to win the lottery and when we're older we'll move, say, to Spain? We'll see what happens, but one needs to live in the here and now – and 'here' means the UK for us at the moment.

How do you find British people?
So far, I've not met with any prejudice against myself, my family, friends or our nationality. I've heard from others that Polish people can be treated differently, for example at the doctor's, because they're struggling with their English. But I've never experienced anything like this myself – so either British people hide it well, or I've been lucky!

The majority of British people I've met are very positive and they say good things about Poles. So it feels normal to live here. Sometimes I'm not sure how honest people are in showing their feelings, but is there really any difference between a British and a Polish person?

Maybe there are differences in general mentality – and the British way is definitely the one that I prefer! By this I mean the interactions with people in shops, on the streets, on buses etc. In the UK people smile a lot more than they do in Poland. In Poland, if you try to smile at strangers, the majority of them will look at you as if something is wrong with you! But, thankfully, it's slowly beginning to change.

What do you see as your contribution to the UK?
I work at a Leeds primary school, where I assist during lunch breaks. On Mondays and Wednesdays, I also help in the Early Years section and Key Stage 1. Sometimes I'm given a group of children to work with; at other times I work on a one-to-one basis. And, on top of that, I help across the school – wherever I'm needed. I'm currently also working towards my Level 3 Teaching Assistant qualification, which will hopefully enable me to get even more involved!

My other main contribution is my work at the Polish Community Centre and teaching the children about Poland – our language, our traditions, how our grandparents and great-grandparents fought so that Poland did not disappear from the maps.

Going to our Polish church with my children is also my contribution to my family, so that my children never forget who they are and where they come from.

Kasia with her family

IMAGE: Klaudia Chilik

CHAPTER 7

Business

This chapter provides many examples illustrating the various ways in which Polish people have made an important contribution to business and retail activity in the UK. It includes some of the pioneers of Anglo-Polish business collaboration, such as Michael Marks, whose company would eventually become one of the most famous British brands in history.

Poles in the UK

The influence of Polish people on British business is so profound that it is likely that a significant proportion of people in the UK currently own a garment of clothing sold by a retail chain which was founded by a Pole. This is primarily because both Marks and Spencer (▶ p. 191) and Tesco (▶ p. 191) were both originally set up by Poles, over 90 years ago.

Tens of thousands of UK businesses now employ Poles, in a wide range of roles, from the factory floor to the board room. Many business owners have gone on record to say how vital their Polish workers are to their companies' success and growth, casting light on the contribution that Poles make to the UK economy. Other British companies, offering services to Polish people setting up their own business, have also seen a major upturn in demand. These businesses, in turn, create new jobs in Britain for people of all nationalities.

The often repeated appreciation of Polish people's work ethic and hard-working attitude is, perhaps, never more at home than when considering their contribution to business in the UK. This is helping Britain's economy remain in a healthier state than most of the countries in mainland Europe.

Did you know?

Polonia Volleyball Club, from London, winners of the title of Champions of England in the 2015-2016 season, was originally founded in 1973 by two members of the Polish YMCA. The club was first established by Polish people for their compatriots, but then started taking part in local English competitions and gained many more nationalities over the years. More information about this successful and diverse Anglo-Polish club, which has business sponsors and will now be competing in Europe, can be obtained at **www.polonia.vc/history**.

CHAPTER 7: Business

Did you know?

Two of the UK's best known retail brands — **Tesco plc** and **Marks and Spencer plc** (M&S) — were both founded by Polish people over 90 years ago.

A 'super' market

The major food and general merchandise retailer Tesco plc is now the world's third largest retailer, when measured by profits. It was founded in 1919 by the Polish-Jewish immigrant **Jack Cohen** as a series of market stalls, in east London.

The 'Tesco' name first appeared in 1924, after Cohen bought a shipment of tea from T.E. Stockwell, and combined these initials with the first three initials of his own surname. The brand took off and is now a household name across Britain.

The first Tesco store opened in Barnet (north London) in 1929, and the company quickly expanded to have over 100 stores across the country by 1939. Originally a food and drink retailer, Tesco diversified in the 1990s into many other areas, including clothing, electronics and toys. There are now over 3,500 Tesco stores of one kind or another across the UK.

Marks in time

In the case of M&S, one of the two original founders of the company was **Michael Marks** (*Michał Marks*), a Polish-Jewish refugee, who arrived in England in the early 1880s. At the time, the area he was born in was under Russian occupation following the Partitions of Poland.

After receiving financial and practical help from the English businessman Isaac Jowitt Dewhirst, Marks set-up a 'Penny Bazaar' on Leeds market. He later teamed up with Yorkshireman Thomas Spencer, from Skipton (who was Dewhirst's cashier), to establish — in 1894 — a permanent stall in the elegant covered hall of the market.

The successful partnership eventually grew into the multi-million pound company known across the world today, which employs tens of thousands of people in Britain alone. It is one of the best examples of Polish-British business collaboration in history.

191

Poles in the UK

A POLISH PRINCE IN LONDON

The colourful 2016 London mayoral candidate **Prince John Żyliński** was born in the city in 1951, to Polish parents. He cherishes his Polish heritage and has become a champion for Polish people, heritage and values since he launched his campaign to become Mayor of London.

Both Polish and English
Although Żyliński describes himself as 'Polish and English through and through', he traces his ancestry right back to the Russian nobility, and is thought to be one of the wealthiest Poles in the UK.

He is, perhaps, Britain's ultimate 'Polish builder', as much of his wealth has been built on property development in London, which he has engaged in for almost 30 years. During this time he has created hundreds of new homes, helping to provide housing for people of all nationalities.

Sword and splendour
His colourful contribution to the mayoral campaign, complete with an elegant sword and a beautiful London palace certainly made Żyliński a memorable candidate for London voters – whatever their heritage.

His famous palace – called The White House – has become popular with photographers and film directors alike. Celebrities such as Rihanna, Rita Ora, Britney Spears, Victoria Beckham and Leona Lewis have had photo shoots at the property, which is similar to one owned by his grandmother in Płock (in central Poland) and burnt down by the communists after World War II. The palace is known also known as 'a Polish Island in the English sea', and has been described as one of London's most interesting buildings by *Time Out* magazine.

Żyliński also supports many charitable activities, and has hosted all sorts of fundraising events at the White House, including opera concerts and numerous ballet performances. Bucking stereotypes, he has even performed in the ballet *Swan Lake* himself, having started taking ballet classes in 2005.

A distinctive voice
During his campaign to be London Mayor, Żyliński made some interesting points about the contribution of Polish people to the UK, both in the war years and more recently. His campaign was targetted at London's 250,000 Poles and at all those who wanted an independent voice for the capital.

Find out more
www.zylinski.london

IMAGES: John Żyliński

CHAPTER 7: **Business**

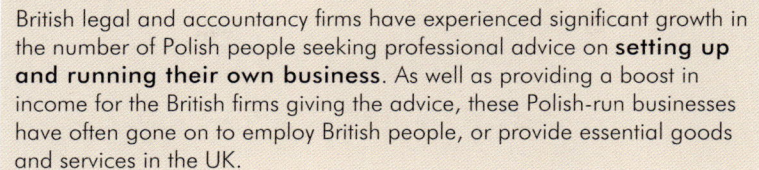

Did you know?
British legal and accountancy firms have experienced significant growth in the number of Polish people seeking professional advice on **setting up and running their own business**. As well as providing a boost in income for the British firms giving the advice, these Polish-run businesses have often gone on to employ British people, or provide essential goods and services in the UK.

Did you know?
At the time of writing (May 2016), three football players from Poland play in the Premier League – the top tier of professional football in England and Wales. They are **Artur Boruc** (goalkeeper, AFC Bournemouth), **Łukasz Fabiański** (goalkeeper, Swansea City AFC) and **Marcin Wasilewski** (defender, Leicester City FC). Of special note is Wasilewski's appearance in several games during his club's extraordinary 2015–2016 season, when they won the Premier League title for the first time in their history. Since the start of the Premier League in 1992, a total of 14 Polish players have played in this league. The Premier League is now big business, attracting huge revenues from television contracts, ticket purchases, merchandising and major sponsorship deals.

> Polish migrants gave the UK Marks and Spencer, victory in the Battle of Britain, the unravelling of the Enigma code, and more recently the world-beating work ethic of the one million Polish newcomers.
>
> Prince John Żyliński

Poles in the UK

Anna Katarzyna Collins's story (28)

IMAGE: Revolve Studios

in the UK, where she would end up giving an amazing gift to fellow British citizens.

Home life in Poland
Anna was brought up in the settlement of Nowy Glinnik in central Poland, among a mixed landscape of industry, agriculture and forests. Every day she would take the four-mile journey to school in the nearby city of Tomaszów Mazowiecki, where English was always her favourite subject (along with geography).

She had ambition and drive from an early age and developed her skills outside the classroom during her time at middle school, when she was the head girl of her school (at age 14). She knew she had to go the extra mile to achieve success and this was the start of Anna's inspirational journey.

Life was not easy for Anna growing up, compared to her friends. She was brought up by her mum and her elder sister Angelika, who was like a second mum to her. Anna's childhood shaped her ambition and she became a product of her environment – a person with a resilient attitude. Any setbacks were seen in a positive light as steps forward and positive experiences for Anna.

Even at the young age of six she remembers that she could not wait to leave her home country to live abroad – in an English-speaking country. This ambition grew stronger throughout her time

Anna Collins's home city is now Leeds in West Yorkshire. She has a new surname, a British passport, many British friends and works for a British company.

Yet nine years ago things were very different for this remarkable young woman. An 18-year-old Anna, then with the surname Kuzia, was about to start a long and lonely journey from central Poland to take up a job in Scotland, before making a giant leap, over the Atlantic Ocean, to the USA. There, she hoped to start a new life.

However, a series of planned events and unplanned coincidences led Anna to plant roots

CHAPTER 7: **Business**

> It has been a pleasure to welcome Anna into my family and this has given her an insight into Bradford family life. My father, especially, enjoys her company at Christmas time, and he likes to tease her about the Yorkshire 'language' – for example, referring to 'ome instead of home! She is a goal setter and strives to succeed, and also is a proud and kind young lady. The age gap does not get in the way of our friendship.
>
> Susan Brown (fellow graduate, Bradford University)

at primary, middle and secondary school, and in 2004 an exciting move to the UK became more realistic when Poland joined the European Union.

However her mum, who works as a nurse, remained reluctant to let her daughter make the move to the UK at the age of 17. It took a generous eighteenth birthday gift from her godfather Mirosław to finally allow Anna to fulfil her dream. Mirosław paid an employment agency to help find his god-daughter a job anywhere in the UK and she ended up in Scotland.

Anna, as a young child, with her mother

IMAGE: Anna Collins

Scotland-bound

So in June 2006 Anna began the 36-hour journey from central Poland to Edinburgh into the unknown world that awaited her. From Edinburgh she travelled north to Gilmerton (near Crieff, Perth and Kinross), where she began working in a hotel and in a bar. It was a very challenging time for Anna; she thought she knew English very well but the Scottish accents were like nothing she had heard before! Answering the phone proved to be a particular problem. But she befriended an Italian girl who also worked at the hotel, and who did not speak English at that time; this enabled her to learn how to carry out basic conversations in Italian. And slowly, they got used to the types of English spoken in this Gilmerton hotel.

> Anna is a very ambitious person who exceeds in her goals and expectations. I have known Anna since university and she always had excellent social skills and was able to manage her time effectively, juggling university and part-time work. We completed many group projects and Anna was very results-focussed and open minded. Anna not only has the business knowledge, she also has the practical mindset to exceed. It has been a pleasure knowing Anna because she is the epitome of a success story.
>
> Sofia Iqbal (fellow graduate, Bradford University)

Anna's time in the Scottish hotel helped her to develop an awareness of different cultures, and also allowed her to improve her verbal reasoning skills.

She had some fun experiences in Scotland. She was taught how to shoot live pigeons and she ate venison (deer meat) almost raw, because

195

Poles in the UK

> Anna is one of the most determined, hard-working and goal-achieving people I know. Once she sets a goal, she will consider and then focus on everything needed to achieve that goal. She also has great social skills, which she demonstrated by organising a university friends' get together, just so everyone could catch up, as we all know life can be too busy at times.
>
> Nkele Manaka
> (fellow graduate, Bradford University)

IMAGE: Bradford Telegraph and Argus

Anna with her team during the 'Positive Bradford' initiative

a cook at the hotel liked to prepare it rare, where the blood was still showing in the middle! She also tried a different type of whiskey each day; it was important for her to be part of the work culture and to learn new things.

Although Anna returned to Poland after three months to sit her *Matura* exam and take her driving test, her eyes were very much fixed on a new life in the UK – and maybe the opportunity of a move to the USA.

A new home in Yorkshire

Anna's next big move took place in June 2007, when she found a new job in Castleford, West

> I have known Anna in a professional capacity for the last 14 months, and it has been a pleasure knowing her. She is a hard-working and dynamic young lady, who is keen to enhance her professional experience. She has an excellent attention to detail and very good professional ethics.
>
> Mashood Akmal (director of Aeroservices Ltd)

Yorkshire. It was very different work to that in Scotland, as Anna found herself on the assembly line and in the quality control department at the Pioneer electronics factory, and it did not suit her.

Anna moved to Leeds, persevered with various jobs and at last started to feel more at home in the UK. And with this, the dream of a new life in the USA was changing into a love of the UK!

She had always wanted to go to university and it now made sense to apply to study here. So she took some more examinations in English, had her secondary school records translated into English and started applying to local universities. The whole process took her a year.

Anna was offered a place to study for a three year honours degree in business and management at Bradford University School of Management, a highly respected place for this course. This eventually worked out really well – Anna enjoyed her studies and made lots of new friends.

She is still in touch with many fellow graduates from her university days and spends Christmases with either the Brown or Pickard family in Leeds and Bradford respectively. She calls Susan Brown and her family her first 'British family', who 'adopted' her.

CHAPTER 7: **Business**

Anna had to earn a living to support herself for much of this period, and carried out a whole range of jobs while at university. She also carried out voluntary work which gave her extra experience, which included interpreting for Polish patients at Pinderfields Hospital in Wakefield and working with young people in Bradford. During this period she learnt to balance both work and education and achieve impressive results in both areas.

Another project Anna was involved in during this time was about making Bradford a better, more positive place to live and work. The aims were to help to put the city on the map and to counter long-running economic and social problems that have been seen in the city for many years. Along with a team of fellow students she designed window stickers to be given out at an event, and Anna also managed the project's Twitter account for a few months.

Anna on her graduation day

IMAGE: Maria Żurawska

> Anna made a distinct impression on me in class in several ways. She was confident, forward and had ideas – that was unusual among the class I was teaching. She took an active role in the modules and helped to lead activities in class. She was one of the best performers in a mock graduate assessment we ran and was a student representative on both the Staff Student Liaison Committee and the School's Management Committee.
>
> Dr Peter Morgan
> (former lecturer, Bradford University)

The super-dynamic Anna also somehow managed to find time to be the student representative for her course for three years and was the undergraduate representative for two years. She went for these roles because she felt she wanted to contribute to student life. The work included talking to senior staff at the university about the concerns of students and helping to get positive changes made.

After graduation – onwards and upwards

Before her joyful graduation ceremony, which was attended by her mother who flew to the UK from Poland especially for the event, Anna started a new job working in the telecommunications industry in Bradford, in a managerial role.

She did not end her studies there, and went on to obtain several other qualifications that would help her progress in her career and develop as a person. These included an interpreting course which would allow her to use her language skills even more effectively.

Anna has always been keen to use her time effectively and for a while she actually had two jobs in Bradford, as well as spending much of her time studying for additional qualifications! Her other job involved interpreting for Polish people at home, in hospitals and in many other locations.

Poles in the UK

> *I always admired Anna's resilience, resourcefulness and hunger for knowledge – and she just gets along with everyone! Her passion for life is truly inspirational and she is forever working towards a positive future, with a down to earth attitude.*
>
> Jackie Robinson (former colleague, Pinderfields Hospital, Wakefield)

The ultimate gift

Recently, Anna has provided perhaps the ultimate gift to fellow Brits: she has donated some of her eggs to help women who are unable to have children due to fertility problems.

The egg donation process is a long, moderately painful and certainly very serious undertaking for any woman. Tests, counselling and lots of paperwork are required, but it is a hugely positive thing that she has wanted to do for many years. So she finally made it happen.

Knowing that she might be able to provide the gift of life was a brilliant and amazing feeling for Anna and she is very happy to have done it.

A new job in Leeds

By June 2015 Anna was looking for a fresh challenge and she was successful in applying for a new job in logistics (in the aviation industry), based in Leeds city centre.

Anna at work in Leeds in her current role

IMAGE: Natalie Wiggins

Anna is always exploring new opportunities and she recently undertook a television presenting course in MediaCityUK, Manchester. She has also carried out a radio producing and presenting course at Radio Aire in Leeds.

She was inspired to do these after getting to know Kasia Madera, a high profile British news presenter for the BBC, of Polish parents (▶ p. 151). Anna had the honour of meeting Kasia in person in May 2013 at New Broadcasting House in London – the home of the BBC.

Anna really admires Kasia for her professionalism and the positive way she represents Poland here in the UK. She feels that both the UK and Poland need more people like Kasia, who is a great role model. Anna and Kasia are in regular touch and the esteemed presenter gave Anna some great tips for how to behave in front the camera, when she auditioned for the BBC last year.

Another aspect of Anna's rich and colourful life has been acting as an extra for ITV's *Emmerdale*, *DCI Banks* and other series. She was recommended to do this by a fellow graduate. This work was tiring and there was a lot of waiting around involved, but it was quite exciting too, especially when she saw herself on screen. That was certainly a new experience!

A new name and passport

Anna has recently taken two important steps that most Polish people who have moved to the UK do not take: she now has both British and Polish citizenship and passports, and she has also changed her surname. This means she is what is called a dual national of the UK and Poland.

Anna decided to take both these steps in order to create a closer bond with her new home country. The process of obtaining British citizenship – and a precious British passport – is a very lengthy and expensive one. It requires

CHAPTER 7: **Business**

Anna after she gained British citizenship in 2014, with a specially commissioned cake

Anna with the British and Polish flag in London in 2015

a lot of documentation, a test, details of previous addresses, employer information, references and all sorts of other things.

Finally, after several years of hard work, Anna found out in November 2014 that she had been granted British citizenship. It was an overwhelming moment for her and she telephoned her mum straight away, breaking into tears with the amazing news!

> *One of the things that has struck me about Anna is her strength and determination as a Polish woman, coming here several years ago and making a successful life here. She also works as an interpreter and of course being bilingual is an excellent asset. I think she is an excellent role model for any young Polish woman and she is a good example of how migration benefits this country. I think only good things await her.*
>
> Liz Aspinall
> (current colleague, Aeroservices Ltd)

Anna now had a further touch of official Britishness – but she had certainly earnt it. Following the wonderful news Anna had a citizenship party, complete with a special cake a friend had made.

Leeds and the UK are very much home for Anna now and she thinks it is significant that she has spent all her adult life in different parts of Britain. She is proud to be a Polish-Brit and feels she has acquired many British characteristics over the last nine years. These include the following, which have helped her to feel more comfortable amongst British people:

- Celebrating 25 December as the most important day at Christmas, rather than 24 December as in Poland
- Having overseas holidays
- Socialising a lot and going out frequently in the evenings
- Following British news and talking about it
- Following the Royal Family!
- Eating Sunday roast for 'tea' (the evening meal in Yorkshire)
- Moaning about the weather!

Poles in the UK

She is so proud of her links with Leeds that she has had a special tattoo inked on her leg declaring her devotion for the city – 'I love Leeds!'

Getting used to Britain – and British people

Although Anna now feels very much at home in the UK, there have been many challenges for her as she adjusted to life here.

She has experienced some racism and hurtful remarks from British people who were rude to her, or did not understand the full reasons why she had travelled here.

Both the Scottish and the Yorkshire pronunciation took time to get used to and the British love of queuing was not something that she was used to from Poland. She also arrived here with an American accent, having been used to listening to US radio stations and speaking only to American native speakers of English, rather than British, for several years.

Anna also sees lots of new things in the UK that she had not noticed much before in her home settlement in Poland. This includes seeing people with different skin colours, vibrant hair colours and unusual hair styles on the British streets.

She also found just being on her own in a new country can be tough. She quickly learnt to be even more independent, to face challenges and go on to explore new things.

In general, despite a few exceptions, Anna has found British people to be laid back, polite and reserved. And they are typically tea drinkers (with milk, unlike in Poland where tea is usually drunk without).

However, now she knows that you can experience all four seasons in one day in the UK, she understands where this obsession with the weather comes from.

Many positive contributions

Anna is a wonderful example of a modern Polish-Brit because of the huge range of ways in which she has contributed to the UK in the nine years that she has been living here. This includes helping to boost the economy, helping people in need, carrying out a variety of voluntary roles and of course the amazing donation of her eggs to help couples with fertility problems.

Anna during a photoshoot in 2014

IMAGE: Revolve Studios

The sky is the limit

Anna's star sign is Aquarius and for her the sky is the limit. She always says that if there's a will, there's a way. Outside work, she loves new challenges and adrenaline, and she has many exciting things to look forward to, this year and beyond. Towards the top of the list for the coming year are the Leeds half-marathon, a tandem skydive and a Segway experience.

Anna recognises that her ambition, drive and hard-working nature is typical of many Polish people, with children in Polish schools having a reputation for constantly exceeding expectations.

Although Anna talks frequently of 'coincidences' in her life leading her to where she is now, she is a classic example of a person who has made her own luck through hard work, determination, a wide network of contacts and being open to new opportunities.

CHAPTER 7: **Business**

Szymon Półtorak's story (40)

Senior Blending Room Operative

Szymon on a recent trip to the Yorkshire coast

Szymon works as a senior operative in a meat-processing factory in Pontefract, West Yorkshire. He has an important role in the factory, helping the company meet its targets and supply the food chain.

Since February 2016, he has also been taking one-to-one English lessons with a private tutor, in order to improve his language skills and pass the IELTS examination. This will ultimately help him to get a better job. It also helps provide an income for his tutor, who is British.

In his spare time Szymon really enjoys adventurous activities, especially skiing and parachuting. He took his first parachute jump in 2008 in Poland, and since then has done almost

a hundred more jumps! He has done many of his jumps at Hibaldstow, in North Lincolnshire. Szymon enjoys the adrenaline rush that comes with parachute jumps, especially the free fall component when you are falling at 50 metres per second and can feel the air rushing past your body.

Szymon lives in Leeds with his friends and his tabby cat Kitka, who is two years old. Although Kitka is a British cat, he has taught her both Polish and English commands, so she is a 'bilingual' cat!

Szymon and his tabby cat Kitka during a recent English language lesson

Szymon about to land back on Earth after one of his first parachute jumps

201

Poles in the UK

Aleksandra Lepczyńska (30)
Contract Coordinator

What's a typical day for you like?
A typical day? I don't have one! Everyday is different. As I'm employed within recruitment, I'm on call 24 hours a day, seven days a week. This has an impact on my private life, but I'm trying to organise my time during the day to make things easier.

At work I have very many responsibilities. They include the following:
- The whole recruitment, registration and induction process
- Processing payroll, assessing performance and managing information
- Liaising with shop floor front-line managers
- Monitoring all agency workers' performance and training
- Completely fulfilling all our customer requirements
- Making sure I'm doing things the right way, for the right reason, ethically and honestly – every time.

I own a lovely dog – a West Highland terrier called Barry. He's my beloved nine-year-old friend, and thanks to him I spend as much time as I can after work on walks. Also, when I'm able to, I try to go to the gym – up to five times a week. In the evening I read books or watch movies. At weekends, I try to spend time socialising and I like going to the cinema, visiting friends and travelling.

In what ways does your Polish language and heritage come in useful in your job?
About eight years ago, I worked in bakery. A Polish man had taken some medicine, which he was allergic to. He was in a really bad condition and he passed out, had a heart attack and also a serious haemorrhage. I was the only person on the whole site who could speak English. I stayed with him on the journey to hospital and then stayed on there as an interpreter, helping with the medical investigations.

At present I'm working as a Contract Coordinator for one of the largest recruitment companies in the UK. A part of my job is to look after the welfare of our workers, who are from Poland and many other countries. As I'm able to understand Polish culture, I can sympathise with the workers. As well as this I use my English language to sort out any issues people are having due to language barriers.

This is recruitment and I deal with people's private lives. Sometimes it's really hard to cope with this, especially when I know that people are thousands of miles away from their families. But it's my responsibility to make sure I treat everyone equally, and I have to evaluate each situation objectively.

What contribution do you think you make to the UK?
I believe that the things I've learned and experienced in Poland help me in my workplace, as I try to make our work easier, by being more creative. I also try to educate British people about our different culture, and at the same time try to show that we're all the same, and part of a multicultural society. I also input into the British economy by doing shopping and paying taxes.

CHAPTER 8

Food and Drink

This mouth-watering chapter presents some of the food and drink classics from Poland, as well as providing examples of the many ways in which Polish people are involved in the UK food and drink sector today. It includes step by step recipes which will allow you to create authentic Polish dishes, from ingredients now sold in UK shops.

Poles in the UK

There is a very high likelihood that, over the course of any week during 2016, a typical British family will come into contact with a Polish person serving in a supermarket, coffee shop, bar or restaurant (▶ p. 212) while going about their day-to-day business. Furthermore, every day, in many schools across the country, expert Polish cooks prepare nourishing meals for Britain's students (▶ p. 215).

Poles have, without doubt, firmly established themselves within the UK food and drink industry, for reasons which are explored in this chapter. However, the Polish contribution to the food and drink sector

Did you know?

Many varieties of **Polish beer** are now proving popular with beer enthusiasts from Britain, such as Angus NcNab, a highly-respected brewer from Shipley in West Yorkshire.

Angus is a self-confessed beer connoisseur, who has only recently discovered the delights of Polish beer. His favourite Polish brew to date is *Warka Strong*, an unusual (and indeed strong – at 6.5% ABV!) sweet concoction produced in central Poland by one of the country's oldest breweries. The distinctive flavour of this beer comes from its roasted malt. Angus especially enjoys *Warka Strong* because it reminds him of Old Peculier, a legendary strong ale from his adopted county of Yorkshire.

Another Polish beer proving popular in the UK is the famous Żubr lager, which is named after the European bison. The primeval forests of eastern Poland support the last surviving wild population of this huge animal, which is distantly related to the domestic cow (▶ p. 49).

CHAPTER 8: **Food and Drink**

HOME-STYLE POLISH CHEESECAKE
(VEGETARIAN AND NATURALLY GLUTEN-FREE!)

Ingredients

5 eggs
250g sugar
100g margarine
1 tsp vanilla extract
750g Polish *twaróg* (half-fat cheese, similar to cottage cheese – available in main chain supermarkets, as well as in Polish shops)
3 small boiled potatoes
A pinch of salt

You can also add roughly chopped pieces of dried nuts and fruit, such as walnuts, figs, raisins, candied orange peel, or anything else you like. Just remember to thoroughly dust any dried fruit or nuts in cornflower before adding to the mix.

Method

1. Separate the egg yolks and the whites – you will need both.
2. Mix the egg yolks with the sugar until creamy and nearly white. Add vanilla extract and mix for another 30 seconds or so.
3. Using a potato masher, thoroughly mash the cheese, margarine and potatoes into a uniform 'dough'. If you have a kitchen mincer you can use it instead of mashing the ingredients manually.
4. With a large spoon, gradually start adding the dough to the sugar and egg yolk mix. Mix it all together with a hand mixer as you do so, until it is even.
5. In a separate bowl whisk the egg whites with a pinch of salt, until stiff. Using a tablespoon, gently add the whisked whites to the previously prepared dough – but do not use a hand-mixer for this, because you do not want the whites to 'melt'.
6. At the very end, if you like, you can add the add the cornflour-dusted nuts and fruit. Just gently mix them into the dough.
7. For baking you will need a baking tray (this could be a round tart tray) that is no larger than 25 cm in diameter, otherwise your cheesecake will be very flat!
8. Grease the baking tray lightly with margarine, and dust with some cornflower – this is so that the dough does not stick to the tray. Pour the dough into the prepared tray.
9. Bake at 200°C (180°C for fan-assisted ovens). Leave it for about 45 minutes, or until nicely golden-brown.

IMAGES: Simona Żukowska

205

Poles in the UK

Did you know?

All the major British supermarket chains now stock a wide range of **Polish food and drink** products, with the variety of produce available increasing every year. The products available in most stores include speciality dried meats, cheeses, vegetables preserved in brine or vinegar, cakes, beer and vodka. Furthermore, budget supermarket Lidl staged a 'Polish Food and Drink Week' in April 2016 to promote interest in their speciality produce from Poland.

Polish food stalls are becoming more common at festivals and special events in the UK. This stall specialising in Polish sausages, at the Victorian Fayre in Otley (West Yorkshire), proved extremely popular with visitors

IMAGES: Brin Best

CHAPTER 8: **Food and Drink**

Shops specialising in Polish produce are now a familiar sight across Britain, allowing people of all nationalities to enjoy food and drink from Poland. The owner of the Polish Shop in Morley, West Yorkshire, reports that currently approximately 50% of their customers Polish and 50% are English.

Beer connoisseur Angus McNab, from West Yorkshire, sampling some of his favourite Polish beer

> *Our range of Polish beers is proving really popular, and not just with the local Polish community – with British people too. All the beers in that range are good sellers!*
>
> Mr Srao, Owner – Cottage Stores, Otley, West Yorkshire

IMAGE: Brin Best

207

Poles in the UK

PIEROGI WITH MEAT (A CARNIVORE'S TAKE ON THE CLASSIC POLISH DUMPLINGS)

Ingredients

For the dough:

500g flour
50g butter
350ml hot water

For the filling:

500g beef (ideally quite fatty)
Two chicken thighs
Vegetables with which the meat is going to be cooked (one carrot, one parsnip, a thick slice of celeriac)
Salt
Black pepper (fresh, ground)

Preparation of the dough

Work the butter in your hands and mix with the flour, gradually adding the hot water. Keep kneading the dough in this way until it is smooth and can easily be rolled with a rolling pin.

Preparation of the filling

Boil the meat and the vegetables. Once cooked through, take them out of the pan and leave to cool. Then get rid of the skin and little bones in the meat. Once this is done, mince the meat with the vegetables in a kitchen mincer. Finally, add salt and pepper, as well as any other spices you usually like to use, according to your taste.

Method

1. Once the dough is rolled out (not too thin and not too thick), use a medium-size glass to cut out circular pieces. Put some filling into each circular piece of dough, then fold the dough in half to create a 'half-moon' shaped dumpling. Now stick the edges of the dough together — remember to use a tiny bit of water on the edges of the dough to make it stick better.

2. As you work your way through the filling, lay out the finished dumplings on a flour-dusted kitchen towel (flour is essential so that the dough does not stick to the surface).

3. Once they are ready, put the first few of your finished dumplings in a large pan of boiling, lightly salted water, and gently stir once. As soon as they rise to the surface, wait for two to three minutes, then take them out with a large spoon, drain, and place them in a large bowl, adding a little bit of butter so it melts and covers the dumplings (so they do not stick to each other). As the water in your pan is still boiling, you can add the next batch of your *pierogi*.

4. Serve your drained and lightly buttered *pierogi* with golden-fried diced onion, or a mixture of onion and small fried bacon cubes (these are called *skwarki*)

Top tips

Once you have mastered the *pierogi* dough-making process, there are so many options! For a delicious summery treat, try filling your *pierogi* with blueberries, strawberries or plums (adding a little bit of sugar to the fruit that goes into each dumpling). Serve them buttered and splashed with light whipping cream, mixed

IMAGE: Szymon Półtorak

CHAPTER 8: **Food and Drink**

with a drop of vanilla extract and a sprinkle of sugar.

For the traditional 'old Russian *pierogi*' (which are, funnily enough, not very common in Russia), the filling is vegetarian. For this delicious version, which is probably the most popular in Poland, you will need 500g of boiled (then mashed) potatoes and 500g of Polish *twaróg* (white cheese, similar to cottage cheese), as well as one finely chopped and fried onion. Mash the cheese, boiled potatoes and onion together, and add some salt and pepper to taste. And that is your filling done. Using a teaspoon, add some filling to each dumpling. The rest of the process is the same as described earlier, regardless of your chosen filling.

Recipe by Marcin Wielicki (with top tips by Maria Helena Żukowska)

in the UK goes far beyond the smiling, friendly Poles who greet customers every day across Britain.

Helped partly by the large increase in Polish restaurants and delicatessens in the UK, traditional food and drink from Poland is now becoming much better known to British people, some of whom are lucky enough to have fresh Polish cuisine prepared for them by their work colleagues or friends. As Polish alcoholic beverages of all sorts are now readily available in the UK, these dishes can be washed down with a choice of high quality beers and spirits from Poland, several of which have intriguing, exotic-sounding names to their British admirers.

The food and drink industry also provides the opportunity for Poles to volunteer in a variety of roles, thereby helping to make a contribution to their local community (▶ p. 220).

British fans of orange-flavoured Jaffa Cakes were thrilled to learn that exotic Polish versions of these sweet treats are also available, including cherry (pictured) and blackcurrant flavour 'Jaffa Cakes'

IMAGE: Birn Best

209

Poles in the UK

Polish restaurants are now established in most British cities, such as here in York where The Barbakan Café and Restaurant serves mouth-watering Polish meals, cakes and snacks throughout the day. This restaurant, which was first set up four years ago, has a clientele made up of approximately 10% Polish people and 90% people from the UK or other countries.

IMAGES: Brin Best

210

CHAPTER 8: **Food and Drink**

Traditional Polish dishes such as Żurek soup (a sour broth, made with fermented rye flour) are being enjoyed by increasing numbers of British people, as their Polish friends introduce them to recipes from Poland

Scrumptious Polish doughnuts are now enjoyed widely across the UK, including by this young Scottish visitor to Yorkshire, who was thrilled to discover them on a recent visit to the county

IMAGES: Brin Best

Did you know?

Polish chefs and cooking have recently featured in high profile programmes on BBC television. The award-winning Polish chef **Damian Wawrzyniak** was featured on *Mary Berry's Easter Fest* (first broadcast March 2016), demonstrating his expertise in making the traditional *babka* cake. This followed the showcasing of Polish cooking and traditional food in the opening episode of the *Hairy Bikers' Northern Exposure* series, which first aired in 2015. This programme saw the chefs and traditional food enthusiasts David Myers and Simon King discovering the culinary delights of Poland, during a road trip around the country.

I work behind the bar in the Bewley's Hotel in Leeds, serving teas, coffees and other drinks to staying guests and other customers, and taking and serving food orders. I'm a cheerful person and enjoy meeting people, so I like my job. We have lots of friendly customers and they often leave me generous tips. I also work part-time as an aerobics instructor, and am hoping to set up my own business in this area in the future.

Natalia Nowicka, Hotel Bartender

Poles in the UK

Karolina Iskra (26)

Assistant Manager at Pizza Express

IMAGE: Karolina Iskra

When did you first come to the UK and what brought you here?
My mum moved to England in April 2005, to live with my auntie in Wakefield. I decided to join them both in June that year, after I finished studying at my Polish secondary school (I was 16 years old). My older sister also came here with me.

Did you know any English when you first came here? And what was it like when you first moved here?
I've been learning English since I was seven years old. But when I came to England for the first time I couldn't say a word! When my sister and I went out for a walk in Wakefield for the first time, we wrote our address down on a piece of paper, just in case. And typically, we got lost! So we approached some people and showed them the piece of paper, instead of asking them for directions. Somehow we could not form a sentence in English.

The first two months were hard, as my mum and my sister worked and I was at home by myself. I wasn't confident enough about my English to go outside. I understood English, but I didn't want to speak it for fear of getting something wrong. I know now that this was unfounded because perfect grammar is not essential to be understood — British people do not necessarily speak 'textbook English' all the time [*laugh*].

How did you overcome the language barrier?
Two months after I arrived in the UK, I started working in a restaurant, just in the evenings. At the beginning my role was to greet clients and to show them to their table. But, step by step, I started taking orders and eventually became a waitress. So I had to start speaking the language.

And how about education? Did you go to school here? The Polish equivalent to GCSEs are not always recognised as the same as the British qualifications.
My mum wanted me to go to secondary school, but when I saw the school and students I thought I didn't fit in there, and my mum accepted my decision. But when I turned 18, I felt tired of working all the time. Also, my Polish friends were doing the equivalent of A-levels in Poland at the time, and they were telling me a lot about their experiences. I thought that I was missing out and felt a kind of a void.

So I decided to go back to school after all. I first did an English for Speakers of Other Languages (ESOL) course, and then an adult 'access to higher education' programme, which combined GSCEs and A-levels. I then completed a degree in tourism and leisure management at Huddersfield University. I later went into the leisure industry, and currently work in the hospitality industry for Pizza Express. As for tourism, I've kept that as my own, personal hobby [*laugh*].

How are things now?
I see the UK as my home now. I went to Poland earlier this year for my sister's wedding, and it felt like a foreign country to me. In the UK, I feel completely natural, comfortable and at home. I love how open the people are. I feel a bit British now. I do sometimes drop by the Polish shop to buy the occasional food product that I suddenly miss, but other than that I live a British life in Yorkshire.

I live in Dewsbury and I love how quiet it is, even though I grew up in a city. Here I have the beautiful Yorkshire countryside right on my doorstep. I get a nice balance, because I commute to Leeds for work. I can absorb all its urban energy before going back to my peaceful town again.

What are your plans for the future?
I don't plan to return to Poland. I thought about going to Canada about three years ago, but the visa process put me off. My priority is for my family to stay together, and I will only move somewhere else if they want to move, too. And they don't plan to leave the UK.

I love my job and I want to succeed as a manager. I previously worked at Starbucks, where I was made a supervisor. I like to lead a team. So, until customer service work kills me, it's what I want to do [*laugh*]. The plan for the future is to set up my own business, which is my sister's idea. We would like to start a catering business, making cakes to order. I think this is a good idea because everyone, and especially British people, love cake!

What do you think about English people and making friends in the UK? Have you come across any prejudice at all?
At first it was hard making new friends, especially as my work was my only activity, so I didn't have many opportunities to meet new people. I never had any problems at work and I was always accepted straight away.

It was different at college. I was the only foreigner on my course, so my classmates didn't know how to approach me. I was my normal self, I smiled, I tried to chat – but sometimes I felt like they thought I was from Mars! It changed after a while, when the other people realised I was just like them. One of the girls only spoke to me for the first time when we were put in the same group for a task in a biology class. We actually got on so well that we are still friends today.

IMAGE: Karolina Iskra

Karolina on her graduation day in 2012, with fellow members of her Tourism and Leisure Management degree class (she is top left in this image)

I only met with prejudice once. Some guys in the park heard me and my mum talking in a foreign language, and they shouted to us to 'get back to our country' and then giggled. But we didn't think much of it. It wasn't worth worrying about, because the majority of the British are not like that.

There is that stereotype of the British being a distanced and closed community. I don't think

Poles in the UK

Some of Karolina's team from Starbucks, which she describes as 'the best team she could have dreamt of' (she is second from right in this image)

mention my recent driving course, where I contributed *a lot* of money to my driving school, because it took me a million lessons to finally pass [*laugh*]! I also did some volunteering at the Thackray Medical Museum in Leeds. I did charity work at a local parish church and took part in a 'cycling for charity' event. I plan my future to be in this country, so I'll still give a lot more, especially when my sister and I launch our business.

Finally, the people I make friends with often tell me 'it was so lovely to meet you' — and I hope they're not lying [*laugh*]! Hopefully, one day some of them will remember me as a good friend and a positive contribution to their social lives.

this is true. It all depends on the person, and not the nationality. I have lots of good friends here now. The British are very friendly, kind and helpful — and they like Polish people!

What's your contribution to the UK?

I've been working for some years now, so there's the contribution to the economy. I took a student loan for my degree, which I'm now repaying — another financial contribution. That's not to

Any interesting stories?

I've had people asking me which part of Africa Poland was in! If it was just one person, I'd have thought they were joking, but this has happened more than once. And secondly, my first encounter with an English bus. I was stuck at a bus stop, wondering why my bus went straight past without stopping; then another one, and another one… That was before anyone told me you need to wave your arm to let the driver know you want to get on!

IMAGES: Brin Best

Last year, Karolina created a hand-made Easter card for a British friend, which she presented with a box of special Polish chocolates. On the card she drew a traditional Easter egg display from Poland

Karolina was well known among her Starbucks customers for her bubbly personality, which led one to design a fun little badge for her on the theme of the 'Little Miss' children's books. This is also a play on words with her surname, which means 'sparkle' in Polish

CHAPTER 8: **Food and Drink**

Renata Wroniecka (40)

Cook at a Leeds Primary School

Agata and Paweł at the Yorkshire Air Museum

When did you first come to the UK and what brought you here?
It was in February 2013. I came first with our two wonderful children, my seven-year-old son Paweł and 13-year-old daughter Agata. My husband, Krzysztof, who is 65, joined us in late March that year. We were all born in Toruń, northern Poland, and our decision to leave the country was very difficult for us all – but mostly for my husband. What brought us here was the hope of a better future. It was the prospect of work, which would provide us with a stable income so that we could make ends meet, from one payday to the next.

What was the beginning like for you?
Our first few months in the UK were tough. None of us knew the language, we didn't know where to start and in what order things should be organised. We couldn't always ask for a Polish interpreter. For us, and I think for many Polish people, it was hard to get used to the fact that there is generally a long waiting time for formalities to be processed. At the same time, many things can be sorted over the phone, whereas in Poland unfortunately only paperwork will get things done. Thankfully, God put many helpful people on our way.

What's your life in the UK like today?
Our lives have changed significantly since we moved to England. We live a lot calmer, slower lives, not running after everything all the time. Although only one of us works (it's not easy for my husband to find employment because of his age and health), we still manage just fine.

The children are doing very well at learning English now. It's a bit harder for us parents, but we're very slowly overcoming the difficulties and learn the language as much as we can.

Agata is in Year 9 at a Catholic secondary school; Paweł is in Year 2 at primary school. This year we're preparing for two important religious events in our family – Paweł's First Communion and Agata's Confirmation.

Thanks to the Polish Catholic Community Centre, we participate in the life of the Polish community, but we also get involved and help build it through our volunteering there. It's

215

Poles in the UK

a great joy to be able to give something back in this way.

How do your children find their English school? And do they enjoy Polish Saturday School?

When the children first went to school, there wasn't a single Polish-speaking student or teacher there. But they've now overcome the language barrier, and so they have no problems studying at their English schools.

Going to the Polish Saturday School is very enriching for them, because it's only there that they can continue to perfect their mother tongue and learn about Polish traditions.

Of course, there are also harder days when they ask us 'why do we have to get up on Saturday mornings to study, when all the other kids sleep in until 10:00 am?!'. But we know that if we stopped going there they'd soon forget their Polish and would only speak in English.

What are your plans for the future?

We don't have a plan as such, but for now we're staying here in the UK. Our children will finish their schools here and get their education, and then we'll see.

What do you think of British people?

We generally think that British people are quite closed as a community. For centuries no-one disturbed their peace and now all of a sudden many people from different countries come here and complicate everything. Even though sometimes they smile, they never seem to show their true feelings. I can say for sure that a Pole is treated differently to a British citizen, for example at work.

What's your contribution to the UK?

I work for Leeds City Council as a cook in a primary school. Together with my colleagues I prepare, arrange and serve children's meals during their lunch breaks. My specialism is preparing healthy puddings and making them a pleasure to look at, so that the children want to eat fruit! I also have a secondary job, cleaning offices at the Leeds Media Centre.

Through our work here in Britain, we pay taxes. Our children will most likely live here permanently. So they, too, will support the economy by paying their taxes and working towards their pensions, therefore supporting British society, which currently has an ageing population.

Any funny stories you would like to share?

Three weeks after we first arrived in England I had to buy a car, because I wouldn't have been able to get home from work on public transport. Shortly after that, I decided to go to a B&Q hardware store. Unfortunately, my satnav died and I had no idea how to get back home. It was awful! Imagine that – driving a car on the 'wrong' side of the road, the vehicle's steering wheel is on the side you're not used to, you don't know the language or the area, and you get lost.

Instead of going towards home in Leeds, I drove in the opposite direction, towards Manchester. Of course, I realised that this was probably not the way, but obviously you can't just hop off the motorway. I took the first possible exit and ended up driving down winding village roads. I couldn't see any people, there was no one to ask, and not even other cars. So I started to pray –

CHAPTER 8: **Food and Drink**

'please, God, give me a hand! Send a police car my way, or someone else who can help!'

And then, finally, a fire engine drove out of a side street and parked. I stopped my car in front of the fire engine and ran out of my car, satnav in hand. I called out to them: 'Help me, please! My navigation is dead, my English is bad. Where is Leeds?' ['bad' pronounced the slightly American way, so that it rhymed with 'dead'].

The fireman laughed at me at first, but then he explained to me exactly how to get to Leeds. I got back in the car and just thought 'thanks, God!'. To this day I always feel a warmth in my heart whenever I see firefighters.

IMAGE: Krzysztof Wroniecki

Renata with children, Agata and Paweł, during family relaxation time

Poles in the UK

Ania with daughter Zosia
IMAGE: K. Wilczek

Ania Jurkiewicz (36)
Kitchen Assistant

When did you first come to England and what brought you here?
I first came to England in July 2004, initially to Preston (Lancashire). This was just after Poland joined the European Union, and the borders opened for us as a result. After I completed my degree studies in Poland I came here in search of work, to improve my financial situation. So, for me it was economic migration. I still had to return to Poland briefly, to pass my final thesis examination, but I had a job in the UK by then. So, after I passed it and graduated, I decided to stay in England.

What was the beginning like – did you come across any problems in England?
One main problem was that I didn't speak any English. I studied Russian and German for a number of years at school, but never English.

I tackled this issue by taking an English as a foreign language course at a college, alongside my work. It consisted of three-hour lessons, three times a week, so was quite an intensive course. I did this for about a year, and my English improved significantly.

Before then, however, it was quite hard not knowing the language. I first arrived with a friend, whose sister had already been living here for a few months, so she helped us find our feet initially. My first job was in a factory – it was very hard work, working in low temperatures all the time (with frozen food). But it was the only kind of work one could find without being able to speak English. A lot of people from different backgrounds worked there – Romanian, Hungarian, Polish – and there was always one person from each nationality who spoke English, so we communicated through that person. Once I improved my English, I moved on to working in a canteen. It was much better because I could now talk to people, I could communicate easily.

How are things now?
I currently work as a kitchen assistant in a popular fish and chip restaurant. My team is very diverse. It's mostly English people, but I also have colleagues from Hungary, Portugal, Turkey, Zanzibar and Poland.

It's a large and busy restaurant, and we also operate as a takeaway. I prepare various dishes, from fish to mushy peas and other delicacies, all to traditional English recipes. I enjoy my job and feel confident in my role.

CHAPTER 8: Food and Drink

However, the plan for the next few years is to change my career path and move on to accounting, when my daughter is a little older and I have a little bit more time, and when I feel brave enough to take on that challenge.
I studied accounting as part of my marketing and management degree in Poland, and I also did a short accounting course here in England some time ago. I would like to get into that again once I feel a little bit more confident to continue studying and to look for a job in that area.

What are your plans for the future?

I don't plan to return to Poland. Zosia was born here and her dad is English, although he comes from a Polish background, as his parents are Polish. His side of the family lives here in England, though. I have a job and I've bought a house here. I have a circle of good friends here, too. I feel settled and at home here in the UK, and I'm used to the British customs and culture. Perhaps I don't feel 100% British, but because I've spent 11 years of my adult life over here, I feel a part of the community and I identify more with England than I do with Poland now. This doesn't mean that I forget about Poland – I obviously still go back sometimes to visit my relatives and friends, but I wouldn't go back to live there. The UK is now my home.

What do you think about English people? Have you come across any prejudice?

I've never come across any prejudice or any racist attitudes. I'm aware that some British people might be prejudiced towards those from other backgrounds, but I've never experienced any such negativity myself. I've been made to feel comfortable and welcome here.

At the very beginning, just after Poland joined the EU, I remember a lot of people asked me questions such as whether we had McDonald's restaurants or things like chewing gum in Poland. So people's ideas about Poland weren't always quite correct, because I think some people didn't realise that Poland is not really that far away from the UK! I found questions like these quite funny.

Of course, sometimes British people refer to me being Polish in jokes, but I know this is just humour, and it's not meant to be offensive at all. Overall, I've always had good relations with Britons, everything is very positive here for me and I like living here a lot.

Poles in the UK

Beata Podolak (43)

Volunteer at Saltaire Canteen

Beata with Duncan Milwain (left, manager of Saltaire Canteen) and Adam Smith (right, a founder and co-director of The Real Junk Food Project)

Beata Podolak works as a volunteer at the Saltaire Canteen, a 'pay as you feel' café in West Yorkshire. We interviewed her there during a break between serving customers to find out more about her work in this ground-breaking eatery.

When and how did you start working at the cafe?
I began working here one year ago. I was attending English language lessons in the nearby town of Shipley, a couple of years after arriving in the UK. I came here to join my husband, who had already been in the UK for a few years. One of the other students there, Monica (from Portugal), asked if anyone was interested in volunteering at the café. My family has always enjoyed helping others, so I decided to give it a go.

What do you do at the café?
I work as a volunteer two or three days a week. I help out with a variety of things, such as setting out tables, serving customers and clearing up. I have occasionally also cooked Polish dishes, helping to bring a European flavour to the menu. And I've helped to bring new customers to the café by publicising it in local schools, churches and other places.

Why do you enjoy working at the café?
There are many reasons. All sorts of people can eat at the café because you only have to pay what you can afford for the food – there are no fixed prices. Some of the people who eat here need a hot meal, but most of the time just cannot afford to eat out. So we provide an important service.

I also love meeting new people and we have a lot of interesting customers and staff. Some of our customers come here because they're lonely and it's nice to get to know them and keep them company. Sometimes they become friends, so there are benefits for staff and volunteers, as well as customers. Several groups now meet at the café every week, including a mother and baby group, a knitting group and four lovely ladies.

What are the benefits of the café?
The main benefit is that we enable people to eat tasty and nutritious meals by using food from supermarkets that would otherwise be thrown away. The café is good for the community and through our work we show respect for food. We are helping to change the way society thinks about food and our work changes us too, so it works both ways.

The café has had some very positive publicity in newspapers and magazines, which is great for all of us who work here. It also helps us to expand our work. We are already working with two local schools to provide free food for the children, as part of a wider project called 'Fuel for School'. This work will be expanding in the future. All this is doing a lot of good in the community; we are really making a difference.

CHAPTER 8: **Food and Drink**

SALTAIRE CANTEEN

Saltaire Canteen, situated within the famous World Heritage Site in West Yorkshire, aims to reduce food waste by transforming out of date and damaged foods into nutritious and tasty meals for local people and visitors. It is part of a large network of similar cafés situated throughout the UK and across the world.

Opened in December 2014, the Canteen has quickly become a popular and lively addition to this historic 'model village', which was built in the 1850s by the industrialist Sir Titus Salt, for the workers from his enormous textile mill. The Canteen is run as a Community Interest Company – in other words it makes profit but all the income is invested in further activities which benefit the public.

Focussed on the community

The Canteen now employs three people and over 20 volunteers, and is guided by two principles:

- To make its meals from a minimum of 90% 'intercepted' food items (that is food that would otherwise have been thrown away, mainly from supermarkets)
- To be run on a 'pay as you feel' basis (except for drinks), meaning that people are given a brown envelope and only pay what they can afford, or think their meal is worth.

Every week hundreds of people from all walks of life are welcomed into the Canteen. Here they find nutritious food, somebody to talk to and the chance to unwind from the stresses and strains of life. Currently, it is estimated that about 15% of the customers of the Canteen go there because they are on very low incomes and simply could not afford to eat out (or indeed eat at all) without being able to take advantage of the 'pay as you feel' rule.

Many of the volunteers at the Canteen are from overseas, and it provides an ideal environment for people to learn new skills and improve their English language capability in a workplace setting. Several people who have volunteered at the Canteen have gone on to find paid jobs after developing their skills as volunteers.

Linking with schools

In January 2016 the Canteen expanded its work by linking up with local schools to provide free meals for children, as part of a new initiative called 'Fuel for School'. A teacher from one of these schools, which caters for many children from underprivileged backgrounds, revealed that one third of their children turn up to school each day without having eaten breakfast. This aspect of the Canteen's work is set to expand rapidly in the future, as additional schools take part in this programme.

Find out more
www.saltairecanteen.co.uk
www.therealjunkfoodproject.org

Saltaire Canteen, and the wider umbrella organisation which it forms part of (The Real Junk Food Project), has the unusual aim of making itself obsolete by forcing all supermarkets to stop wasting so much food.

PART THREE
THE BRITISH ON THE POLES

CHAPTER 9

The Polish Contribution to the UK

I SPEAK POLISH WHAT'S YOUR SUPERPOWER?

The final chapter presents the personal perspective of British people of all ages on the many Polish contributions to the UK. It also includes some general conclusions, looking back over the other chapters of the book, on what Poles have done for Britain. The chapter demonstrates, in a powerful and often personal way, why Polish people and culture are valued by so many across Britain today.

The British on the Poles

The preceding 221 pages of this book have provided the opportunity to explain in detail the very many ways in which Polish people, and those with Polish heritage, have made a positive contribution to the UK over the ages, in war and in peace time.

These pages have revealed, through interviews and accompanying text, the various contributions of Polish people to Britain, across the following key areas:

- The sciences
- The arts
- Public services
- Business
- The food and drink sector.

Building upon this powerful testimony, this concluding chapter provides further examples of British people's views on their Polish colleagues, friends or relatives, helping to quantify what these people mean to them.

As will become clear, Poles are appreciated in the UK today for much more than simply their practical contributions to the country in a broad range of areas. They are also valued for their positive cultural values; they have brought a fresh mindset to the country, enhancing or building on the values that most Britons already hold dear to their hearts.

The UK is embracing a new era during which Polish people, and those with Polish heritage, will occupy a more significant role in the country than ever before. Working and living alongside their British colleagues and neighbours, another exciting new chapter for Poles in the UK is about to begin.

> *My Polish friend can always be relied on for wise words and clear guidance in a crisis.*
> Chris Ottewell

> *I've been friends with Kamila for over seven years, having first met her back in secondary school, and then carried on to college with her. What I will always remember about her is how confident and head strong she is.*
> Kennedy Craven

CHAPTER 9: The Polish Contribution to the UK

MY POLISH FRIEND TONY

I was six when I first met Tony. He was from Dundee, on the east coast of Scotland, where I was living at the time.

Tony was in my class at primary school. He used to play rugby with Dundee Eagles and I started to enjoy playing rugby with him and then training with the team myself.

I was new to the school and he started to show me around because he was my buddy. He was a nice friend. Sometimes I met him after school to play in the park too.

Tony taught me some Polish words and he brought some Polish foods into class, such as special Polish chips. He made me feel more at home and settled at my new school – he helped me a lot.

Tony was an epic friend!

Soham Handa (age 9)

IMAGE: Brin Best

Did you know?

Figures published by Her Majesty's Revenue & Customs in May 2016 showed that recent EU migrants had paid £3.1 billion in income tax and National Insurance contributions in the UK in the tax year to April 2014, but have claimed only £556 million in benefits. This means that they have made an overall contribution to the British economy of more than £2.5 billion.

The figures also showed that foreign national migrants working in Britain now make up 10.6% of the workforce. However, the rise in oversees workers in the UK happened at the same time as a 185,000 rise in the number of Britons in work, suggesting that overseas workers are not simply 'taking all the UK jobs'.

I think Polish people have brought a lot of positive things to the UK, but I do worry about the future of Poland, and the 'brain drain' effect that the country must now be experiencing, with about 800,000 Poles living over here.

Jenny Rogers

The British on the Poles

'AN ICE-CREAM CORNET PLEASE MR KUBIAK!'

My earliest experiences of talking to a Polish person are closely linked to my earliest experiences of eating ice-cream. This is because the ice-cream man who visited my street in Manchester in the 1970s was a kind Polish man who I came to know as Mr Kubiak.

The aftermath of war

After World War II many ex-soldiers, and other Polish people who had been forced to leave their country, settled in Manchester. Many of them found it hard to get work because Polish people were discriminated against in the same way that Irish and black people were.

But some, like Mr Kubiak, *did* manage to get jobs and 25 years after first setting up home in Manchester he was a familiar face in my neighbourhood. He was especially familiar to me because my favourite treat was ice-cream!

Waiting for the music

So on weekends, when I was allowed to buy an ice-cream, I would sit on my doorstep in the late afternoon. I was hoping to hear the distinctive music Mr Kubiak played from his van to let people know that he was about to arrive. Children from many of the houses on my street would run out excitedly to meet him when that music played!

My top ice-cream choice then (as now) was always a cornet with a generous dollop of vanilla ice-cream, topped off with bright red syrup. Mr Kubiak always asked me if I wanted raspberry syrup and I always said yes. It was a little game we played.

A generous man

Mr Kubiak was a generous man with a kind face. He would sometimes give me little gifts, such as sweets or even balloons. He told jokes and made me laugh. Sometimes he even did a little magic trick. I always looked forward to seeing him on Saturdays.

Me and Mr Kubiak had an unlikely friendship. I was a little British boy who loved ice-cream; he was a World War II veteran, who fought for freedom for his and my country alongside people like my granddad. And he served me my ice-cream treat once a week.

Occasionally Mr Kubiak would mention his time as a soldier, but he never went into much detail. There are so many questions that I wish I could ask him now.

A lasting legacy

Mr Kubiak probably had no idea that his weekly visits to my street created a lasting legacy. Because without his friendship and kindness I would never have ended up with my lifelong fascination for all things Polish – which has led to the writing of the book you currently have in your hands.

Brin Best

CHAPTER 9: The Polish Contribution to the UK

The Great Polish Map of Scotland

My favourite contribution of Polish people to the UK is the 'Great Polish Map of Scotland', one of the world's great three-dimensional scale maps, which was the brainchild of Polish war veteran Jan Tomasik. The map, which covers an area of 50 m by 40 m, is laid out in the grounds of Barony Castle Hotel near Peebles, Borders, and was completed in 1979. Also of interest is that nearby Edinburgh formed a formal partnership with the Polish city of Kraków in 1995.

Mark Roberts

My Polish tutor really helped me learn some important phrases in the language, which has helped to break down barriers in my job as a police officer in West Yorkshire. Being able to communicate with Poles in their mother tongue has made the world of difference.

Bryan Birbeck

The Polish nurse who looked after my injured son could not have been kinder. She knew exactly what to say and do to make him – and me – feel better about his broken arm!

Sarah Broom

The British on the Poles

Polish families and groups of young Poles mix with British people and those of many other nationalities during a sunny May Bank Holiday weekend in Ilkley, West Yorkshire. Britain today is a country where Polish and British people rub shoulders on a day-to-day basis, inside and out of the workplace

> *There's no doubt that we couldn't run our vegetable-picking operation here in the Fens of Lincolnshire without our Polish workers. They're punctual, reliable and extremely hard-working – what more could an employer want?*
>
> Dennis Butters

Housing offices in cities such as Leeds (pictured) now display welcome notices in Polish and many other languages, reflecting the multicultural nature of so many of Britain's cities today, which brings with it many benefits

IMAGES: Brin Best

CHAPTER 9: The Polish Contribution to the UK

LET'S THANK THE POLES

The Poles have influenced Great Britain massively. In fact I'd suggest they, and the other external influences to our culture, are exactly what earned us the 'Great' title.

The British Empire at one point covered much of the globe; places were eventually earned or given back, as we accepted we have no place to rule other cultures.

I think this is largely forgotten by most Brits, but well remembered by the rest of the world. I'm a firm believer that multiculturalism is the only way forward in our modern, ever-developing world, and that there is in fact much to be learned from cultures different from our own.

One thing I've learned through my experience of Polish people, both friends and strangers, is that I have found that there's an unspoken bond between them – but also with us, if you're open to it.

My Polish friends took me into their home in my time of need; the Polish chef at work looks after me with some of the best food. Even those I don't know still greet me with open arms and a smile on their face, something that I've yet to see much from locals or 'natives'.

Having worked with several Polish people, I've noticed that a work ethic unparalleled in Britain exists in most of them. Unlike us, it doesn't seem to have been 'drummed into' them. It was actually refreshing to have worked with individuals such as Karolina Iskra (▶ p. 212) and Michał Bryś at Starbucks who, like I, feel that working your hardest is simply how work should be done. This is a suggestion many British people seem to shrug off on their way to sign-on, or enter their 9–5 'rat race'.

For me it's about perspective. I think many of us Brits have become jaded to the world we've helped create. The opportunities we're taking for granted are often seen to others as incredible and rewarding, hence their move to the UK.

The media slander of the Polish and other immigrants is horrific to me, as in fact this group have often been some of the nicest, kindest and hardest-working individuals I've ever met.

It seems that having been living in such 'quality' for so long, we forgot the real value behind things, and it became wasted on us. It has, therefore, been snapped-up by others less fortunate than us, who see our country as a shining beacon of support for their already incredible attitude and work ethic.

I think Britain should say thank you to the Polish people who come here, firstly for their support, but secondly not for 'coming over here and stealing our jobs', but rather bringing themselves and their mindset to set the bar, and an example for how things should really have been done all along.

IMAGE: Ben Parker

Find out more

Ben's Soundcloud music page can be visited at: **www.soundcloud.com/parkerbenjamin**

Ben Parker, creative, business-person and musician

The British on the Poles

MARRYING INTO THE POLISH COMMUNITY

From my experience, the Polish community have helped the UK economy in many ways.

My knowledge of the Polish community in Stratford-upon-Avon began in 1959, when I first met Polish men in a metal-processing company. They had arrived during World War II, had learnt sufficient English to 'get by' and were genuine, friendly, happy people.

Many bought their own homes. Others, mostly single men, who worked within the Ministry of Defence sites (as engineers), lived within camps.

In recent years, many young people have come over to the UK, married, raised a family and worked in all parts of the economy – including engineering, medical areas, transport and tourism (especially in hotels and restaurants).

From a cultural perspective, the Polish nation has over a thousand years of history. Much of its history is found in its culture, such as dance, music and its strong sense of Christianity.

So, the Polish community adds a new and varied dimension to the UK, as its culture is so much different to ours. Poland's influence in this country, through its history, culture and language, makes us all more interested in, knowledgeable about and tolerant of all peoples. Special mention from my perspective would be the contribution Polish culture has made through its dance and music.

I've read lots of books about Poland and Polish culture. However, reading books does not give you that in-depth feeling, that knowledge and immersion into a 'subject'. Meeting the people and living the 'subject' is totally different to reading about it. I'm therefore really proud to be part of the Polish community.

John Green

IMAGE: John Green

> *I was recently refurbishing my bar and employed a small group of Polish builders for the task. They did an excellent job, were very punctual and every morning they greeted me with a smile and a handshake!*
>
> Bar owner, West Yorkshire

CHAPTER 9: The Polish Contribution to the UK

AN AWARD-WINNING NOVELIST

I met my Polish friend Dorota through the website Fan Fiction (www.fanfiction.net). She was reading some stories I put up. She said it was to keep up her English skills, but she spoke (and wrote) better English than some locals I know!

Dorota was struck by the line in one of my pieces of writing, 'I am not a friend of Dorothy!' (Dorota is the Polish equivalent of Dorothy) and that's when she started writing to me.

She'd been a student in the UK when the Polish borders closed in 1981 and she got stuck here – a teenager with no money, and only one family member in the country. It was hard for her, being away from her parents, but it left her with amazing language skills. She also speaks fluent German and enough Russian to be able to sort out a problem I was having with a pirate e-book site.

At the time, I had some dual-language English-Polish children's books that I'd written, and I was able to send them for her children to read. She was keen that their skills would be as good as hers – her whole outlook is very international.

As I moved from children's writing to adult romance, she became a valuable beta reader for me. She picked up grammatical errors (oh yeah!), but because she'd travelled so extensively, she was able to give me advice that helped flavour my stories.

In one book, I had my characters riding a motorcycle down the coast of Italy. She criticised my description of the sea colour, saying it wasn't really like that, and she also told me which wine my characters would have drunk.

To say she was outward-looking would be to misunderstand her. She's a European, and proud of that fact. I'm proud to call her my friend. And I love how the internet can break down barriers of distance and foster friendships instead.

Jane Harvey-Berrick

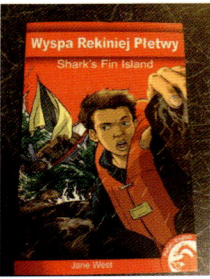

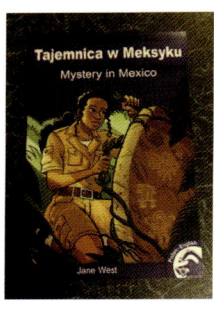

IMAGES: Jane Harvey-Berrick

The British on the Poles

❝ *I was certainly very grateful when a Polish motorist on the M1 alerted me to the flat tyre on my car, which I had overlooked. He even took the trouble to speed up alongside me to point out the problem, after I overtook him. I'll never know his name, but he did a very kind thing that day, and when I see a Polish number plate I always remember his good deed.*

Jarvis Hayes

❝ *The older generation of Polish pilots who work for the Polish airline LOT are the best in the world. These mainly ex-military pilots are so good because they trained in gliders. They're excellent at landing planes in difficult windy conditions. I know from experience, having lived in Poland for a while!*

Elizabeth Marshall

❝ *I have so many laughs with my Polish friends. It's amazing how similar their sense of humour is to mine, despite the distance between our two countries. I think that a good sense of humour is one thing that links people in the UK and Poland together.*

Martin Fisher

Index
Places and physical features

Aberdeen 22
Alsace 95
Altai Krai 89
Archangelsk Oblast 143
Argentina 91, 146,
Auschwitz 97–99, 124, 152
Australia 91, 146
Austria 25–27, 29, 99

Baltic Sea 21–23, 40–41, 43, 104
Barnet 191
Belarus 16, 33, 42, 89, 93–95, 112, 146, 154, 162
Belgium 27
Berlin 33–34
Berwick-upon-Tweed 85
Białowieża Forest 49, 109, 112
Biebrza Marshes 111, 113
Bieszczady Mountains 36, 46
Birmingham 94, 110, 120
Bolton 99
Bombay (Mumbai) 90
Bradford 183, 187, 195–197
Brandenburg, Margraviate of 18
Brest 23
Bristol 100, 185
Bug river 90, 93

Cambrian Mountains 144
Cambridge 94, 110, 154
Canada 91, 146, 213
Cardiff 154,
Carpathians, Polish 48
Caspian Sea 90
Castleford 196
Checkendon Camp 88, 92

Ciechocinek 51
Cieszyn 98, 176
Chepstow 99
China 166
Coventry 99–100, 174
Czech Republic 16, 19, 42, 99
Czechoslovakia 99
Czocha Castle 67–68

Denmark 18, 104, 163
Dewsbury 213
Dundee 65, 227
Dunedin 170
Duszniki Zdrój 46, 51, 52

Ealing 152
East Germany 34
Edinburgh 66, 85, 95, 195, 229
Egypt 84–85, 166
Elbląg Canal 44–46

Falmouth 87
France 27, 42, 80, 95, 106, 108, 120

Gdańsk 22–23, 31, 34, 55, 60–62, 108, 114, 116, 151, 170, 187
Gdynia 30, 60, 62, 74, 119, 121
Germany 25, 29–34, 42, 78–81, 86, 96–99, 114–115, 143
Giewont massif 47
Gilmerton 195
Glasgow 65
Gniezno 16
Grunwald 20–22, 128

Habsburg Empire 25, 29
Hamadan 84
Hańcza lake 42
Harrogate 177
Hastings 22
Hebden Bridge 66
Hibaldstow 201
Huddersfield 175, 212
Hull 23
Hungary 19, 25, 121, 175, 218

Ilkley 230
Illinois 115
India 88–91, 95
Indian Ocean 92
Iran 84, 88, 90, 143
Iraq 84, 88, 90
Ireland 146
Israel 90, 138
Italy 26, 31, 42, 84, 90, 119, 233

Jamaica 119
Jamestown 24

Kaliningrad Oblast 42
Kampala 143
Karkonosze Mountains 48, 50
Karpacz 50, 52
Kazakhstan 90, 143
King's Lynn 23
Kolhapur 90
Kraków 18–19, 22, 35–36, 44, 55, 57–60, 66, 85, 94, 102, 109, 112, 124–125, 128, 157, 183, 229
Krewo 20

235

Książ Castle 68
Kudowa Zdrój 51

Lake Windermere 74
Leeds 65, 103, 122, 125, 127,
    140–142, 155–156, 158–160,
    162–172, 174–175, 177–183,
    185–188, 191, 194, 196,
    198–201, 211, 213–217, 230
Legnica 19
Liberia 74
Libya 90
Lithuania 33
Liverpool 65
London 23, 44, 79, 81, 86–87,
    91, 93, 99, 119–120, 138,
    140, 142, 151–152, 155,
    162, 174, 190–192, 198–199
Loughborough 170
Lublin 22, 93, 114
Luniniec 89

Łeba 43
Łowicz 69, 94
Łódź 53, 68

Malbork 20, 44, 53
Manchester 143, 145–146, 163,
    198, 216, 228
Masuria Lake District 36, 42,
    44–45
Mauritius 166
Mexico 146
Mongol Empire 18
Monte Cassino 31, 84–85, 90
Morley 207
Moscow 115–116
Motława river 60, 62

Nettlebed Camp 92
New York 79
New Zealand 91, 146, 170–171
Newcastle 99
Nogat river 53

Norfolk Broads 144
Northern Ireland 144
Northolt, RAF 81, 83, 87
Norway 18, 50, 74
Nowogródek 94–95
Nowy Glinnik 194

Oder river 63
Olza river 98
Ostrołęka 113
Otley 180, 206–207
Ottoman Empire 23–25

Pahlevi 143
Pakistan 166
Palestine 84, 90
Paris 27, 106, 120
Peebles 229
Peenemünde 79
Persia 90, 143
Pieniny Mountains 48
Płock 192
Polish-Lithuanian Commonwealth
    23, 37, 162
Polish People's Republic 94
Pontefract 201
Portugal 218, 220
Poznań 79, 113, 116
Prague 99
Preston 218
Prószków 40
Prussia, Kingdom of 25–27, 29

Ravensbrück 97–98
Reading 88, 92–93, 95, 108
Riga 28, 31
Romania 25
Rome 67, 84
Russia 16, 23–27, 29, 42, 74,
    96, 146, 151
Russian Empire 29

Saltaire 44, 220–221
Sandomierz 67

Scotland 22, 85, 120, 144,
    194–196, 227, 229
Second Polish Republic 29, 37
Shepherd's Bush 152
Sherbourne 99
Shipley 204, 220
Siberia 28, 88–90, 93–94, 98,
    145
Siedlce 40
Skipton 191
Slovakia 19, 42
Słowiński National Park 43
Smoleńsk 152
Sochi 135
Sopot 60, 62
South Africa 64, 146
Soviet Union 19, 29, 31, 33, 80,
    84, 88–90, 110, 143, 146,
    151
Spain 42, 188
Stołowe Mountains 50
Stratford-upon-Avon 232
Sudety Mountains (the Sudetes)
    46, 48, 50–52, 65, 68
Sulejówek 97
Sweden 23–24
Syria 84
Szczecin 74, 104

Śniardwy lake 42
Świętokrzyskie Mountains 67, 73
Świnoujście 43

Tatra Mountains 42, 46–47, 80,
    157
Tehran 84, 91
The Alps 80
The Bahamas 74
The Netherlands 109, 112
Tilbury Port 90
Tobruk 90
Tomaszów Mazowiecki 194
Toruń 44, 51, 53–54, 103, 215
Tricity 60

Turkey 74, 218

Uganda 143
Ukraine 16, 24, 33, 42, 65, 110, 146
USA 24, 74, 78, 91, 115, 119, 132, 194, 196
Usedom 43

Valivade 89–90
Vienna 23, 25, 94
Virginia 24
Visegrád 19

Vistula river 22, 28, 32, 57, 104

Wakefield 166, 197–198, 212
Wales 95, 99, 114, 154, 179, 193
Warsaw 25, 28, 30–33, 36, 42, 55–57, 69, 79–80, 93–94, 96–98, 106, 108, 113, 115–116, 122, 127, 135, 143, 148, 157, 176
Wawel Castle 44, 58
Wieliczka 44, 60
Wolin 43

Wrocław 36, 55, 63–65, 67, 70, 128, 180

York 210

Zakopane 47
Zalesie 116
Zalipie 66
Zamość 44, 89
Zanzibar 218

Żywiec 176

People

Adele 142
Al-Janabi, Mariam 184–185
Ali, Monica 144
Akmal, Mashood 196
Amirian, Kari 125
Anders, General Władysław 90, 92–93, 95
Andre, B.E. 121, 143–147
Aspinall, Liz 199
Austen, Jane 144

Bacciarelli, Marcello 19
Bagiński, Tomasz 135
Barry the dog 202
Beckham, Victoria 73, 192
Bella the dog 180
Bellotto, Bernardo (Canaletto) 55
Berry, Mary 211
Betton, Keith 112
Best, Amanda 109
Bieniek, Joanna Ewa 114–116
Birbeck, Bryan 229
Birenbaum, Halina 152
Björk 121
Bohusz-Szyszko, Marian 174
Bolesław I the Brave 17, 18
Bolesław II the Generous 23
Bolesław II the Horned 23
Bolesław III the Wrymouth 17, 23
Bolesław IV the Curly 23
Bolesław V the Chaste 23
Bonaparte, Napoleon 26
Boruc, Artur 163, 193
Borysiewicz, Sir Leszek 154
Boznańska, Olga 119, 133
Broom, Sarah 229
Brown, Susan 195

Bucholc, Marek 165
Butters, Dennis 230
Byczyński, George 185

Campbell, Thomas 27
Carr, Katy 123–124
Chełmoński, Józef 128
Chopin, Fryderyk 27, 55–56, 118, 120
Churchill, Prime Minister Winston 79, 87
Cieśluk, Anna 164
Clarke, Dr Mike 113
Clooney, George 132
Cohen, Jack 162, 191
Cohen, Leonard 169
Collins, Anna Katarzyna 194–200
Conrad, Joseph 27, 118, 132
Cooper, Gary 34
Copernicus, Nicolaus 21, 23, 54–55, 102–103
Craven, Kennedy 226
Cruz, Idalia Maria 165

Davies, Norman 93
Dejewska, Kasia 159, 186–188
Del Rey, Lana 169
Dewhirst, Isaac Jowitt 191
Dobrawa (princess) 18, 163
Domzal, Czesia 89, 93
Domzal, Zygmunt 93, 95
Domzal-Karpowicz, Barbara 88–95
Dmowski, Roman 29
Duda, Andrzej 151
Dudek, Jerzy 163
Dylan, Bob 92

Eljasz-Radzikowski, Walery 16
Enya 169
Eysenck, Hans Jürgen 115

Fabiański, Łukasz 193
Faith, Paloma 142

Gaudasińska, Elżbieta 157
George, Boy 73
Gergiev, Valery 138
Gierymski, Aleksander 128–129
Gilmour, David 65, 126
Golding, William 144
Gostomski, Monsignor Bronisław 152
Green, Adrianna 161
Green, John 232
Green, Zygmunt 178–179
Grottger, Artur 128, 137
Grudziński, Piotr 126
Grzegorzewska, Wioletta 150

Hamilton, Basia 119
Handa, Soham 227
Harvey-Berrick, Jane 233
Hayes, Jarvis 234
Haylock, Julian 139
Hendrix, Jimi 124
Henry the Bearded 23
Henry II the Pious 23
Hirsch, Jerry 115
Hitler, Adolf 82, 90
Hough, Teresa 160, 182–183

Iqbal, Sofia 195
Iskra, Karolina 212–214, 231

Jadwiga of Anjou 18
Jan III Sobieski 25
Jastrzębska, Maria 33, 121, 148–150
Jones, Jade 181
Jurkiewicz, Ania 218–219

Kaczmarek, Jan A.P. 123
Kafka, Franz 144
Kamiński, Marek 104–105
Karpowicz, Maja 40, 43, 47, 55, 58, 60, 64, 67–69
Karpowicz, Szymon 90
Karpowicz, Dr Zbig 110–113
Kazimierz the Great 19
Kazmierski, Marek 150
Kennedy, Nigel 119, 124–125
Khan, Batu 18
Khan, Genghis 18
Kieślowski, Krzysztof 123
Kilar, Wojciech 123
Kolator, Radosław 164
Komorowski, Bronisław 116, 151
Konrad I of Masovia 20
Korzeniowski, Apollo 27
King Canute 17–18, 163
King, Simon 211
Klecki, Alexander 155
Kossak, Juliusz 128, 131
Kossak, Wojciech 128, 131
Kotsis, Aleksander 128, 130
Kreffta, Kinga 140–142, 166–169
Kulikjan, Michalina 162
Kulmaczewska, Agnieszka 170–172
Kulmaczewski, Rafał 170–172
Kuszczak, Tomasz 163
Kwaśniewski, Aleksander 100
Kwiecień, Mariusz 151

Lee, Harper 144
Lem, Stanisław 132
Lenin, Vladimir 29
Lepczyńska, Aleksandra 202

Levy, Andrea 144
Lewis, Leona 192
Little, Tasmin 138
Louis I of Hungary 19

Łaski, Jan 162
Łempicka, Tamara 136

McNab, Angus 204, 207
Maddocks, Fiona 139
Madera, Kasia 151–152
Madonna 73
Makowski, Tadeusz 121, 133
Malczewski, Jacek 128
Małecki, Matt 180–181
Malka, Zuzanna 165
Manaka, Nkele 196
Marks, Michael 162, 190–191, 193
Marshall, Elizabeth 234
Matejko, Jan 17, 21, 128, 134
McEvoy, Captain Theodore 83
Mela, Jan 104–105
Michałowski, Piotr 127–128
Mickiewicz, Adam 94, 116
Mickiewicz, Anna-Maria 150
Mielcarek, Tomasz 150
Mieszko I of Poland 17–18, 163
Mieszko I the Tanglefoot 23
Miłosz, Czesław 132
Milwain, Duncan 220
Milton, John 169
Mokrzycki, Jan 96–100
Morgan, Dr Peter 197
Moskal, Wojciech 105
Mrożek, Sławomir 94
Mulley, Clare 81
Myers, David 211

Needham, Kathryn 84–85, 87, 155, 157
Nowicka, Natalia 211

Olech, Arek and Robert 103

Ora, Rita 192
Ottewell, Chris 226

Paderewski, Ignacy Jan 29, 163
Panufnik, Sir Andrzej 138
Panufnik, Roxanna 118, 138–139
Parker, Ben 231
Paszkowska, Agnieszka 179
Paterek, Kasia 185
Penderecki, Krzysztof 123
Peterkiewicz, Jerzy 93
Piechowski, Kazimierz 124
Piłsudski, Józef 29
Podkowiński, Władysław 133
Podolak, Beata 220–221
Pope Gregory IX 20
Pope John Paul II 31, 35, 119, 165
Pope Pius IX 35
Półtorak, Szymon 201
Prus, Bolesław 144

Queen Elizabeth II 100, 160
Queen Victoria 29, 163

Rasiak, Grzegorz 163
Rejewski, Marian 79
Reymont, Władysław Stanisław 132
Reynolds, Quentin 86
Rihanna 121, 192
Ritter, Stephen 139
Roberts, Mark 229
Robinson, Jackie 198
Rogers, Jenny 227
Roy, Arundhati 144
Różycki, Jerzy 78

Salinger, J.D. 144
Salt, Sir Titus 221
Saganowski, Marek 163
Sapkowski, Andrzej 135
Saunders, Dame Cicely 174
Sawicka, Zuzanna 173–175
Schafernaker, Tomasz 108

., 151
, 132
, 144
80–81
ie, Maria 102,
, 164
Smith, A m 220
Smolarek, Iza 150
Solny, Emilka 163
Spears, Britney 192
Spencer, Thomas 191
Stalin, Joseph 29, 88–89, 143
Steinbeck, John 144
Stirling, Jane 120
Stoss, Veit 58
Strelau, Professor Jan 114–116
Suchocka, Hanna 31
Sweyn Forkbeard 18
Szykuła, Wiktoria 162
Szymańska, Dominika 164
Szymborska, Wisława 132

Świętosława (princess) 18

Tokarczuk, Olga 93

Tomasik, Jan 229
Tomaszewski, Professor Tomasz 115
Trotsky, Leon 29
Tubacka, Laura 163
Turing, Alan 79
Tusk, Donald 151
Tuwim, Julian 94

Urbanowicz, Witold 86

Vetulani, Tadeusz 109

Waits, Tom 169
Wajda, Andrzej 123
Wałęsa, Lech 31, 34, 60, 119, 152
Wandzel, Jacek 176–177
Wasilewski, Marcin 193
Wawrzyniak, Damian 211
White, Jack 121
Wielicki, Marcin 208
Williams, Robbie 73
Witkiewicz, Stanisław Ignacy (Witkacy) 118, 136

Władysław I the Elbow-high 23
Władysław II Jagiełło 20
Władysław II the Exile 23
Władysław III the Spindleshanks 23
Wodzińska, Maria 120
Wojniakowski, Kazimierz 26
Wojtek the bear 31, 84–85, 124
Wojtyła, Karol Józef 31, 35
Wragg, Tamsin 168
Wróbel, Aleksy 150
Wroniecka, Renata 215–217
Wyspiański, Stanisław 128, 133, 136

Yang, Pati 125–126

Zanussi, Krzysztof 123
Zarzycka, Basia 120
Zygalski, Henryk 79
Zygmunt II Augustus 24

Żurawski, Maciej 163
Żyliński, Prince John 192–193

Further reading and information

The following reference sources will allow the reader to learn more about some of the main topics explored in this book. They supplement those mentioned in specific sections of the book.

Books

Olson, L. and Cloud, S. (2004) *The Kosciuszko Squadron – Forgotten Heroes of World War II*. Arrow.

Radzilowski, J. (2003) *A Traveller's History of Poland*. Interlink Books.

Sebag-Montefiore, H. (2004) *Enigma: the Battle for the Code*. Phoenix.

Valentine, I. (2004) *Station 43: Audley End House and SOE's Polish Section*. Sutton Publishing.

Zamoyski, A. (2015) *Poland: A History*. William Collins.

Websites

Poland's Official Travel Site:
www.poland.travel/en-gb

Polish Ministry of Foreign Affairs Information Site:
http://poland.pl

Museum

Polish Institute and Sikorski Museum
www.pism.co.uk
20 Prince's Gate, LONDON, SW7 1PT
(Situated in South Kensington, near to the Royal Albert Hall)
Tel. 0207 589 9249

About the authors

Brin Best

Brin's first encounter with a Polish person was in childhood, when his Manchester street was regularly visited by a kind ice-cream man called Mr Kubiak. He has subsequently had several life-affirming friendships and other links with Polish people of all ages, which have led to the writing of this book.

He has 25 years' experience as teacher, educational consultant and author. He worked as a teacher, head of department and school development officer, before joining the advisory staff of a local education authority in Yorkshire.

During his career Brin has worked with hundreds of Polish children and young people of all ages and abilities, as well as those with mixed British and Polish heritage.

He has written 26 previous books for a range of national and international publishers, including many best-selling and award-winning titles. Several of his books have been translated into foreign language editions in Europe and the Far East. He has also appeared on several television and radio programmes in the UK as a specialist consultant or contributor.

Brin is also a trustee of the British Polonia Foundation, the charity which has published *Poles in the UK*. He has been involved in helping to run a range of charitable organisations for the last 20 years, and has been the trustee of two other charities in Yorkshire. He also served for four years as a trustee and executive council member of the Royal Society for the Protection of Birds – Europe's largest environmental organisation.

Brin was elected a Fellow of the Royal Geographical Society in 1992 following his expeditionary research in Ecuador, which won the BP International Conservation Prize in 1989. He was later awarded a Millennium Fellowship for his ground-breaking environmental education work with young people.

You can learn more about Brin's work by visiting his website at **www.brinbest.com**.

Maria Helena Żukowska

Maria's interest in all things creative started early and developed in *gimnazjum*, Polish secondary school. Here, she was editor-in-chief of a school magazine and her writing won her a seat of MP in the Polish Parliament of Children and Young People in 2006.

The fond memories of her own education and the opportunities her *gimnazjum* offered her are what makes Maria passionate about inspiring young minds today.

Maria is an English Literature graduate from Leeds Beckett University. She was awarded the Prize for Best Dissertation in 2013 for her BA thesis on Eastern Europe in Gothic literature.

While still at university, Maria wrote her first book – an A-level study guide on John Milton's *Paradise Lost*, which was published by ZigZag Education.

She then went on to study for an MA in Contemporary English Literatures at the same university, and graduated in 2014 with a distinction. Maria is currently adapting her highly-regarded MA thesis (exploring the representations of 'Eastern' Europe in fiction and film) for publication.

Maria remains closely related with the higher education sector. She works as an Education Service Officer at the University of Leeds, supporting students and tutors throughout the entire academic process, from enrolment to graduation.

Alongside her main occupation, she does short academic translations from Polish into English, including for works published by the Institute of Literary Research of the Polish Academy of Sciences.

She also volunteers at the Polish Saturday School in Leeds. Here, she is always busy preparing for various events which aim to maintain and celebrate Polish culture and language, as well as strengthen Anglo-Polish ties.

Finally, Maria has had a lifelong passion for music, which she combines with her literary work, and is a singer-songwriter in her spare time.

...utors

B.E. Andre was born in Manchester, the child of Polish post-war refugee parents. She was educated at Stretford Grammar and Loreto College, read French, German and Swedish at UCW Aberystwyth, and then completed further post-graduate studies in Manchester. This was eventually followed by a Masters degree in Critical and Creative Writing at the University of Winchester. She is the proud mother of three grown-up sons and lives in Northwich, Cheshire. With *Blood and Scars* was her debut novel. Visit B.E.Andre Author on Facebook.

Maria Jastrzębska is a Polish-born poet, editor and translator. Her most recent book is The Cedars of Walpole Park, a bilingual collection of her selected poems, translated into Polish by Anna Błasiak, Paweł Gawroński and Wioletta Grzegorzewska, and published by Stowarzyszenie Żywych Poetów. Her work appears in many anthologies, including *Piękni Ludzie* (Poezja Londyn IBIS) and *Hallelujah for 50ft Women* (Bloodaxe), and she has co-edited several anthologies, including *Queer in Brighton* (New Writing South). She teaches creative writing and has worked as a bilingual assistant with Polish children and as a community interpreter. **www.mariajastrzebska.wordpress.com**

Specialist contributors

Amanda Best studied Ecology at the University of East Anglia in Norwich, and has worked in the nature conservation field for 27 years. She is currently a Biodiversity Technical Specialist at the Environment Agency. Amanda loves wildlife and is passionate about the aquatic environment, and has a particular interest in the creation and management of wetland habitats.

Joanna Ewa Bieniek studied Pedagogy at The Siedlce University of Natural Sciences and Humanities in Poland. Her course included modules on psychology, where she first came across, and was inspired by the work of, Jan Strelau. She moved to the UK in 2006 and hopes to start a psychology Masters course in the UK in the near future.

Katarzyna Dejewska is a teaching assistant at a Leeds primary school and a volunteer teacher at the Polish Saturday School in the city. She specialises in Early Years education. She is passionate about working with and supporting the youngest learners, both one-to-one and in a group setting. At the Polish School, Kasia's mission is to help her students develop their Polish language skills and learn more about their Polish heritage.

Teresa Hough is an experienced English teacher and Head of the Leeds Polish Saturday School. She has worked in the British Education sector for over 30 years, supporting student learning at a variety of levels – from primary to further education. She has also taught English as a foreign language. Teresa has been actively involved in the continual development of the Polish Saturday School in Leeds since 1986, and she takes a keen interest in teaching Polish-British students about Polish culture and language.

Maja Karpowicz is studying English with Creative Writing at the University of Birmingham. Being a third generation Anglo-Pole, she has always had a deep love and passion for her Polish heritage. She attended Polish Saturday School in her teens and achieved a GCSE in the language, and hopes to write about her Polish family history in the future. After completing her degree she plans to work in television/film, in the hope of giving Poland – and all those with Polish heritage – a strong, inspiring and individual voice in Britain.

Kinga Kreffta is a singer-songer and singing teacher based in Leeds. She has a passion for Polish-British history, and was the joint leader of a workshop for children from the Leeds Polish Saturday School, which explored the contribution of Poles in the UK.

Kathryn Needham is an experienced secondary school teacher who now has an interest in the wider education of all, including primary-age children and adults. She first became interested in Polish heritage when supporting adult learners within the community to develop their English language skills. Kathryn was a contributor to a book about the teaching of geography, published in 2014 by Bloomsbury.

Marcin Wielicki has a passion for Polish food and cooking. Trained in physiotherapy and based in Leeds, he is hoping to begin his own physiotherapy business in the near future.

Simona Żukowska works in the construction industry. A French philologist by trade, she takes a keen interest in social issues and is passionate about all things creative, including Polish and international art and culture. According to her daughter, Maria, Simona bakes the best Polish cakes; she has contributed her home-style cheesecake recipe to this book.

Student collaborators

The following 38 students from the Leeds Polish Saturday School contributed to the planning of the book, during a workshop held in October 2015 (and/or completed work on the same theme following the workshop*).

Mariam Al-Janabi, Piotr Bogacz, Marek Bucholc*, Ania Cieśluk*, Idalia Maria Cruz*, Julia Damanskis, Hubert Dembowski, Miłosz Dembowski, Franek Fortuna, Natalia Gostyńska, Dawid Kłos, Radosław Kolator*, Natalia Kosiada, Alex Kowalski, Michalina Kulikjan*, Paweł Liszkiewicz, Fatima Łobocka, Tomasz Łuczak, Laura Madaj, Konrad Madzia, Zuzanna Malka*, Anastasia Mazzella, Karol Natanek, Mikołaj Natanek, Ania Paszel, Szymon Seńkowski, Zuzia Siudek, Emilka Solny*, Ola Szatkowska, Adam Szcześniak, Krystian Szwichtenberg, Wiktoria Szykuła*, Domin[...] Szymańska*, Laura Tubacka*, Bartłomiej Wiśniewski, Maksymilian Włodek, Sebastian Włod[...] Agata Wroniecka.

THE BRITISH POLONIA FOUND[

9 Throstle Nest Close
Otley
West Yorkshire
LS21 2RR
UK

The British Polonia Foundation is a UK charity which aims to forge links between British and Polish people, building on the shared history of the two countries.

In addition to publishing *Poles in the UK*, the Foundation is carrying out a range of work in schools and other places to improve understanding of British-Polish history, and of the Polish contribution to the UK.

The Foundation's work is informed by the important historic links between the two countries through the ages, including the vital cooperation which occurred during World War II. It also recognises the contemporary contribution that Polish people are making to the UK, in all walks of life.

The Foundation works all over the UK from its base in Yorkshire. Its trustees come from British and Polish backgrounds, with wide experience in education, communications and business.

facebook   The British Polonia Foundation

THE BRITISH POLONIA FOUNDATION

9 Throstle Nest Close, OTLEY, West Yorkshire, LS21 2RR, UK

UK REGISTERED CHARITY No. 1168711